ALL THE HORRORS OF WAR

ALL THE HORRORS OF WAR

A JEWISH GIRL, A BRITISH DOCTOR, AND THE LIBERATION OF BERGEN-BELSEN

BERNICE LERNER

JOHNS HOPKINS UNIVERSITY PRESS
Baltimore

© 2020 Johns Hopkins University Press
All rights reserved. Published 2020
Printed in the United States of America on acid-free paper
2 4 6 8 9 7 5 3 1

Johns Hopkins University Press
2715 North Charles Street
Baltimore, Maryland 21218-4363
www.press.jhu.edu

Library of Congress Cataloging-in-Publication Data

Names: Lerner, Bernice, author.
Title: All the horrors of war : a Jewish girl, a British doctor, and the
liberation of Bergen-Belsen / Bernice Lerner.
Description: Baltimore : Johns Hopkins University Press, [2020] | Includes
bibliographical references and index.
Identifiers: LCCN 2019027983 | ISBN 9781421437705 (hardcover) | ISBN
9781421437712 (ebook)
Subjects: LCSH: Genuth, Rachel—Biography. | Holocaust
survivors—Biography. | Hughes, Glyn (Hugh Llewelyn Glyn),
1892–1973—Relations with Holocaust survivors. | Bergen-Belsen
(Concentration camp)—Biography. | Ex-concentration camp
inmates—Biography.
Classification: LCC D805.5.B47 L47 2020 | DDC 940.53/18092 [B]—dc23
LC record available at https://lccn.loc.gov/2019027983

A catalog record for this book is available from the British Library.

The map on pages x–xi is by Kelly Sandefer, Beehive Mapping.

Cover and interior design by Amanda Weiss

*Special discounts are available for bulk purchases of this book. For more
information, please contact Special Sales at specialsales@press.jhu.edu.*

Johns Hopkins University Press uses environmentally friendly book materials,
including recycled text paper that is composed of at least 30 percent post-
consumer waste, whenever possible.

FOR

Isla, Ruby, Sidney, and Caleb

I thought that most of us who survived would never be human again. We were treated worse than animals, we were so dehumanized, and with so little to hope for, I just could not imagine ever getting married and having a family.

RACHEL GENUTH, liberated in
Bergen-Belsen on April 15, 1945

Belsen was unique in its vile treatment of human beings. Nothing like it had happened before in the history of mankind. The victims of this infamous behavior had been reduced to a condition of subhuman existence, and there we were, a mere handful of war-weary men trying to save those who could still be saved and to allay the sea of suffering and the depths of agony.

BRIGADIER HUGH LLEWELYN GLYN HUGHES,
in Sam Bloch, ed., *Holocaust and Rebirth 1945–1965*

CONTENTS

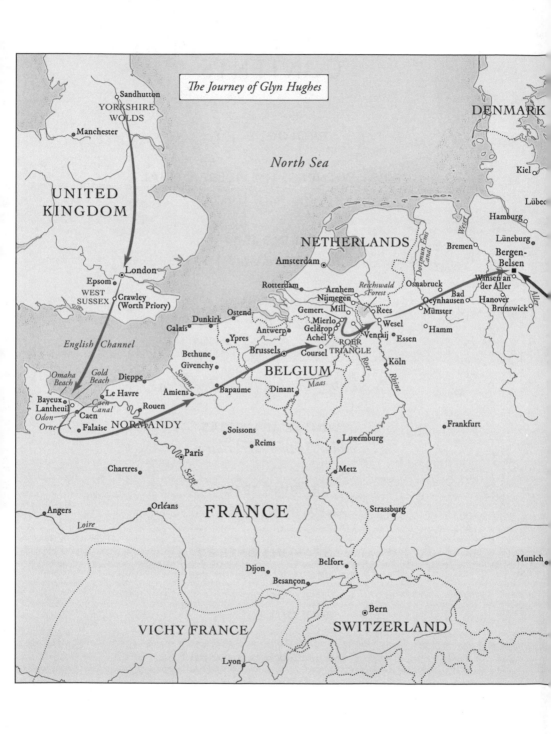

The Journey of Glyn Hughes

The Journey of Rachel Genuth

ALL THE HORRORS OF WAR

PROLOGUE

The beginning of the end of Rachel Genuth's childhood may be traced to an afternoon in early September 1940. It was during the harvest, the time of year when Rachel helped her father, Moshe, a produce trader, lift crates of fruit to be sold to retail vendors. All summer long, the tomboyish ten-year-old accompanied Moshe on trips to orchards; she mounted wagons full of watermelons, climbed trees, and with her pocketknife cut swirled apple peels that when tossed behind her formed the first initial of the man she would marry—usually an *S*. (She hoped it would be Sruli, her bookish neighbor who once, seeing her try to sweep a floor, had taught her the correct way to do the job.)

On what began as an ordinary day, Rachel and her friend Raize walked two miles to an orchard on the outskirts of Sighet to bring Moshe his lunch. As a dozen laborers worked the grove and Rachel and Raize wove through rows of trees, everyone suddenly heard a military band approaching from the direction of the former Czechoslovakia (now under Hungarian rule). The nearby border had been crossed. At the sound of gunshots, Moshe told Rachel and Raize to run and hide in the attic of the estate's villa. They could come back down when the soldiers passed.

The villa's stairwell was narrow, and its attic dingy but not dark—light shone in through two small windows. Surveying the space, the girls spotted a dull copper cylinder, an object unlike any they had ever seen. They took a closer look but dared not touch it.

As the Hungarian troops marched toward the orchard, the sounds of brass wind instruments and gunfire grew louder; after the band and soldiers passed, the noise tapered. Rachel ran down to tell her father about the unusual object. Hugging her close, shuddering at the unthinkable,

Moshe explained that the cylinder was a live grenade. He speculated that the Romanian landowner, anticipating the prospect of Hungarians confiscating his orchard, had planted a weapon. The landowner likely knew of Hitler's recent edict awarding northern Transylvania to Hungary, which it had ruled before World War I. The strategic territory included beautiful Sighet, surrounded by mountains, nestled between the Tisza and Iza Rivers.[1]

Not everyone felt as the Romanian landowner did. Walking home, Rachel and Moshe saw people lining the streets, welcoming—with flowers and cheers and Hungarian flags—uniformed soldiers led by officers. When they relayed the news to Rachel's mother, Blima, she also rejoiced. Like others of her generation, she had been educated in Hungarian schools; she spoke the language, knew the history, and could recite Magyar (ethnic Hungarian) poems. In this land of changing borders and nationalities, she would now be able to help her children with their homework.

Little did Blima know that her children's schooling would soon be the least of her concerns.

A few weeks later, while Rachel slept at her grandmother Chaya's, a blackbird pecked insistently on the bedroom window. Chaya rose to listen. The bird, she said, was bringing good news: Rachel's aunt Malcsi and her family were on their way. Sure enough, before officials closed the border between Romania and Hungary (on October 2, the Hungarian parliament officially incorporated northern Transylvania into its land), Rachel's aunt Malcsi, her husband, Mano, and their two children—eight-year-old Baibe, who had won a Shirley Temple look-alike contest, and six-year-old Heime, her clever brother—left Brasov, Romania's second-largest city, for Sighet. Perhaps they feared the murderous Iron Guard—Rachel overheard her parents talking about "Greenshirts" killing Jews. In any event, no border would separate the family.[2]

It was a happy day when aunt Malcsi and her family appeared. Rachel remembered their earlier visits, when they showered her and her siblings with expensive toys (which Blima promptly sold). Aunt Malcsi and Uncle Mano had also sent packages of chocolate, fish oil, and vitamins—items manufactured in their factory. After Rachel's older sister, Elisabeth, spent the summer with them in 1939, she could not stop talking about their elegant apartment with indoor plumbing; their maid, who cleaned, washed, and ironed; and the shopping excursions they took her on. Rachel thought her sister had been terribly spoiled. And she hoped that she too might one day visit Brasov.

But this was not to be. After Hitler's edict, Aunt Malcsi and Uncle Mano sold what they could and left their comfortable cosmopolitan life. They rented a large apartment in Sighet and unpacked what they brought with them, including never-before-seen gadgets that made life easier. Rachel's mother had only a wooden bowl and chopper, whereas Malsci had a meat grinder. Blima made stew; sophisticated Malcsi made hamburgers.

Others of Rachel's relatives were also well off. Her uncle Nachman, who in his youth had tried to make his way in Palestine, had returned to Sighet and married a woman whose dowry enabled him to open a butcher shop and goose-down business. In addition to his sizable home and two rental apartments, he built a synagogue for his local community. Its garden contained plants with enormous leaves; Rachel showed his three little girls how to use these as sunshades.

In June 1941, less than a year after the Hungarian takeover, the Germans invaded Soviet territory. In the ensuing chaos anti-Semitic leaders, motivated by the recent unwelcome influx of Jews from Galicia and Bukovina (regions on the northern slopes of the Carpathian Mountains) and Poland, decided to deport all foreigners. The National Central Alien Control Office would "resettle" those Jews who could not prove continual Hungarian citizenship—for themselves and their ancestors—going back ninety years. On July 8, 1941, Dr. Gabor Itai, lieutenant governor of the District of Máramaros, in which Sighet was located, promised Jews with "unhinged status" a "new life" in Galicia.[3]

Though born and bred in Sighet, Rachel's aunt Malcsi and her uncle Nachman had each lived away from the town. One July night, gendarmes stormed Nachman's home. They dragged the businessman to the police station. As he had lived in Palestine in the 1920s, Nachman was unable to produce papers verifying that he had continually resided in the area that was now part of Hungary. The next day officers came for his wife and children. Rachel's aunt Malcsi, uncle Mano, and their children—having lived for a time in Brasov—were ousted from their home in the same terrible way.[4]

Among the several hundred "foreign" Jews thus rounded up and expelled from Sighet was Moshe the Beadle (the synagogue caretaker). Several months later, he returned and told what happened. No one believed him. Not even Elie Wiesel, his devoted pupil. "They take me for a madman," Moshe the Beadle told the young Wiesel.[5]

Freight trains brought sixteen thousand expelled Jews from Hungary and seven thousand from Poland to a camp in Kőrösmező, on the Hungarian-Soviet border. From there, trucks transported one thousand a day to Kamenets-Podolsk, in Ukraine. A few weeks later, the deportees were forced to march with the city's indigenous Jews to a forested area with large craters created by bombings. For three days beginning on August 27, the *Stabskompanie* (staff company) of Friedrich August Jaeckeln, SS-*Obergruppenführer* (higher SS and police leader), assisted by Order Police Battalion 320, Einsatzgruppe C, and Ukrainian auxiliaries, compelled their prey to undress and lie head-to-toe, "sardine-style," in the massive pits. They shot each man, woman, and child. Some were but wounded. (Investigators who later opened the pits found that 35 percent had been shot dead on the spot, 50 percent were injured, and 15 percent had been buried alive.) The perpetrators made no effort to conceal their crime—the first large-scale Nazi massacre of Jews—from the local population, many of whom saw the earth move up and down for days.[6]

Moshe the Beadle had taken a bullet in his leg and lay still as the drunken Nazis finished their work.[7]

As for Rachel's relatives, it is likely that they reached Kamenets-Podolsk in late July; lived under inhuman conditions abated only slightly by the beneficence of local Jews who shared what meager food and shelter they had; then met their fate on August 27 or 28, following the joint German-Hungarian meeting on August 25, when the Nazis agreed to kill Hungary's "alien" Jews by the month's end. The other possibility: Rachel's aunts, uncles, and cousins—including Baibe with the blonde curls—were murdered in a similarly barbaric way somewhere on the way to Kamenets-Podolsk.[8]

In *Night*, Elie Wiesel wrote, "The deportees were soon forgotten." Days, weeks, and months passed. "Life had returned to normal."[9]

Not for Rachel. Not for her parents. Not for Chaya, whose "stars had been taken from her eyes." The brokenhearted mother and grandmother now lived only to fulfill her daily obligations. This was why, since the summer of 1941, either Rachel or her sister Elisabeth slept beside Chaya, who cried herself to sleep. Rachel's heart ached. Had something terrible happened to her aunts and uncles and to her five little cousins? Would she ever see them again?

In an effort to console Chaya, someone sent her letters ostensibly from Nachman and Malcsi. These said that they had been resettled in the Ukraine, that they were well but could not write much. Chaya was not convinced. Nor could she believe Moshe the Beadle.

Who could believe Moshe the Beadle? How could the most cultured of peoples—the Germans—kill innocent human beings for no reason? How could such barbarism occur in the twentieth century?

Rachel saw her mother and Moshe the Beadle speaking in the yard. Blima did not think the man mad; she slumped in sorrow.

FIRST WITNESS,
THE BELSEN TRIAL

Fall 1945

On September 18, 1945, Brigadier H. L. Glyn Hughes, who had led relief efforts at Bergen-Belsen, entered a converted gymnasium forty-eight miles northeast of Bergen, at 30 Lindenstrasse, in the outskirts of Lüneburg, Germany. Called upon to serve as first witness at the Belsen trial, he steeled himself for the weighty role. His testimony and bearing would set the tone of the first international war crimes trial, immediately preceding the Nuremberg trials.

In Britain, there was enormous public interest in the trial. Since April 22, cinemas had been showing a film clip, "In the Wake of the Hun," depicting the aftermath of the concentration camp's liberation. Such horrifying accounts caused an outcry: the perpetrators must be punished. After King George issued a Royal Warrant entitled "Regulations for the Trial of War Criminals," the general officer commanding 30 Corps summoned a military court to try Josef Kramer and forty-four other Nazi guards, all charged with having committed war crimes as part of a system of ill treatment and murder of inmates at Bergen-Belsen between October 1, 1942, and April 30, 1945. Among the forty-five defendants was a group also charged with committing these same crimes, during this same period, at Auschwitz-Birkenau. All summer long, affidavits had been taken and evidence amassed. (In the chaotic conditions right after the liberation, it was difficult to collect evidence. The trial, originally scheduled for July, was postponed until September.)[1]

Now, two British trucks, led and followed by armored cars manned by Tommies (British soldiers) with machine guns, brought the accused from a nearby jail to the courtroom. Curious Germans flanked the road. Children pointed at Irma Grese, calling out her name. The *Aufseherin* (female SS guard) in a pressed and tailored tunic (in contrast to other SS guards' wrinkly gray uniforms), wearing a hairstyle accented by blond ringlets, reveled in the attention. She would be watched closely throughout the trial, during which she would turn twenty-two.[2]

Shortly before 10:00 a.m., a voice over a loudspeaker announced that the court was about to enter. All stood, doffing their hats. Following the lawyers, judge advocate—in a gray wig and black robe—and officers came the accused, escorted into the courtroom by red-capped military police.

A gallery lined three sides of the courtroom, brightly lit by powerful electric lights. At one end, beneath a cinematographic projector, approximately two hundred press correspondents sat at desks. Below them sat officers for the prosecution. Under the screen at the opposite end sat German and Polish interpreters, stenographers, and official guests. A specially built three-tiered defendant's dock contained the accused Nazi functionaries; high on their chests hung tie-on squares of white cloth, each with its own large black number. In front of them sat the defense lawyers. In the first days of the trial, many of the four hundred seats available for onlookers would be occupied. Thereafter, many would remain empty. (Apart from being preoccupied with their own losses, Lüneburg's citizens carried a dark past—they had elected Hitler, and their town's state psychiatric hospital participated in his euthanasia program; two hundred to three hundred children had been murdered in its children's ward.)[3]

The military court, comprising five British officers and the judge advocate, would bend over backward to allow the defendants to testify and mount their defense. In addition to one Polish and eleven British regimental officers with legal qualifications, they would be represented by Colonel H. A. Smith, a former professor of international law at London University, who argued that the murderers were merely abiding by German law, obeying superior orders that required them to imprison and mistreat certain "German nationals by annexation." In refutation, Colonel T. M. Backhouse—one of four prosecutors of the legal staff of headquarters, British Army of the Rhine—cited provisions of both the Geneva Convention and the Hague Convention regarding the treatment of internees. Speaking in a clipped, precise manner, he gave a picture of mass starvation, beatings, filth, disease, and cannibalism. He announced that Brigadier Glyn Hughes would be the first of many witnesses to make evident that Kramer and his forty-four aides were guilty of unbelievable cruelty.[4]

Glyn Hughes stepped into the plain wooden witness box in the middle of the room. Standing rigidly, his voice steady, he described the medical crisis in the camp upon its liberation on April 15. At one point, projected film footage—the first to be admitted as evidence at a war crimes trial—depicted rotting corpses being pushed into a pit by a bulldozer. All of the defendants but one appeared solemn—gum-chewing, insolent Grese fixed her hair and blew her nose.[5]

When asked about Kramer's attitude upon turning the camp over to the British, Hughes told the court that the SS officer had been indifferent and unashamed. When an interpreter translated Hughes's response, Kramer hung his head.[6]

Beyond the unprecedented role he shouldered at Bergen-Belsen and his knowledge of the complexities of evacuating and treating multitudes of patients, Hughes's authority derived from a host of personal attributes. The man in the witness box was a quick and confident decision maker, commanding loyalty and respect from subordinates. Though generous of spirit, he insisted on discipline, imparting with a curt word or piercing look his disapproval of unseemly behavior. For Hughes, there was always a right and a wrong way of doing things; he led by example and held others to high standards. He treated men of all ranks with equal respect and could not "see an injustice . . . without doing something to try and put it right."[7]

In appearance, Hughes was striking: tall and dark, with strong features. His distinctive walk engendered certainty and hope in others. Rabbi Isaac Levy, a military chaplain he met in Bergen-Belsen, considered him "a man of great proportions, both physically and spiritually." A friend who knew the scope of his life's work said, "He had the gift of healing, not only in his hands and in his head, but in his heart."[8]

Hughes opened his testimony by providing precise information on the layout of the camp and the number of inmates found in each of five compounds. Owing to the lack of food and water, everyone was suffering from starvation and gastroenteritis. Owing to the lack of lavatory facilities, "the compounds were absolutely one mass of human excreta." Without sanitation, "conditions were absolutely suitable for disease," of which there was every form, including typhus and tuberculosis. "I have been a doctor for thirty years and seen all the horrors of war," Hughes said, "but I have never seen anything to touch it."[9]

Piles of corpses of various sizes were lying all over the camp. In the most crowded huts, six hundred to a thousand people occupied a space built for one hundred. Uncountable numbers of dead putrefied among the living. The living did not have room to lie down. Many of them "were so weak they could hardly raise themselves on one elbow." Even as he exhibited photos, including one of a naked man sitting on a pile of corpses, Hughes maintained, "No description nor photograph could really bring home the horrors that were there outside the huts, and the frightful scenes inside were much worse."[10]

Near the crematorium, Hughes had seen signs of filled-in mass graves. To the left of the bottom compound was an open pit half-full of corpses. It had just begun to be filled.[11]

The brigadier said that, of the forty-one thousand surviving Camp One inmates, 70 percent had required immediate hospitalization. Of these, he estimated that ten thousand would die before they could be placed in a hospital. Ten thousand who had died in the previous days and weeks, in all stages of decomposition, had to be buried.[12]

Glyn Hughes's testimony went on for hours. Fifty-three years of age and no longer the athlete he once was, he might have given in to fatigue. But he refused to sit. Authoritative, straightforward, he contradicted the argument of the defense, which was that the volume of incoming transports and increasingly deplorable conditions had pushed matters beyond Kramer's control.[13]

On March 1, Kramer had written a letter to the head of Department D of the SS Administration Department in Oranienburg, SS-Gruppenführer (group leader) and concentration camps inspector Richard Glücks, describing the dire situation. He explained that, when at the end of January *Stabsarztführer* (chief medical officers) inspected the camp, they had agreed that thirty-five thousand detainees were beyond what it could hold; this number had already been exceeded by seven thousand, with another six thousand two hundred on their way. The barracks were overcrowded, spotted fever and typhus epidemics had broken out, and the daily mortality rate, which was sixty to seventy at the beginning of February, was now up to two hundred fifty to three hundred per day. It would increase under the prevailing conditions. He wrote that there were practically no supplies in the area as well as problems with transporting whatever supplies did exist to the camp. He noted the need for boilers, a delousing machine, a sewage installation, and beds, blankets, and eating utensils for approximately twenty thousand internees. Knowing his superior had "even greater difficulties to overcome," he nevertheless implored him to help.[14]

Hughes argued that vast resources were readily available and could have been deployed. Upon their arrival, his men found large stocks of medical supplies in an administrative building. Within a short time, they collected an additional 135 tons of medical supplies in the area. They found a "most beautiful" German military hospital with doctors, nurses, orderlies, and more than a thousand beds a mile and a half from

Camp One. They found large numbers of Red Cross boxes sent by Jewish associations, with meat extracts, biscuits, and food of all kinds. A bakery capable of producing thousands of loaves of bread a day was located within two miles, and a civilian dairy was also nearby. During cross-examination, Captain E. W. Corbally asked whether it was easier for the British army to provide more than a starvation diet because it had more food. Hughes answered, "The main reason was we saw that it was done . . . [W]e made an effort which was not made before."[15]

Hughes told of challenges he faced. The war was not yet over when he arrived at the camp—battles were still raging in northwest Germany, and few Second Army units were available. He began his work with but one casualty clearing station, one light field ambulance, and two hygiene sections, bringing the total number of medical and other personnel to a mere 361 (including only twenty doctors) on April 17.[16]

In addition to providing food and water, the liberators managed to eradicate typhus within two weeks of their arrival. This was accomplished with only sixty-eight men. Kramer had many more personnel at hand—neighboring barracks contained an estimated fifteen hundred Hungarian guards, and large numbers of German troops were in the area.[17]

Hughes described the attitude of Klein, the camp's only doctor, as "callous and indifferent." He told how Kramer, who had shown him around the camp, did nothing when SS men shot at prisoners who tried to get at guarded potatoes. He himself had to put a stop to the killing, which had become a matter of habit at Belsen.[18]

Defense attorney Captain Phillips asked, "What would you say was the principal cause of the indescribable conditions at Belsen?" Hughes replied, "Neglect to keep the ordinary humanitarian rules, to feed [the prisoners], to keep them clean, to provide sanitation." And when asked what should be done for a person near death who is apathetic, starved, and ill, Hughes answered, "Feed him, wash him, and see that he is perfectly comfortable. Cases like this require almost individual attention—feeding with small amounts frequently and [doing] everything which can possibly be done for them. They should not be made to make any muscular effort."[19]

Following Hughes's testimony came that of Lieutenant Colonel James Johnston, who commanded 32 Casualty Clearing Station and served as senior medical officer at Belsen. Johnston stated that "all those in any way responsible for ordering, or carrying out orders, which resulted in the state of affairs hereinbefore described, must inevitably have known that it was bound to result in deaths on a gigantic scale."[20]

Glyn Hughes had persuaded Dr. Hadassah Bimko to testify. Bimko had maintained a protected ward for a hundred and fifty children, had walked Hughes through Bergen-Belsen soon after his arrival, and was appointed administrator of its nearby hospital by him. On September 22, the fifth day of the trial, the courtroom went silent as the Polish Jewish dentist, who had endured fifteen months in Auschwitz and five months in Belsen, recounted with tears and in a sometimes cracking voice how her father, mother, brother, two sisters, husband, and six-year-old son were murdered in Auschwitz. Walking slowly along the dock, the short, stocky woman calmly looked at each defendant.[21]

The most notorious among them was Kramer, who had supervised the gassing of thousands at Auschwitz before earning the moniker "Beast of Belsen." Executing any order with the "greatest unconcern," the massive, narrow-eyed man casually shot twenty-two prisoners the day before the British arrived. Dr. Fritz Klein, who in Auschwitz had made daily inspections of naked prisoners to decide who should be sent to the gas chamber, had served as Bergen-Belsen's doctor. Peter Weingartner had been in charge of Vistula, a severe Auschwitz *Kommando* (work unit). Among other practices, he had brutalized and murdered women in his charge by setting guard dogs on them. Franz Hoessler had met incoming trains in Auschwitz-Birkenau and assisted in loading those selected for the gas onto trucks. Juana Bormann, at fifty-two the oldest of the nineteen female defendants, had watched with pleasure as her dogs tore prisoners to pieces. Elizabeth Volkenrath, head *Aufseherin* and "the worst-hated woman in the camp," had been so ruthless that witnesses came forth with abundant evidence of the beatings she administered. Irma Grese, who at nineteen had been in charge of a compound of eighteen thousand women, beat, tormented, and murdered thousands. When a British officer found her in a barn a few miles from Bergen-Belsen, she brightened while telling him of the pain she inflicted on inmates. She had worn heavy boots and carried a braided cellophane whip. (She admitted using it on Auschwitz prisoners, but "for some reason," she said, "I always used my hands at Belsen.") Her physical attractiveness rendered her an especially curious case—how could one so young and beautiful commit such heinous crimes?[22]

Others charged with odious crimes in both camps were Ilse Lothe, Hilde Lobauer, Heinrich Schreirer, Stanislawa Starotska, Georg Kraft, Herta Ehlert, and Ladislaw Gura. Though defending officers appealed to separate the Belsen charges from the Auschwitz charges on the grounds that there was no connection between the two camps, the prosecutor insisted that "these two cases were a continuation of a series," and that, with the exception of Starotska, all those indicted on both charges came from Auschwitz to Belsen. The court overruled the application for separating the two charges. In fact, cruelty, sadism, torture, and murder were ubiquitous at both camps. The difference between the hells, in the words of survivor Rachel van Amerongen-Frankfoorder, was that "death was more visible in Belsen . . . At Birkenau entire groups disappeared . . . If they wrote down your name . . . your time was up. Death was very efficient and neat there. At Bergen-Belsen nobody said good-bye, people died slowly from disease, exhaustion, cold, mostly from starvation . . . At Bergen-Belsen death lurked everywhere."[23]

Bimko pointed out fifteen of the defendants by name. Her eyes locked with those of Grese, who averted her gaze.[24]

Bimko explained how the system at Auschwitz-Birkenau operated, how the Jewish *Sonderkommando* (special squads) were forced to bring bodies from the gas chambers to the crematoria. She said that she saw

Josef Kramer kicking and beating sick prisoners. She said she saw him, Dr. Klein, and SS officer Hoessler participate in the selection of victims for the gas chamber. She said she saw Irma Grese watch ailing patients being loaded into trucks bound for the gas chamber. And she identified Karl Francioh, supervisor of the cookhouse at Belsen, as the man who shot an inmate through the stomach the day before the British arrived.[25]

In cross-examining Bimko, defense counsel Captain C. Brown suggested that she fabricated statements about Kramer's brutality. The thirty-year-old dentist responded that it was she and not the defending counsel who "was present . . . during those conditions." Stony-faced Grese burst into laughter. Herta Ahlert, the *Aufseherin* sitting next to Grese, followed suit. Some spectators joined in. Major General Berney Ficklin, president of the court, announced that he would not tolerate such disturbances.[26]

Captain Brown expressed frustration at Bimko's elaborate and emotional responses to his yes and no questions. Bimko challenged him further: "If counsel who only knows things by hearsay can speak, why am I, a real witness, not allowed to speak?" When asked whether medical stores were available once Dr. Klein was made senior doctor at Belsen, two or three days before the arrival of the British, Bimko declared, "The world should know that [because the British troops were just arriving,] the stores were made available."[27]

After Bimko's testimony, Hughes and members of the court traveled south from Lüneburg to Bergen-Belsen, where the brigadier pointed out what British troops found in and around Camp One. But he knew no one could imagine the filth and ordure, the stench of disease and death, the Second Army had met just six months earlier.

SPRING 1944
March, April, May

In Bergen-Belsen, inmates died of starvation and disease under deteriorating, chaotic conditions. One year earlier, the Nazis had a well-ordered strategy for mass murder.

In the spring of 1944, as the main Allied powers (Great Britain, the United States, the Soviet Union, and France) entered the final stages of planning the most ambitious military invasion in history, Hitler's henchmen began to effect the largest and most rapid mass murder in history. While the immense buildup of Allied soldiers, vehicles, and supplies transformed southern England into a gigantic armed camp, the SS at Auschwitz-Birkenau prepared to receive 437,000 Jews from the Hungarian provinces; they increased the number of *Sonderkommando* (prisoners who worked in the anterooms to the gas chambers and moved bodies from the gas chambers to the ovens) to one thousand, made sure the gas chambers were in good repair, equipped the ovens with new parts, and built a railway spur that would bring arrivals under an arch and directly into Birkenau. Instead of trudging from the railway ramp between the Auschwitz main camp and Birkenau, those immediately selected for death would now walk only a few minutes to the gas chambers. In a separate section of the camp—Birkenau II—the Nazis would hold "depot prisoners" (approximately 20 percent of mid-May to mid-July arrivals). These able-bodied Hungarian Jews constituted the largest remaining reserve of slaves; some might serve German industries in desperate need of labor.[1]

That March, while Glyn Hughes, deputy director of medical services (DDMS) of the British Second Army's 8 Corps, reviewed top-secret documents pertaining to the impending D-Day invasion, fourteen-year-old Rachel Genuth was caught in the Nazis' murderous web. Her hometown's mayor, deputy prefect, and gendarmerie commanders attended a top-secret conference to detail procedures for concentrating and expelling Sighet's Jews.[2]

✹ ✹ ✹

Officially designated a "follow-up" formation, 8 Corps, comprising 60,244 men belonging to two armored divisions and one infantry division, was to follow assaulting Allied troops onto the shores of Normandy as soon as possible after D-Day. By the spring of 1944, 8 Corps was ready. Its leaders had studied its future role from every angle. It had trained well. Several large-scale exercises, lasting as long as two weeks, had been carried out in northeast England as if it were occupied France, testing lines of communication and the endurance and fitness of troops for battle. During Eagle, the most recent and final exercise, all arms of 8 Corps participated in a realistic representation of a winter campaign, breaking out of an imagined bridgehead in severe weather. Several troops, while playing the part of the dug-in enemy awaiting the attack, died on account of the conditions.[3]

For such exercises, DDMS Glyn Hughes had all medical corps formations set up simulation facilities. Imagining an atmosphere of congestion in surgical areas, they would hold "patients" on the operating table or in the treatment department as long as they would when in action. They would rapidly set up and take down tents and makeshift operating rooms, breaking large installations into blocks for quick loading and transport. Casualty clearing station (CCS) nurses would put up their own tents and execute other tasks unusual for women. (When they later impressed other units, they would proudly "[stick] their chests out and [say]—but we are 8 Corps.") Personnel likely to land "wet-shod" rehearsed landing moves. Hughes had no patience for anyone who did not take training seriously. When a field ambulance

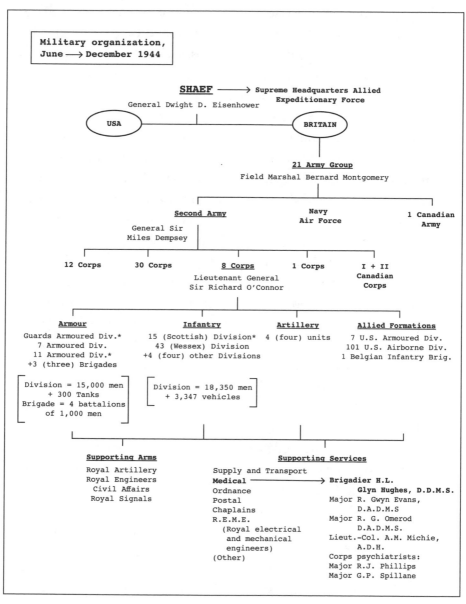

Military organization, June–December 1944.

Design credit: Emily Hoadley

commander dismissed practice as a "mere token," Hughes knew his unit would perform poorly overseas (which was exactly what happened).[4]

Beyond training, Hughes insisted that medical personnel gain knowledge required of combatant troops, such as how to waterproof vehicles and how to detect and clear mines. He convinced army powers that doctors ought to be both advisors *and* students of military tactics—force commanders needed considered medical opinions on an area's terrain and facilities and in turn medical officers needed to be informed about battle plans. "The moral," said Hughes, "is that senior medical administrative officers . . . must at all times be forward and in close touch with the ground situation as only the earliest information may avert a disaster." The Royal Army Medical Corps could then "weave frayed ends into an orderly rope" for those coming up from the rear.[5]

Hughes embodied the qualities of both healer and soldier. Though he rarely spoke of his service in World War I, when as a regimental medical officer he took up arms and led men in battle, his proclivities were apparent. Now, he would oversee medical care *and* give expert advice on military matters. When a difficult technical question or complicated tactical problem arose, a cry went up at 8 Corps Headquarters: "Send for the DDMS—he'll know the answer."[6]

Glyn Hughes had come a long way since the beginning of the war. In December 1939, at the age of forty-seven, he stood before medical personnel as commanding officer of 11 General Hospital at the port of Le Havre. In riding breeches, with hands on hips and a small cane dangling at his side, he explained how to use a Thomas splint, ameliorate the effects of poison gas, and prevent frostbite.[7]

When Germany invaded France in May 1940, Hughes supervised lieutenants in charge of stretcher-bearers and casualty clearing stations for 141 Field Ambulance of 5 Infantry Division. His division navigated Ypres, where the British had fought so hard in World War I. And Avion, where Hughes saw dozens of farm animals tied up and refugees moving in all directions. And Givenchy, where he witnessed the bombing of a refugee convoy just as it approached and where he lost an ambulance and thirteen men from Company A. Fighting then broke out at Vimy Ridge, another World War I battle site. Hughes noted that neighboring Neuville-Saint-Vaast, a stepping-stone to operations at Vimy, was precisely where British trenches ran in 1916. His efforts to conserve medical manpower while providing prompt treatment of casualties would end eight months into this second war, when the German army beat British, French, and Belgian troops in "a colossal military disaster." Hughes and his unit drew back toward Dunkirk, the French port city from which more than three hundred thirty thousand British and French troops were to be rescued.[8]

In the early dawn of June 1, Hughes, with four other members of the last division to escape the German assault, boarded an old barge. Unlike those who had had to wade from the shore and stand shoulder-deep in frigid water for hours before they could board any type of vessel or fatigued stretcher-bearers who lifted badly wounded men onto rolling boats on gusty nights, Hughes and his comrades did not get their feet wet. The waters were "calm as a millpond." Above all, they were lucky for having dodged brutal treatment or even death at the hand of violent captors—the fate of many who were left behind.[9]

Now, four years later, Hughes was about to again cross the Channel—for an operation and in a manner that was a far cry from what he had experienced at Dunkirk.

By the spring of 1944, Hughes had instituted the systematized treatment of large numbers of wounded as assistant director of medical services (ADMS) of the newly formed Guards Armoured Division, attended administrative conferences on "broken battle conditions," and assumed his current post with 8 Corps, which had absorbed the Guards Armoured Division in 1943.[10]

By the spring of 1944, the plan of the chief of staff to supreme Allied commander (COSSAC) for the cross-Channel invasion was expanded upon by the Supreme Headquarters Allied Expeditionary Force

Ramsgate at last. Finally, on June 1, at 11:15 a.m., after an eleven-and-a-half-hour voyage from Dunkirk aboard an old barge that normally carried chalk for a china clay factory from the Isle of Wight to Portsmouth, which sailed among merchant marine boats, fishing boats, and other vessels bringing British and French troops to safe shores, Glyn Hughes and his group landed at the Ramsgate Quay. All Hughes had was his uniform and some gear. At 11:30 a.m. the men devoured the most delicious sandwiches they had ever eaten, and by noon they were on their way for an unknown destination, which turned out to be Manchester. *Photo from the Museum of Military Medicine. Helen J. McCarrick,* Nursing Times *(London), March 4, 1969.*

(SHAEF); two artificial ports, "Mulberry harbors," had been designed and built; Normandy was selected as the point of attack rather than the more strongly defended Pas-de-Calais (where, owing to the Allies' elaborate and ingenious deception plans—including fake army camps and partly concealed dummy tanks—the Germans concentrated their powerful Fifteenth Army); and every conceivable contingency had been planned for.

Hughes regularly visited the guarded planning flat at Sandhutton Hall, home of 8 Corps Headquarters. From this location in the verdant, undulating countryside of the Yorkshire Wolds—an ideal training ground—an escorted officer traveled daily to Second Army Headquarters in London to collect and bring back top-secret information and orders.[11]

Poring over documents and maps, Hughes identified problems. He voiced these during discussions with other planning staff. Operation Overlord, the Battle of Normandy, would begin with dangers attending the voyage over the Channel: seasickness, casualties from the loss of or damage to any craft (and the imperative to collect and carry survivors), shortages of medical personnel and equipment. High rates of casualties were expected during the landing: at least five thousand the first day and twenty-six thousand by D+14 (fourteen days after D-Day). The assault force would suffer the greatest number of wounded before it would be possible to get enough medics, hospitals, and equipment onto the crowded beachhead. The beach medical organization would have to cover all surgical needs until large medical organizations came ashore.[12]

Hughes weighed methods of evacuation of casualties, by hospital carrier and by air, both during the initial stage of landing and in the long term. He anticipated the need for field hygiene and sanitary sections, and he created a scheme for the correct phasing in of all medical units.[13]

In the weeks before D-Day, the already proud 8 Corps received extra encouragement. In a large meadow adjacent to Sandhutton Hall, General Sir Bernard Montgomery paraded down a square lined by the Guards Tank Brigade, pausing intermittently to speak to soldiers. The commander in chief of British forces then moved to the square's center. Climbing atop a jeep, he motioned for the troops to gather around him. A tremendous rush. "Three cheers." A cavalcade then followed Montgomery, who pulled away in a Rolls Royce sporting a large Union Jack.[14]

Other morale boosters followed. On March 23, the king, queen, and Her Royal Highness Princess Elizabeth met with soldiers of the elite corps. One week later, Winston Churchill visited Sandhutton.[15]

✻ ✻ ✻

Field Marshal Bernard Montgomery (FAR RIGHT) and Prime Minister
Winston Churchill (FOREGROUND) visit 8 Corps troops, spring 1944.
The Museum of Military Medicine.

Twelve hundred miles east of the Yorkshire Wolds, an isolated Carpathian mountain town was about to feel the full effects of Hungary's
alliance with Hitler. Sighet's ten thousand five hundred unsuspecting
Jewish inhabitants, nearly 40 percent of the town's population, were
more vulnerable than they could imagine. They were unaware of the
Warsaw ghetto uprising, mounted in the spring of 1943. They did not
know about the death camps in Poland, including Treblinka and Sobibor, where hundreds of thousands were murdered and where revolts had
taken place within the past year. Those who heard "rumors" of killings
of Jews in Ukraine hoped the war would be over soon and they would
remain safe.

Rachel Genuth, the second of six children, lived with her family in
Sighet's center, near shops, a movie theater, and churches. The Genuths'
apartment was one of several attached residences stretching from Timár
utca (Tanning Street) to serpentine Kigyó utca (Snake Street). Each
apartment had its own shed, outhouse, and if room allowed, a garden.
Rachel's maternal grandmother, Chaya Davidovitz, conveniently lived
at the start of the long yard—Rachel and her siblings ran to her whenever Blima, their mother, scolded them.

In mid-March 1944, as the Allies launched air attacks in German-occupied northern France, disrupting the enemy's transportation and fuel infrastructure, while Hitler summoned Hungarian regent Miklós Horthy to his Austrian mountain palace, allowing German forces to invade the country holding Europe's last untouched mass of Jews during their leader's absence, the Genuths prepared for Passover. Rachel helped scrub every surface of their three-room apartment. Blima gave the walls a fresh coat of paint and washed and pressed the shelf liners and curtains. Kitchenware, brought in crates to and from the attic, was exchanged; unmatched porcelain dishes replaced unmatched everyday dishes. Having saved all year, Blima and Moshe now bought their children new clothes and shoes.[16]

Rachel looked forward to the seder meal, to enjoying some of her favorite foods—roasted goose, soup with flanken (tender beef), and potato latkes. Most of all, she appreciated that her family would be together.

Two years earlier, Moshe, having just turned forty-one and with a sixth child on the way, was called up for *munkaszolgálat* (forced labor). Among fifteen thousand other Jewish men from northern Transylvania, he would serve troops of the Hungarian army, deployed to fight the Soviets in Ukraine.

Shortly after Moshe's conscription, Chaya woke one night to the sound of a knock at her door. Blima's second sister, Rachel's aunt Gizi, had returned to Sighet with her husband, Joseph, and their two small boys. Rachel remembered her aunt's wedding several years earlier. Blima and Chaya had spent weeks preparing, home-baked treats were served, and Rachel and Elisabeth wore new patent leather shoes. Gizi and her handsome husband then moved to Nitra, the capital of western Slovakia, where they opened a commercial bakery. Now Rachel met her adorable cousins with dark hair and big brown eyes. She wanted them to stay, but it was dangerous for Chaya to harbor "foreigners."

Gizi and Joseph had already known terror. Fleeing Slovakia—where authorities confiscated their property and closed Jewish-owned businesses; where Jewish men, then whole families, were being hunted down and deported to Majdanek or Auschwitz—they paid smugglers who might have stolen the money and valuables they had on them or killed them. They dressed as peasants and drugged their children so they would not wake up and cry. (When traveling by wagon, they covered the boys with hay; when walking through woods, they carried them on their backs.) Having come all the way east to Sighet, they would have to backtrack; last Rachel heard, they made it to Budapest, where they hid in a Jewish cemetery.[17]

During his absence, Moshe missed another momentous event. In September, Blima went into labor. Rachel ran for the midwife, and the Genuths welcomed Rózsi, their fifth girl. While Rachel and Elisabeth helped their grandmother Chaya, who took over Uncle Nachman's butcher shop, Blima tried to make ends meet by serving as a wet nurse for a wealthy family. Rachel and her brother Yitzhak stacked wood planks at that family's parquet tile factory, tedious work that earned them a pittance.

Then ten, Yitzhak acted as the man of the house. When he was younger he would buy a box of candy, sell individual pieces to his classmates, and eat the profits. That was before Moshe taught him about reinvesting. With saved money, Yitzhak then had bought and bred angora rabbits. With proceeds from the sale of the rabbits' fur, he had purchased a milk-producing goat.

Winter arrived and frigid temperatures took hold. Occasionally, a neighbor stopped by to see how the Genuths were faring. A view into the kitchen reassured the visitor—there was always a pot of soup on the stove. Between their stock of goose fat, Yitzhak's goat, and Blima's creativity, the children did not go hungry.

✳ ✳ ✳

May 1943. Moshe had been gone for more than a year. Blima received an official telegram—her husband was in a hospital; she could come and pick him up.

No event before or since could match in joy that of Rachel's mother returning with her father. As Moshe saw his baby daughter for the first time, amid hugs and kisses and tears of happiness, Rachel noticed that, though he appeared well, her father had lost parts of three fingers on his right hand.

Word of Moshe Genuth's homecoming spread far and wide. Of the thousands of men drafted into *munkaszolgálat*, almost no one had come back. Women and children, many from distant villages, came to ask Moshe whether he had seen their father, husband, son, or brother. He comforted all his callers—their loved one was okay; they should not lose hope.

Rachel sat by Moshe's feet or on a nearby stool, listening in on every exchange. Her heart broke when she heard him tell his cronies, a few older men from the synagogue, the truth. Hungarian overseers tortured the laborers for the most trivial offenses or none at all. Those who gave up their watches or gold rings for the promise of some bread were instead given twenty-five lashes on their naked bodies. The men slept on lice-infested straw. Deprived of adequate clothing and food, those unaccustomed to hard work died early on. Moshe wheeled an officer's bicycle. Through snow and freezing rain he held its icy handlebars. Frostbite caused the damage to his fingers.[18]

Severely weakened, many of the laborers contracted typhus. In April 1943, Hungarian officers set up a "hospital" in a large barn for six hundred seventy healthy and sick men, in the Ukrainian village of Dorosics. Those too sick to crawl out could not get anything to eat. Those who were feverish and stricken with abdominal pain moaned and begged for water. Dozens died each day; corpses lay in stacks next to a nearby stable.[19]

The officers surrounded the entire quarantined area with a barbed-wire fence. On April 29, just after Passover's end, they secured the barn

doors from the outside with wire, poured gasoline around the structure's perimeter, and set it on fire. Bedlam. Shrieks. Living "torches"
leaping through collapsing planks. Machine gun fire took down those
who tried to run away.[20]

As Moshe described to his confidants how he climbed out of—and
helped two of his compatriots escape from—the burning building,
Rachel trembled. Her father was one of the few who survived the ten-
minute conflagration and slaughter. He and the two men managed to
reach woods, where they met partisans who laid out a choice for them:
they could go to Russia, where they would be safe, or they could go
back to their hometown, where the Jewish community, given Hungary's
alliance with Germany, was imperiled. Moshe and his fellow townsmen
wanted only to return to their families. Seeing their poor condition, the
partisans helped them get to a hospital.[21]

April 7, 1944. One year after his return, Moshe sat at the head of the
seder table, a pillow symbolizing freedom at his side. Sixteen-year-old
Elisabeth sat at the end nearest the door, and Blima sat next to Moshe,
near the counter and stove. Next to Blima sat Chaya, who, together
with Rachel's mother, spoke of the wondrous liberation of the Israelites.

Between Chaya and Rózsi—eighteen months old and in her high
chair—sat Rachel. Opposite Rachel sat six-year-old Faige, whose eyes,
blue like those of all the Genuth children, appeared large in her round
face. Ten-year-old Judy sat between Faige and Aunt Zseni—eight
months pregnant and unsure of the whereabouts of her husband,
Yossel, who had been drafted into *munkaszolgálat*. Her baby slept in
the nearby crib. Twelve-year-old Yitzhak sat between Moshe and Faige.
He chanted the four questions, the first of which asks why this night is
different from all others.

After the festive meal Yitzhak found the afikomen, the hidden piece
of matzoh. Everyone sang "Chad Gadya," the song about a little goat.
Though tired, the children watched with eager anticipation as Elisabeth

rose to open the door for the prophet Elijah. As they continued to talk
and sing, through the now-open door staggered their janitor, the man
who lit the fire for them on the sabbath. He came straight to the table.
Pounding it with his fist, he spoke loudly, almost screaming. "Good
folks," he said, "do not worry, the war will be over in one year." Blima,
Chaya, and Zseni recoiled. The children cowered in fear. But their
father, Rachel noticed, remained perfectly calm. He gave the gentile a
goblet of wine and, after the man drank it, escorted him out the door.
Back inside, Moshe told his family that when a drunk speaks, he speaks
the truth.

By the time the Jews of Sighet celebrated Passover, SS-Obersturm-
bannführer (Lieutenant Colonel) Adolf Eichmann had gained the cooperation of the Hungarian gendarmerie and secretaries of Hungary's
Ministry of Internal Affairs. He had marked Sighet's Jewish institutions
on his map, and local authorities had chosen the site of the ghetto. It
would be in the mostly Jewish district, encompassing four main streets
and several small side streets. Jews from neighboring villages would be
deposited in the smaller ghetto in Ober-Yarash, a slum-suburb consisting of tiny alleys. Close to thirteen thousand Jews would be concentrated in the delimited areas, with as many as ten people crowded into
a midsized room and twenty occupying larger rooms.[22]

On the seventh day of Passover, Rachel, following the beat of the
town crier's drum, gathered with neighbors to hear the latest news—
Jewish shops must close; Jews must abide by curfews; Jews must turn
their valuables over to the authorities. These same messages, with
warnings to Christians who dared hold valuables given them by Jews,
resounded in newspapers and on posters.[23]

On April 15, the last day of Passover, while Moshe and Yitzhak attended services at the Machzikei Torah synagogue and Rachel counted
the hours until she could have popcorn (a snack prohibited during the
holiday), Lajos Tóth, the chief of police, held a meeting of Sighet's

officials. They established twenty commissions, each comprising a police officer, two policemen, two gendarmes, and one civil servant. These men would be responsible for rounding up the Jews.[24]

On April 20, several thousand Jews from twenty-six villages in the region were given less than two hours to move to Sighet. They could bring with them only bedding and clothes weighing up to fifty kilograms and food for fourteen days. They came by foot or by lorry. Every room in every building within the small and large ghettos, including cellars and attics, was now filled. One hundred and forty of the community's leaders—who might have organized resistance to the measures—were imprisoned, with no food or water. Ferenc Hullman, the government's "expert advisor on Jewish affairs," rejected almost all of the Jewish council's requests for aid. Hungarian persecutors, who arbitrarily subjected Jews to violence and forced labor, tortured religious men, forcing them to cut off their beards and *peyot* (sideburns). Fifty gendarmes guarded the main ghetto's barbed-wired perimeter, surrounding streets including Timár utca, where Rachel's home was located. The Genuths' apartment was already crowded; no one moved in with them.[25]

Despite the conditions, ghetto inhabitants displayed a spirit of mutual assistance and solidarity. Despite or because of fearful premonitions, grown-ups acted kindly toward children. (And they did not overly mourn those who perished, for, at least in Sighet, the dead would be ensured a proper burial.) Rachel experienced the "eerie, dreamlike quality" of the ghetto in her own way. Yes, a yellow star had to be sewn onto her coat. Yes, there was an evening curfew. But it was springtime, and, with no work (the authorities forced Chaya to close her business), she could gallivant and play. True, the windows of her friend Szilvi's house, facing outside the ghetto, had to be painted: all windows of buildings bordering the ghetto were whitewashed—no one was allowed to interact with anyone from the free world. But the Genuths' janitor and his wife, who could have left their small apartment for better housing elsewhere, refused to move. With passes that enabled them to leave and reenter the ghetto, they brought the Genuths provisions from beyond its border.[26]

Sighet's Jews knew that Miklós Horthy, Hungary's regent, was anti-Semitic. That he might relocate them to Transdanubia, the agricultural region west of the Danube River, was plausible. It was also rumored that they would be taken to work in Germany or resettled outside of Europe, perhaps in Africa. No one could imagine what their government was about to do to appease Hitler. Had they known, they would have acted differently. They would have dispersed. They would have hidden. As it was, the Jews carried on as best they could.[27]

Preparing for "resettlement," Blima had never been busier. For days, she boiled fruit for jam and made noodles. She toasted bread and egg barley (a traditional barley-sized noodle). Moshe filled their ceramic-lined metal container with goose fat. With a small amount of goose fat and Hungarian egg barley, they could make a nourishing meal.

At the end of April, Adolf Eichmann, Hungarian state secretary László Endre, and Lieutenant Colonel László Ferenczy of the royal gendarmerie headed up a delegation of Ministry of the Interior employees and doctors to observe the conduct and state of mind of Sighet's Jews. How aware were the Jews of what awaited them? What degree of cooperation could be expected during the impending deportation? What inefficiency was in need of correction? The behavior of families like the Genuths might have indicated to them that the deceived would, without panic and restiveness, follow orders.[28]

Mid-April 1944. While the Jews in the Hungarian provinces were being segregated, the Second Army's 8 Corps moved from the Yorkshire Wolds to various locations in Sussex and Surrey. Corps headquarters was set up in a Roman Catholic school called Worth Priory, midway between London and the coast. Within the fine house, a heavily guarded planning flat held a sand model of the future area of operations. A rocky massif with two high points of strategic significance dominated the three-dimensional rendering of the Normandy countryside. General Richard O'Connor, who would guide soldiers through the hardest fighting overseas, pondered the sand model and maps covering the flat's walls in endless deliberation. Upset by reports of the last-minute intensification of anti-invasion preparations, particularly the increasing German tank buildup opposite the British landing area (which already expected the lion's share of the enemy's counterattack), O'Connor pressed for a greater allocation of Sherman Firefly tanks and rounds of sabot shells.[29]

Except for officers with passes, no one could gain access to the planning flat. Barbed wire and whitewashed windows further protected the secrets of when, where, and how the invasion would take place.[30]

With D-Day looming, 8 Corps received its marshaling and embarkation instructions. General O'Connor addressed all three divisions in person; General Henry Crerar of the Canadian army and General Dwight D. Eisenhower, commander of SHAEF, visited; and General Montgomery addressed corps officers, speaking of his faith in the invasion despite alarming threats from German field marshal Erwin Rommel of underwater obstacles (such as barriers and chains, in addition to naval mines).[31]

In May, more than two million British and other Allied soldiers were concentrated in southern England. Before being sequestered with no further communication with the outside world, before troops were given maps with fictitious place names and the topmost levels of the armed forces were briefed on the exact date and location of the landings, London beckoned. It was not far to the city for an evening's entertainment.[32]

Occupied with his responsibilities as DDMS, Glyn Hughes had little time for amusement. Besides, there was no longer a home for him in London. For one, his family's four-story domicile on Stanford Road had been destroyed during the Blitz (the German bombing campaign

of 1940–41). A bomb had then flattened the second residence to which
the Hughes family intended to move. His wife, Armorel, and fourteen-
year-old son, Michael, had left for rural Chagford, where Hughes had
once enjoyed life as a country doctor; and his daughters, Diana, aged
twenty-one, and Jean, aged nineteen, now attended boarding schools
outside the city.[33]

After World War I, after completing medical school, Hughes had
married Armorel Swynford Jones, an attractive VAD (voluntary aid
detachment) he met while at University College Hospital. They had
been happy during their years in Chagford, where the young doctor
treated poor, grateful patients and played rugby for the team at nearby
Exeter and Armorel participated in the village's parish-centered life.
In 1928, Hughes moved his family to Kensington, where his children
could attend fine schools and where he assumed a private practice as
an obstetrician-gynecologist. It was not long before he worked with
renowned surgeons, treated celebrities, and earned the honor of being
a physician to the queen. It was not long before the family adopted
an upper-middle-class lifestyle, including a crew of hired help, a vaca-
tion home, dinner parties for the parents, and a nanny for the children.
Trappings of success—frequenting Trumper's, the expensive men's hair-
dresser; spending evenings at the sports-themed Bath Men's Club; enabling his wife to shop at Barkers and other posh stores—meant a great
deal to Hughes. He had known adversity.[34]

Hugh Llewelyn Glyn Hughes was born on July 25, 1892, in Ventersburg, South Africa, a backwater with fewer than seventeen thousand
residents, few homes and businesses, a telegraph office, and a small
school. The nearest railway stop was at a farm eleven miles away. Two
years earlier, his father, Dr. Hugh Griffin Hughes, had moved with his
wife to this Orange River colony in what would become part of the
British Empire to seek his fortune. Two years later, Dr. Hughes accidentally stabbed himself with a contaminated needle while performing
surgery. Within forty-eight hours he died of septicemia. His bereaved
wife returned with their son to Europe, where she and the boy lived in

poverty and where Hughes eventually attended a preparatory school in South Wales.[35]

When Hughes was seven, a doctor diagnosed him with a spinal deformity and told his mother he would forever be puny. Prescribed horizontal rest and confined to a spinal carriage (similar to a pram), he had to be wheeled about like an invalid. Years later, a second doctor found no reason for restricting his activities. Hughes's childhood enfeeblement had an effect on his psyche. An intolerance in himself of any weakness or vulnerability remained at the core of his personality—never would he give in to pain and suffering.[36]

Hughes's physical liberation preceded deliverance of another kind. In October 1903, the Epsom College council resolved that he be admitted as a foundation scholar; his application, submitted nineteen months earlier, was finally accepted following confirmation of his mother's meager means and a sudden, unexpected vacancy. Hugh Llewelyn Glyn Hughes, a "disadvantaged son of a physician," would receive a quality education at the school's expense.[37]

At the venerable school for sons of medical men, the boy defied his prognosis. He achieved athletic prowess and academic success. By his senior year Hughes was head prefect, captain of the rugby team, and sergeant of the military's Rifle Corps. He was on his way to realizing his childhood dream of becoming a soldier—of being among men, in the thick of action, oblivious to danger.[38]

Hughes's dream came true after World War I broke out. Five years after graduating Epsom, before completing medical school, he served as a regimental medical officer. Eventually, he would display aspects of his military training and patriotic sentiments as head of a household. While even-tempered and fair, he made clear that discipline ruled. He expected his children to take classical courses and do well in school and to have good manners. Mornings began with a cold bath. At breakfast, everyone took his or her regular seat, Hughes farthest from the dining room entrance, Jean always to his left. Buried in the London *Times*, the veteran, when reading of events in Germany, railed against the "Hun."[39]

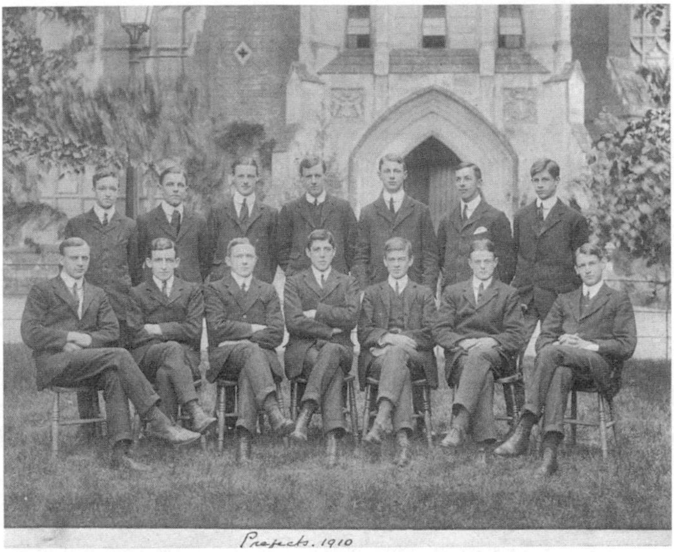

Epsom College prefects. Glyn Hughes, head prefect (CENTER FRONT).
© *Epsom College Archive.*

As the years went on, as continental politics roiled, Hughes and Armorel experienced marital discord. So different in temperament and disposition, each failed to consider the other's needs.[40]

✡ ✡ ✡

Before World War II broke out, Hughes volunteered for active service. Now, five years after enlisting, he was among the highest-ranking medical officers in the British Second Army. On May 2, he held a conference for commanders of 8 Corps' medical units in order to relay the latest information on plans for Operation Overlord. Two days later, he attended a meeting at the office of 21 Army Group's director of medical services. On May 9, he joined other corps deputy directors of medical services for a conference at Second Army medical headquarters. And, on May 31, he visited the headquarters of 1 Airborne Division, to discuss 8 Corps' medical responsibilities. Privy to details concerning the imminent invasion, he anxiously awaited word of its hour. Impatient with slow deliberations and delays, he hoped it would be soon. He gave his full attention to the weather, the conditions upon landing, and how best to treat soldiers risking their lives in battle.[41]

He knew little about Auschwitz.

✡ ✡ ✡

Rachel knew nothing about the Allies and the Axis (the alliance of Germany, Italy, and Japan), but she knew of activities that eluded the local authorities. In preparation for the impending deportation of the Jews, they strove to ensure that no valuable property left Hungary. A team of torturers, including Lajos Tóth, the chief of police; Colonel Sárávari, commander of the gendarmerie; and József Konyuk, head of the local firefighters, beat well-to-do Jews in a building called the "mint," in front of their spouses and children, until they told where their property was hidden. The police registered confiscated money, gold, cameras, and other items. Despite the risks, Rachel realized that people would not easily give up their valuables; much would remain secreted away.[42]

To avoid arrest, the Genuths turned over their brass candlesticks. But Moshe buried his pocket watch and cigarette case. Chaya buried objects from her son Nachman's home. And early one morning Rachel saw her neighbor Rószi and her father digging a hole near their shack. Into this space and their dry well went their family's heirlooms.

Rachel, Elisabeth, Judy, and Faige sat one at a time as their mother styled for them flattering short haircuts. To console Rachel, Blima stored her shiny black braids on the armoire's top shelf for her to one day return and find the souvenir. Blima and Moshe gathered by the door all they had readied for the impending departure: double pillow-cases filled with food, blankets, clothes, pots, and utensils. And their container of goose fat.

Blima and Moshe insisted that the children wear their leather boots for the journey—there might be a lot of walking. Even Elisabeth, who preferred dainty shoes (never mind that they pinched her toes), had to comply.

On May 15, at 5:00 a.m., Hungarian police banged on the door. It was a warm, sunny Monday. It was the darkest of days. Rachel wore two pairs of underwear and three cotton print dresses, one atop the other. Over all was her only coat, an embarrassment on account of its patches. One of its pockets held the black book in which Rachel had listed customers' outstanding payments for poultry orders. She would at the first opportunity collect the more than 1,000 pengős owed.

Though ordered to leave their apartment open, Moshe turned the key in the padlock. He tried to maintain composure, but his eyes welled with tears. Blima cried. Elisabeth cried. She at first refused to carry anything, a sixteen-year-old rebelling against the world. She had no choice—even six-year-old Faige had to carry a bundle. Rachel cried. Twelve-year-old Yitzhak cried the hardest. The boy with auburn hair and freckles begged the janitor to take care of his goat and angora rabbits, each in its own cage in the shack.

Through Rószi Katz's yard, out the back fence, the Genuths went. They huddled closely on increasingly crowded Kigyó utca. By noon hundreds of Jews were sitting on the street, ten in a row, their belongings next to or under them. Rachel realized that the Hungarians knew precisely how many Jews lived in each apartment, for they constantly counted the assembled and ran back and forth from homes to make sure no one was missed. (They had a copy of the list of each street, building, and resident—meticulously prepared by young Jewish men who believed the census would be tied to the allocation of food.) Escape was impossible. People who stayed back for any reason were summarily shot. Rachel understood why they were waiting so long: the numbers were not adding up right. Some of the area's Jews were unwell and in the Talmud Torah, the small synagogue on Timár utca that had been converted into a temporary hospital. Such was the case with Aunt Zseni. Nearly nine months pregnant, she went there with her first baby to await the birth of her second. Rachel's grandmother Chaya then left their ghetto to tend to a sick cousin alone in Sighet's other ghetto. No, the numbers would not tally.[43]

Ten-year-old Judy and six-year-old Faige had been excited about taking a trip, but the charade quickly disintegrated. Having to sit in the street for hours was intolerable for anyone, let alone hungry and thirsty children. Hungarian officials occasionally allowed someone to bring drinks of water or go to an outhouse in one of the yards.

The start of what was to come was going badly. The hot sun turned baby Rószi's little face bright red. She writhed in agony. Blima put wet cloths on her face but could not keep her from crying.

Finally, at 4:00 p.m., everyone rose and started to walk to the Machzikei Torah synagogue. During the half-mile trek, people dropped what was too cumbersome. There went the Genuths' container of goose fat. There went some of their pillowcases filled with toasted bread and bundles of blankets. It was more than enough for Blima to carry Rószi, still crying, and Moshe to carry Faige, who could not walk far. Elisabeth, Rachel, Yitzhak, and Judy each carried what they could.

By the time they arrived, the Machzikei Torah synagogue was filled to the rafters. Forced to continue on, they moved in misery toward *Die Alte Shul*. Though it was almost dark when they reached the beautiful old synagogue, they were counted again. Officials ordered everyone to relinquish any valuables that had not yet been surrendered. The Jews would be leaving the country, but their property should stay in Hungary.

Rachel despaired. Where was *Die Alte Shul's* famous rabbi, who was always surrounded by students and sages and whose wisdom people came from afar to seek? Where were his beautiful wife and his four young children? Rachel had been in their home delivering orders for her grandmother. Now, the adjacent sanctuary did not appear holy at all. Men, women, and children of all ages occupied every inch of space in both the upper balconies and the lower hall. No one was allowed to leave.

The Genuths squeezed into a corner. Rószi was crying now from both hunger and pain. Blima gave her aspirin, but it did not help for long. Everyone took turns trying to soothe her. Moshe broke out some toast and jam. Someone distributed water. Beset by the relentless wailing, Rachel was sure that no one except some of the younger children slept that night.

Finally, dawn. Hungarian officers ordered everyone to gather their belongings and line up. No one could change their clothes, brush their teeth, or wash. Nevertheless, it took a long while to assemble thousands and ensure that nothing of value was about to leave Hungary.

Blima had to surrender her two gold rings. An officer clipped off Rachel's earrings with small red stones; soldered, of one piece, they had been a part of her since she was two weeks old. Each of Rachel's sisters had her earrings taken the same way.

Moshe again carried Faige, and Blima, Rószi. The rest of the Genuth children carried their coats and bundles. They walked in rows of ten as the gendarmes, with rifles at the ready, enforced silence. Moving down the middle of the wide, tree-lined boulevard leading to the train station, Rachel looked wistfully at the modern homes to which she had delivered poultry orders. She could only imagine what would become of Jewish property.[44]

Alongside the train platform, a line of cattle wagons awaited the exhausted throng. Rachel ducked into the station to use the facilities. Splashing water on her face, she experienced a private moment of grief. What a horrible way to leave her home and town, which she had never left before and where she had been born and had lived happily with her family and friends.

May 16, 1944, late afternoon, the Sighet train station. Hungarian gendarmes shoved eighty people into each wagon. They chained and padlocked the doors. The Genuths wedged in among others. Knees pulled to their chests, Elisabeth and Rachel tried to sit near their peers and socialize. Yitzhak drew close to Moshe, who assured his family that things would be okay. Judy and Faige snuggled up against their mother and the baby.[45]

Mortified at the thought of urinating in public—especially in front of Karchi Katz, her friend Szusi's older brother—Rachel held back as

Sighet train station. This photograph, taken in 2019, shows how narrow the train platform is—Hungarian gendarmes pushed and shoved the more than three thousand Jews in each of four transports into awaiting cattle cars. The track closest to the station, used to deport the Jews to Auschwitz, is no longer in use.

long as she could. Finally, Blima held up her coat, behind which Rachel went in one of the wagon's two pails. The second pail held water to be rationed during the trip.

After traveling a whole day, the train stopped at a station. By this point the water was gone, and both pails contained urine and feces. Someone emptied the contents and filled the pails with water. The elderly and the children were the first to drink. Revolted, Rachel swore she would never again drink water.[46]

The train rambled on. It grew longer—once a day it stopped at a station where additional filled cars were attached. The old people moaned. The children cried. Some adults shared food and tried to sing and tell stories. But nothing could distract the forlorn for long. The heat and stench were so oppressive that at one point Moshe lifted Rachel so she could take in a bit of fresh air at the small, barred, high-up window. At that moment, the train passed a meadow where cows grazed freely. Moshe explained to Rachel that there were varieties of cattle; Holsteins were angular, white with large black patches, and could be counted on to produce much milk. Rachel also saw peasants in fields. They stopped what they were doing and stared at the cattle cars carrying people.

The train came to a halt. The station's sign: Kosice. Rachel detected Moshe's grave concern; they were crossing the border into Poland. At the next stop, the wagons' doors did not open. From the sounds of the commotion outside, some realized that the Hungarians were transferring their human cargo to the Germans.

Reminiscing, Moshe and Blima spoke of how, as teenagers during the last war, they lost parents, struggled, and learned they could endure hardship. They laced stories of difficult times with an implicit message: the future is uncertain, but one can withstand adversity. Before the train's final stop, Moshe spoke directly to Rachel. "I have confidence in you," he said. "You are strong and capable. You will be okay."

When their three days of confinement in a stifling box came to an end, there was no time to say more.

The first transport of Hungarian Jews arrived in Auschwitz less than three weeks before D-Day. German army field marshal Rommel, the bold and aggressive World War I hero and expert on infantry attacks, had been determined to drive the enemy invaders into the sea. His goal would not be realized, and not only because he would miscalculate the date and place of the Allied landings.[47]

Beginning on May 15, four trains, consisting of thirty-five to forty freight cars each, transported approximately twelve thousand Jews to Auschwitz daily. Even with problems of conveyance caused by Allied bombings, these same trains could have been used to transport men and supplies to repel the Allied attack, bolstering Germany's defense in western Europe. But the Nazis had their priorities.[48]

When the cattle car's doors opened, Rachel saw impeccably groomed SS officers with guns and German shepherds. They barked orders: "Raus!" "Everyone out!" They then gave instructions and assurances. Rachel clung to her mother but was ordered to go with the young women, so she joined Elisabeth. Blima's last words to her eldest daughters: try to stay together. She then went to the left with Rachel's three little sisters; Moshe and Yitzhak were directed to another line. No goodbyes. No panic.

Rachel found herself in a row of five among hundreds, marching along a paved road. Wires connected closely spaced electrical posts. Though it was dusk, the strange place was so brightly lit there was not a shadow in which one could hide.

After marching a short distance, the group entered a large building. Rachel felt a collective shyness when ordered by male German officers to undress. Some girls cried. They were told to stop or they would be shot. Most tried to hide their private parts with their arms and hands.

The next command: lift your arms as you walk between two women who will shave your armpits—and every other place you have hair. Rachel heard a lot of sniffles. Shorn of their beautiful tresses, all the young women and teenagers looked quite horrible, unrecognizable.

Forced into an adjoining hall, a well-lit room outfitted with showerheads, Rachel sensed intense fear from others around her. No one knew what to expect; some suspected something terrible. When tepid water rained down on them, these women cried with relief. Though there was nothing with which to dry herself, Rachel did not feel cold. Back in the anteroom, she ran for her boots, now her only tangible connection to home. Then she stood in line to receive a uniform—a gray sack dress.

Everyone had the same burning question: When would they be reunited with their loved ones? Someone kind said "tomorrow." A Polish prisoner, an old-timer, said, "See the smoke coming out of those chimneys over there? Smell that stink? There are your loved ones, they are burning this very minute and you will never see them again." Someone else said, "Don't listen to her, she is very mean. They don't burn people. Those are laundry chimneys. You will surely see your family again. They are in a separate camp."

Benumbed, neither Rachel nor most other newcomers registered that they had landed in a death camp. Rachel could not fathom that her mother, Judy, Faige, and Rószi, that her father and Yitzhak, that her grandmother, the most industrious and large-hearted woman of Sighet, who had been caring for another and therefore came to this place with a different transport, were being gassed and cremated or burned alive.

She could not know that she and other females were being kept, provisionally, as depot prisoners (or "transit Jews"), for possible transfer to other camps.[49]

There are men in there, she thought, as they passed by barrack windows. But what the glass reflected was the women's own shaven selves. Inside the wooden structures, triple-tiered cubicles lined opposite walls. Rachel hoisted herself onto a top shelf. Nine others crammed in beside her. The women pressed close to each other because they had to and for softness and warmth—there were no blankets and nothing covered the hard boards beneath them. Their orders: be quiet and go to sleep.

Rachel silently said her prayers and fell into an agitated slumber. A few hours later, shouting: "Raus!" "Out! Five to a row!" This, Rachel learned, was how each day would begin. Before dawn, *kapos* (prisoner functionaries) would wake the roughly thirty-one thousand female prisoners in the women's camp in Birkenau. They would indiscriminately mete out blows while ordering everyone to the vast, dusty parade ground. There the tortured would know further torment. Big greasy ashes floating in the air would land on them as they stood, however wobbly on their feet, and waited. And waited. And waited. Until the SS arrived and counted them all. Until the barracks had been checked and anyone not able to make it to *Zeil Appell* (roll call) had been marked for extermination.[50]

Women at Auschwitz-Birkenau. This photo came from the *Auschwitz Album*, a collection of 193 rare photographs documenting the arrival, selection, and processing of one or more transports of Jews from Subcarpathian Rus (Carpatho-Ukraine), then part of Hungary, in the latter half of May 1944. The photographs were taken by SS-Hauptscharführer Bernhardt Walter, head of the Auschwitz photographic laboratory known as the Erkennungsdienst (Identification Service), and his assistant, SS-Unterscharführer Ernst Hofmann. Rachel was not among these women but went through similar processing, including having her head shaven. These "selected" women were temporarily spared. *Yad Vashem (public domain). Source Record ID: FA 268/168.*

Famished, enervated, some fainted. This was how Rachel—who for three days could not find Elisabeth—eventually located her sister.

The SS and *kapos* were at a distance when she heard a muffled cry, "Berszi [Elisabeth] fainted!" Looking in the direction of the voice, Rachel saw, several columns to the left, two women on either side of Elisabeth propping her up.

After reuniting, Rachel and Elisabeth tried to stay together. During the *Appell* they would stand in a row with either three sisters or a mother and her two daughters, all from Sighet. Their compatriots helped Rachel persuade Elisabeth to eat. At home, Elisabeth would not touch her soup after her brother dipped his spoon in it. Here, five people sipped dirty liquid from one chamber-pot-sized bowl. At home, Elisabeth loved to bring food to those less fortunate. In this place, if you did not consume your disgusting ration—cooked grass or black bread with a spread of tiny, moving worms or snails—you could not survive. When coaxed, Elisabeth at first protested, saying she did not care to live. You must eat, the women told her, for Rachel's sake.

After the *Appell*, the women could go to the latrines, where groups of fifty would relieve themselves over rows of holes in a long wooden box. Opposite the box, faucets dispensed water into gutters. The overpowering smell of chlorine reinforced Rachel's decision in the cattle car—she would never again drink water.

During the hours in which women languished outside the barracks—starving, filthy, longing for their suffering to end—Rachel wandered. At this place that held Jews from all over Nazi-occupied Europe, where inmates asked new arrivals where they were from and whether they knew a particular relative or friend, she and Elisabeth met their mother's stepsister. Their grandmother's second husband, a widower, had had two daughters. Here, outside a barracks in Birkenau, was the artistic one, who had moved to Paris. She asked about Blima, Chaya, and her sister who lived in Sighet, who had two little girls with whom Rachel had played.

On another day, Rachel came to an area of the camp in which she saw children who seemed to be well cared for. Through the barbed-wire fence, she spotted Suri, her school friend, with her older sister. They had told the SS they were twelve-year-old twins, and they were now subjects of Dr. Josef Mengele's experiments. They begged Rachel not to give them away.[51]

SUMMER 1944

June, July, August

It was too late—for Rachel's family, for nearly all the Jews from the Hungarian provinces. Rudolf Vrba and Alfred Wetzler, Slovakian inmates who had managed in April to escape from Auschwitz—an extraordinary feat—had tried, through various channels and a detailed report, to warn Allied powers and Jewish leaders of the impending massacre. But the account of two who had worked for so long in the camp, who had seen and heard and kept track of so much, would have to be believed, translated, and transmitted in record time. The escapees' efforts and those of others who wanted to stop the deportations were no match for the speedy and ferocious German killing machine. Vrba sank into a depression. By the time word reached top British and American officials, the action was underway.[1]

While the SS terrorized the thousands of daily arrivals in Birkenau, while gaunt prisoners whispered directives to those who might say or do something to try to save themselves, and while the *Sonderkommando* stoked the ovens with masses of individuals gassed to death, Allied soldiers anticipated the unknown—how would the "beginning of the end" unfold?[2]

On Sunday, June 4, at a church parade at Worth Priory, 8 Corps commander Richard O'Connor spoke of the coming hardships and difficulties of battle, stressing that a headquarters exists as the servant of the fighting troops. The afternoon saw sports events and a fete, including wives and friends. To cap off the day was a dinner at which Glyn Hughes received a message he could not share, especially as there were guests at his table: D-Day was being postponed twenty-four hours.[3]

On June 5, the DDMS entered "Should be D-Day" in his diary. Like many others of 8 Corps, he may have driven down to the coast to see for himself the high winds and choppy seas that delayed the start of the cross-Channel invasion. When Eisenhower decided—despite the blustery forecast and against the wisdom of the leaders of the navy and air force—to sail on June 6, Hughes thought the supreme commander, "for a time, saved the world." Had they not crossed then, they would have had to wait two or three weeks, and the Germans might have learned of their plans and mobilized accordingly. As it was, the bad weather helped the situation; the Germans did not think the Allies would "brave it."[4]

Hughes spent part of D-Day listening to wireless bulletins and discussing reports on how operations appeared to be going. It was hard to get an accurate picture. More than a hundred and fifty-five thousand Allied soldiers belonging to eight divisions and three armored brigades faced grave obstacles as they landed along an eighty-kilometer (fifty-mile) stretch of the Normandy coast. The DDMS held a conference of medical personnel, including assistant directors of medical services and commanding officers of casualty clearing stations. He described the Second Army's plan and possible roles of 8 Corps, and he issued "Medical Operation Instructions No. 1." Filled with anticipation—he could not sleep—he jotted on slips of paper lists of essentials, such as medical equipment, transport orders, ablutions, and cookhouses.[5]

On June 7, Hughes moved with the first of three 8 Corps convoys to the designated marshaling area. He learned that *boche* (German soldiers) resistance was stiffening, particularly around the port city of Caen, the Allies' first, ambitious objective. He drafted a field service postcard, instructing soldiers to "cross out what does not apply and not to write anything more." Options on the cryptic-by-design card:

I am quite well.
I have been admitted into hospital
   sick

wounded
    and am going on well and hope to be out again soon
I am being sent down to the base
I have received your
    letter(s) dated _____.
    telegram dated _____.
    parcel dated _____.
I will send you a letter as soon as possible.
I have received no letter from you
    lately
    for a long time.

SIGNATURE ONLY
Date _____ [6]

For the next several days, Hughes entered both encouraging and worrisome news in his diary. On June 11, loading day, he beheld more craft than he had ever seen off the coast. That no thought had been given to an actual boarding place seemed to him incredible.[7]

A chronicler of matters large and small, the DDMS would go on to record impressions (for example, the six-mile Mulberry harbor off France's Arromanches beach was "an amazing sight"), frustrations (waiting all day for a conference that never materialized), and escapades (patrols hearing "sounds of feminine laughter" at night). He described his visits to medical facilities (like an impressive, well-stocked field dressing station), as well as horrors of war (Canadian soldiers, shot by the SS, tied together, holding photos of their families in their clasped hands).[8]

✳ ✳ ✳

By the time General Richard O'Connor led 8 Corps overseas on D+6 (six days after D-Day), the Allies had gained a foothold in all five landing zones, securing a lodgment on the coast of western Europe. They had begun to build up vast amounts of supplies. But they had failed to take Caen. For this, Britain's tired 1 and 30 Corps, having carried out the original D-Day assault and having seen ever fiercer fighting since, awaited 8 Corps, the "battering ram needed for a breakthrough."[9]

On the foggy night 8 Corps Headquarters sailed, a Liberty ship came straight toward the middle of its landing craft tank (LCT); Hughes breathed a sigh of relief when the helmsmen turned their respective vessels in the right directions in the nick of time. The LCT finally landed at 11:00 p.m. at the mouth of the Orne River, at a small seaside resort. Hughes and the other officers moved along the road bordering the Caen Canal and, after a night out in the open, found lodging six miles northwest of Caen, at Château de Lantheuil. The owner, a French count and former naval officer under the Vichy regime, gave them a cool reception (the Royal Navy had sunk part of his fleet). Hughes thought the count "neutral" and went with him on a tour of his garden. He noted a similar reserve among the local populace, who gave few "spontaneous smiles."[10]

The next day, Hughes commandeered a six-hundred-bed hospital in relatively untouched Bayeux, the medieval city five miles inland from Gold Beach—the southernmost of the three beaches at which the British landed on D-Day. Its proximity to Mulberry B, the artificial harbor used to offload men and supplies from cargo ships, made it a logical choice. Six days later he took three other hospitals in the area.[11]

Hughes facilitated the organization of medical tasks: collection (at the divisional level), treatment (on a large scale, in the corps area), and evacuation (in the army area). In the forward areas, each of the Second Army's four corps would be assigned field transfusion teams and one or two CCSs to handle surgical treatment. Five surgeons, each of whom could handle fourteen cases in twenty-four hours, working eight-hour shifts and taking one hour and forty-two minutes per case including the induction of anesthesia, were to staff each CCS. One or two smaller units would filter and remove from the CCSs the walking wounded, the sick, and other minor cases.[12]

Hughes worked closely with the Royal Air Force (RAF) and the Royal Navy in planning the evacuation of casualties to England. He oversaw transport to area hospitals and sited the locations of medical installations, which at times had to be dismantled and moved. Other of the DDMS's concerns included obtaining adequate reserves of trained personnel of all ranks and massive supplies of blood, plasma, and penicillin. Like Second Army commander Miles Dempsey, Hughes got to the point quickly and paid meticulous attention to the smallest detail.[13]

There was great store in capturing Caen. Less than eighty kilometers (50 miles) from the Seine and two hundred kilometers (124 miles) from Paris, it would serve as a gateway to the open and rolling countryside and as a pivot for future operations. When told on June 10 that 8 Corps "may be wanted to take it," Richard O'Connor ordered senior officers to study approaches to the city. He planned for 8 Corps to advance on a six-kilometer (3.7-mile) front, force crossings of the Odon and Orne Rivers, then establish itself on high ground northeast of Bretteville-sur-Laize.[14]

On June 19, at a conference at the *mairie* (town hall) in Creully, a village near Lantheuil, between Caen and Bayeux, General Dempsey revealed the new phase of operations. Now that the Allied foothold with twenty divisions and more than a half million men in Normandy was firm, the German High Command would assess the threat to "Fortress Europe" and try to reduce the Allied bridgehead (the secured position from which they would advance) by means of counterattacks. Reports indicated that two SS Panzer Corps that had successfully halted the Russians in Poland were on their way to France. The Allies had to come up with "some quick stroke . . . to retain freedom of action." First, the British would attract as much German strength as possible to the Caen area so the Americans could more easily break through and sweep around to the Seine and Paris. Dempsey announced that, on instructions from Montgomery, 8 Corps would carry out a major attack "with its fresh, if untried troops"—Operation Epsom was scheduled, provisionally, for June 23.[15]

Infuriated that the army committed just-landed troops to battle, Hughes argued that the "show should not be mounted for 48 hours after the arrival of the last combatant unit." How could 8 Corps achieve success without at least twenty-four hours of reconnaissance and practice in back areas? How could units mount an attack before having had a complete day of rest?[16]

The plan was postponed. For one, the worst June storm in forty years delayed the arrival and disembarkation of tens of thousands more men and urgently needed supplies. By the time Epsom launched, on June 26, US forces, after a shaky start on Omaha Beach (where twenty-five hundred of six thousand invading troops were killed), had linked up with the British Second Army (which, together with the Canadians, saw three thousand casualties on D-Day and during the first two weeks after). And the enemy had prepared, with great ingenuity, for 8 Corps' impending assault.[17]

✳ ✳ ✳

One day after the Allies landed in Normandy, Gerd von Rundstedt, commander in chief of the German army in the west, wrote off the Bay of Biscay and southern France as possible invasion points. He now knew Germany needed to move as much manpower and armor as possible to the Channel coast.[18]

By mid-June, Hitler realized that the campaign in the west would determine the war's outcome. He moved from his headquarters at Rastenburg in East Prussia—where he focused on the eastern front—to Soissons, France, where he met with von Rundstedt and Field Marshal Rommel. They told him that, despite huge losses on the beaches, the Allies had strengthened their bridgeheads and poured in more troops and supplies. Rejecting their advice to withdraw his armies beyond the River Seine, Hitler ordered that Normandy be held at all costs.[19]

But there was a cost he was unwilling to pay.

Instead of preparing to aid forces repulsing the enemy invasion, the SS was busy moving Jews. By June 7, one day after the Allied invasion, 289,357 Jews from Ruthenia and Transylvania—including Sighet, Rachel's hometown—had arrived in Auschwitz. The first phase of the Hungarian deportation plan had been completed in twenty-three days. Then, between June 7 and 16, 23 trains brought approximately 50,805 Jews from northern Hungary to Auschwitz, bringing the total to 340,162 deportees since May 15. The 168 trains used for this massive undertaking could have transported at least seven infantry or Panzer divisions—almost a full army of at least one hundred and nine thousand combat soldiers—as well as tanks, fuel, and ammunition—to Normandy.[20]

By June, the industrialized genocide at Auschwitz-Birkenau rivaled that of Operation Reinhard, during which with great speed (and highly coordinated deportation train schedules) three death camps in Poland—Belzec, Treblinka, and Sobibor—collectively murdered more than 1.7 million people in 1942 and 1943. (In August, September, and October 1942, 15,000 were murdered each day in these camps.) Even with its new incinerator ovens and five enormous, recently built trenches for burning the overflow of corpses, the remains of tens of thousands of recent Auschwitz arrivals lay decomposing in crude pits.[21]

In the shadows of this obscenity, fourteen-year-old Rachel took chances. Calculated risks.

One morning, after *Zeil Appell*, a *kapo* asked for volunteers, workers who at the day's end would receive a piece of bread. Believing any activity preferable to hanging around the barracks feeling the intense emptiness in her stomach, Rachel stepped forward. Elisabeth followed her lead.

The sisters became part of 103 Kommando, assigned to road construction. Wearing dog tags with numbers on them, the slaves walked from Camp B to another camp where they cleared ground, loaded lorries, split rocks, and set small stones. Guards (some of whom were political prisoners) beat those who did not work fast enough. Every day, at least thirty of the five hundred *Kommando* laborers got sick or died. Every day, the SS selected replacements to build their city on the fields of Birkenau.[22]

After retrieving rocks from heaps, Rachel and Elisabeth sat on their knees, chopping the edges of one stone with another, forming three-inch squares that fit into a semicircular section of a wide, sandy road. The hot sun beat down on their bare heads, exacerbating their misery.

At a certain hour of the day, Rachel observed women wearing red or white headscarves walking down the nearby main road, returning from shifts in which they sorted clothes, food, and other items that arrived with the transports. She kept her eye on the *kapo*. When her tormentor turned away, Rachel dashed toward the privileged workers. Sidling alongside one of them, she asked whether the woman had anything to spare. It did not happen often, but occasionally a kerchief-wearer surreptitiously passed her a treasure. A sugar cube. A few grains of salt. In one instance, a needle (which could be traded for a piece of bread).

A *kapo* caught Rachel's friend Jolan Szabo trying to pull off the same daring act. She beat her so hard and for so long that she was unable to stand. Then, while Jolan lay bloodied on the ground, the *kapo* trampled her face.[23]

Struggling to survive another day, Rachel had little awareness of what was taking place outside the confines of the barracks area, the dusty *Zeil Appell* grounds, and a punishing Birkenau work site, let alone elsewhere on the continent. But events in Normandy would bear on her fate.

The heaviest fighting of the entire campaign in the west began on June 26, a grim, overcast Monday on which roughly sixty thousand men from 8 Corps—mainly from 15 Scottish Division, 11 Armoured Division, and 43 Wessex Division—attacked to the west of Caen. Their aim was to establish a bridgehead south of the River Odon, advance to the

River Orne, then occupy the deep salient southwest of the city, thereby threatening Germany's position in Normandy.[24]

A great disappointment: steady weather deterioration in England meant they would not have the full promised Royal Air Force support.[25]

A grim realization: Panzer units had for three weeks built up deadly defenses in the French bocage. This land of broken contours, with thick rows of high hedges and tree-lined pastures, protected German soldiers, who planted mines, wires, and booby traps in fields and groves.[26]

Though well trained and eager, the men of 8 Corps had no prior battle experience. Now they were up against Germany's most brutal and tenacious troops. The most celebrated of Waffen-SS divisions in Normandy—12 SS Panzer (Hitlerjugend [Hitler Youth]) Division and 21 Panzer Division—displayed a "moral will to fight"; they would go to the limits of endurance for the *Volk*, Führer, and Fatherland. Commanded by Sepp Dietrich, a personal friend of the Führer's—who in peacetime had created and commanded the Leibstandarte Adolf Hitler (Hitler's home guard regiment)—the seventeen- to nineteen-year-old recruits, chosen based on rigid physical and racial criteria, "fought brilliantly," usually in a spearhead role.[27]

Most of the fighting (against 15 Scottish Division) took place at close range, with the Nazi soldier sitting in thick cover in his "slit trench" until the advance flowed past and he could shoot ready targets, then quickly change position. He would employ this strategy of "inverted infiltration" unless, of course, he was attacked, knocked out, or overrun.[28]

To British soldiers, "the Germans seemed everywhere." Dug-in and camouflaged snipers sprang up and shot them from the rear with machine-gun fire. Wooded areas concealed small parties of enemy infantry, supported by often dug-in tanks and anti-tank guns. During the rapid advance of 15 Division Scots, when a man was shot down in the pale green wheat, his comrades marked his position by ramming his rifle—with fixed bayonet—upright into the ground, topped by his helmet. Such markers showed medical orderlies where to find the fallen.[29]

Care began as quickly as possible. Stretcher-bearers carried capsules of morphine resembling small toothpaste tubes. They would insert a needle on one end, find a vein, push the needle in and squeeze out one milligram per dose. With a pencil or with the man's blood, they would mark on his forehead the number of doses given—one or two. They then took the wounded soldier to the regimental aid post, the stop before one of the bridgehead's CCSs.[30]

Though the Germans did not have nearly as strong an artillery arm as did the British, they made effective use of their most sinister weapon—the dreaded Nebelwerfer. This multibarreled, simply constructed, mass-produced mortar was accurate up to about six thousand yards. It took a heavy toll on 8 Corps (and would cause more casualties to the Allies than any other weapon in the western campaign). It had a loud, screeching whistle. A Scottish Division "Highlander" described the effects of "Moaning Minnies":

> The fury of artillery is a cold, mechanical fury . . . but its intent is personal. When you are under its fire you are the sole target. All of that shrieking, whining venom is directed at you . . . You hunch in your hole in the ground, reduce yourself into as small a thing as you can become, and you harden your muscles in a pitiful attempt at defying the jagged, burning teeth of the shrapnel. Involuntarily you curl up into the foetal position except that your hands go down to protect your genitalia. This instinct to defend the place of generation against the forces of annihilation was universal.[31]

Troops discharged a litany of swearing. One smart, warlike soldier, curled up in shock on the floor of a farmhouse cellar, howled, made bleating noises, and cried for his mother.[32]

If not hit by a Nebelwerfer, one could fall into a Panzer trap. Pressing on with the Worcester Regiment as it moved into the village of Cheux, a young stretcher-bearer saw a large truck in a farmyard; in its high cab, over its steering wheel, was a 15 Scottish Division driver, his head sheared off (presumably by a high strung hidden wire).[33]

Hughes had disdained the *boche* since World War I; he now could not help but also admire the ardent soldiers his corps faced. They seemed resistant to the most pervasive and vexing of medical problems confronting the British Second Army—"exhaustion," the insidious World War II version of shell shock. In June and July, months that saw the large-scale offensives aimed at liberating Caen, nearly a quarter of casualties fell into this category. Even the most disciplined formations suffered from it. Hard fighting, fear of tripping into mines and booby traps, and Moaning Minnies frayed nerves.[34]

Why, Hughes wondered, was there practically no exhaustion in the German army? He theorized that Nazi troops were psychologically prepared for war; they knew that desertion was punishable by death. This was no longer the case in the British army. (During World War I "absence without leave" warranted the death penalty.) He had other explanations for why so many exhibited this malady: During World War I, in which there were far greater dangers and casualties than currently seen, serving in propinquity with comrades in trenches and in the advance bestowed confidence and increased morale. Fighting in the open in separately defended areas conduced terror. A corps psychiatrist and commander of a light field ambulance confirmed that the main victims of exhaustion were in infantry units. Tank crews, protected by armored vehicles and part of close-knit groups, were far less likely to "collapse." Exhaustion was attributed as well to the fact that troops were "bogged down" in the beachhead and bridgehead. Static battles of attrition caused a higher rate of breakdown than mobile fighting.[35]

And yet another cause of exhaustion, explained by a soldier: "Ignorance—stupefying, brutalizing ignorance. You never knew where you were, where the enemy was, or what you were supposed to achieve."[36]

✾ ✾ ✾

Observations and interrogations of captured German doctors and soldiers proved to Hughes that exhaustion—despite the intensity of British shelling and aerial attacks—was practically unknown in Panzer, SS, and Wehrmacht troops. Both British and American psychiatrists were likewise struck by the apparently few cases of "psychoneurosis" among German prisoners of war. Did German military authorities refuse to acknowledge the existence of the condition? Did eleven years of Nazi propaganda ready soldiers for battle?[37]

Panzer troops were fed lies. Captured German prisoners said they received a "pep talk" before going into action—they were assured there would be a victorious end to the war as their V-1 bombs had destroyed London and killed twelve million English. SS Engineer Battalion specialists had been warned that the British always shot their prisoners. They fought desperately to avoid capture. When their wounded met British medical personnel, they acted as would trapped, injured wild beasts, "backing to the limits of [their] cage, snarling at all comers." As for soldiers traumatized by the Allied assault, German psychiatrists told them they were suffering from physical rather than mental complaints. Treatment often included electroshock therapy.[38]

Knowing the reasons for British soldiers' exhaustion did not stop Hughes from believing that the situation could be otherwise. He had witnessed dangers and casualties in World War I that were far greater than even the frightful battles in which the Allies were now engaged. In the first three days of the Battle of the Somme, losses amounted to 54,334 out of 420,000 men, at Loos 37,802 out of 260,000. And yet, in the three years he served as a regimental medical officer (RMO), fewer than nine men in his battalion suffered shell shock. What a contrast to what was happening now, where one division of fifteen thousand men lost one hundred to exhaustion in one day.[39]

✾ ✾ ✾

Thirty years earlier, while a medical student at University College Hospital—where he was a "glutton for work" on the rugby field, where athletes developed an attitude and approach to the game that they would display on the battlefield—Hughes underwent rigorous training to become an RMO. Shortly after his twenty-third birthday, on August 6, 1915, he was posted to 1 Battalion Wiltshire Regiment, 7 Infantry Brigade, Headquarters 25 Division; appointed ("gazetted") a temporary lieutenant RAMC (Royal Army Medical Corps), Hughes's duty was to provide primary health care for troops and to comfort the sick and wounded.[40]

It would not be long before the young doctor ventured beyond usual RMO duties, such as checking the condition of billets (soldiers' quarters), inoculating men against typhoid, and instituting rigorous measures to prevent "trench fever" (a serious general infection caused by lice) and "trench foot" (caused by standing for long periods in cold and wet mud).[41]

Like all RMOs, Hughes had a choice: he could stick to his aid post or frequent the firing trenches. The stationary doctor might be perceived as detached, while occasional visits to the trenches reminded soldiers that medical care was near and readily available. If not too close to the thick of the fighting, some RMOs would go out and treat badly injured soldiers. However, to run into battle and recklessly risk one's own life to attend to a single casualty was an act of "mistaken gallantry"—the army needed medical officers to remain unharmed to continue to serve their regiments.[42]

Hughes began his habit of going to the trenches during his first winter of service, in Ploegsteert Wood (in the Ypres salient). A comrade recalled how he calmed soldiers' nerves in the moments before battle. As he moved among them, word passed around: "The Doc's here—we'll be alright now boys." He would then go "over the top" with the men (he knew all six hundred by name) during an attack, attending to them as they were wounded. Lieutenant Colonel Hayward later said, "It's

August 1916, 1 Wiltshire Regiment after battle near the village of Thiepval, on the Somme. Glyn Hughes, RMO (BOTTOM ROW, FIFTH FROM THE RIGHT). *The Museum of Military Medicine.*

impossible to think of France in World War I without remembering Glyn Hughes . . . By rights he should have been back in the regimental aid post waiting for casualties to be brought back. But not him."[43]

The doctor's presence on the front line not only reassured jittery fighters but also, in the words of another enthusiastic RMO, had a "tremendous moral effect upon the men during a push." One month before he was shot and killed in the line of duty, that RMO justified his stance: "I make a point of entirely disregarding fire when it comes to . . . seeing to a wounded man . . . After all, I always think if one is killed doing one's duty, one can't help it and it is the best way of coming to an end."[44]

Hughes similarly acted without hesitation or thought of himself. (Had not his doctor father died in the line of duty?) Once, while amputating a German sergeant's foot, a shell came over, killed his patient, and missed him. (After this and other near misses, he thought he had a charmed life.)[45]

Hughes would serve as RMO to 1 Wiltshires for more than double the time most medical officers served. If not for a debilitating wound, he would have continued on in that gratifying role—one that enabled him not only to provide care but also to inspire courage in men who faced death.[46]

Given his proud past, it was no wonder that Hughes considered the role of RMO the "most stimulating and least impersonal" of staff opportunities. In trainings before D-Day, he urged RMOs to get to know their men individually and collectively; to have talks with them during quiet times, making known that plans are in place for various eventualities; and to instruct them in first aid, increasing their self-reliance. It was the RMO's responsibility to take precautionary measures against malaria, frostbite, and other serious conditions. And to weed out men who might not stand up to—or who might undergo personality changes under—the strain of war.[47]

It was the RMO who could, by controlling infectious panic, ameliorate the rate of exhaustion. To illustrate the importance of checking contagion, Hughes told a group of RMOs a story:

A very beloved Company Commander in the Coldstreams was blown to bits in front of his own men, and a Corporal and 12 men were so shattered that they went off on their own to the Field Ambulance supporting their Brigade. There was a very wise M.O. in charge and he simply found them accommodation and sedated them. They stayed some time and then the Corporal realizing the enormity of their action, without a word to anyone marched the whole lot back to his unit.[48]

Tough and ruthless, gentle and kind, Hughes moderated tensions in his personality to effectively address the troubling post-invasion medical issue. He hired "commonsense" psychiatrists at the army and corps level who had served as RMOs in the most forward medical units— they would understand the psychological effects of Panzer weaponry and tactics. He arranged for divisional medical officers to take short courses in psychiatry. He ordered combat officers, stationed at forward

medical units, to screen each soldier who claimed "exhaustion"—had he
been granted leave from his unit officer? Careful supervision and assessment of those likely to recover quickly would determine who should be
kept in the division area and soon be returned to service.[49]

The DDMS also encouraged a new scheme allowing deserters to
make amends. After receiving a long sentence (of at least eighteen
months), each case would be reviewed after three months by a small
board that included an army psychiatrist. Every man who returned to
full duty had a chance of rehabilitation. Nothing made Hughes happier
than when he learned of returned cases who did so well in battle they
earned medals.[50]

In a document on protocols for medical officers, Hughes outlined the
functions of field ambulances, principles of major river crossings, and
the relationship between medical problems and tactical developments
(for example, difficult ground for troops makes for even more difficult terrain for evacuating casualties). Beyond practicalities, he stressed
the importance of morale. Quoting Napoleon, who said that physical
force is but one-quarter of waging a war, the remaining three-quarters
a matter of morale, he highlighted the influence of medical services—a
man's sense of competence, power, and worth is tied to his physical and
mental health.[51]

Soon he would see cracks in German soldiers' morale.

On June 29, the third and last day of Operation Epsom, Hitler
insisted—despite General Paul Hausser's plea to wait two days—that
22 Panzer Corps attack 8 Corps. The result: "murderous fire" from
British artillery and naval guns in the Channel destroyed the bulk of
the German attacking force right in its assembly area. And now that the
weather had turned favorable, the RAF began to realize the commander
in chief's plan to "win the air battle first." The Allies' "enormous material superiority," evident in their "twin weapons of air and artillery,"

made it seem, to Baron Heinrich Freiherr von Luttwitz, commander of 2 Panzer Division, as though they were "waging war regardless of expense." Dejected soldiers kept asking, "Where is the Luftwaffe?"[52]

Captured Germans told of their disadvantaged position from the start. Units had hastily been moved—by rail and by lorry, around bridges destroyed by the RAF—to the Normandy front, where they were haphazardly flung into battle in a frantic attempt to halt 8 Corps' advance. They found themselves "caught in the . . . barrage . . . surrounded by tanks of furious Scotsmen throwing grenades."[53]

By the end of Epsom, German losses were significantly greater than those suffered by 8 Corps. And, whereas the British Second Army replenished its armor, supplies, and men of all ranks, Panzer divisions entered the campaign below strength and were unable to make up deficits. Hughes and other 8 Corps leaders were satisfied—their troops had withstood strong opposition, widened and consolidated their bridgehead, and advanced more than six miles through the most difficult country and finally over a considerable water obstacle. The men's rigorous training in England "paid a handsome dividend in action." German leaders were worried. *Feldgendarmerie* (military police) detachments tried to deter desertion. They seized stragglers at bridges and hanged them from nearby trees, as a warning to anyone contemplating the deed.[54]

On July 1, Field Marshal Wilhelm Keitel, chief of Hitler's combined staff, called Field Marshal von Rundstedt. Their precious Panzer divisions were doomed to a costly battle of attrition. "What shall we do? What shall we do?" Impassive, von Rundstedt replied, "What shall you do? Make peace, you idiots, what else can you do?" Twenty-four hours later, on an order from Berlin, Field Marshal Günther von Kluge, "the apostle of victorious defence" replaced von Rundstedt as supreme commander in the west.[55]

By this point, the situation for the Germans had gotten out of control. No longer could they hope to drive the Allies back into the sea. They instead thought only of containing them and stopping any further advance. Resorting to "fire brigade tactics," they plugged gaps created by Allied thrusts by rushing mobile divisions to wherever the situation seemed most threatening. In early July, they dug large numbers of weapon pits along 8 Corps' entire front.[56]

On the evening of July 7, Hughes and his entire 8 Corps "had a grandstand view" of the first heavy bombing of the campaign (Operation Charnwood) in immediate support of a major land assault. Two waves of heavy bombers—more than four hundred fifty aircraft—blasted the northern defenses of Caen. The whole horizon lit up simultaneously—a "vision out of Dante" that could be seen from six to seven miles away. Early the next morning, the main infantry assault began. After twenty-four hours of bitter fighting, 1 Corps took Caen. Though more than three-quarters of its population left and most who remained stayed in deep cellars, several hundred died and thousands were wounded. The basilica and other valuable buildings were destroyed; heaps of rubble littered the streets. And yet most of the German positions around the northern fringe of Caen were still standing.[57]

Among hundreds of terrible injuries seen at CCSs that day were legs without feet, knees without kneecaps, shoulders without arms. With half his head blown away, one sergeant major was still conscious. The medical officer said, "Give him two grains of morphia; it'll finish him quickly." But it didn't.[58]

In field dressing stations those doomed to die were taken to a designated tent and injected with morphine. Medical staff worried about the shortage of blood for transfusions. And they were horrified by the ignorance of soldiers who moved those with severe fractures rather than wait for stretcher-bearers to splint them up.[59]

From July 10 through 12, 8 Corps engaged in Operation Jupiter, in which 43 Wessex Division tried to seize Hill 112, the strategic rise that overlooked the River Orne from the east, and Maltot, a village southwest of Caen between the Rivers Odon and Orne. The "bloody merry-go-round" that was the struggle for the hill (the British pulled out before they should have; the Germans reoccupied the knoll) produced hundreds of exhaustion cases among the thousands who suffered the effects of German "flaks" (antiaircraft and anti-tank artillery guns) and mortars. The main objectives were still not won when, finally, 8 Corps passed into reserve.[60]

On July 15, Field Marshal Rommel wrote to his superiors in the High Command, who had no conception of the crisis facing German divisions in Normandy. (They had by this point lost ninety-seven thousand men and gotten only ten thousand reinforcements; in contrast, 8 Corps' strength—despite its losses in killed, wounded, and missing— had risen to more than one hundred thousand men.) His hopeless message: "We must reckon with the fact that the enemy, within a measurable time, will succeed in breaking through our thinly-held front . . . and in thrusting deep into France . . . The [German] Army is fighting heroically everywhere but the unequal combat is nearing its end." But only upon inspecting the battlefront would Field Marshal von Kluge, the new chief, realize the seriousness of the situation.[61]

According to British field marshal Montgomery's plan, Second Army divisions were to break through enemy defenses and secure ground from which their forces could strike south and southeast; American forces would thrust eastward to meet them. The men would now be fighting on terrain resembling the rolling hills of the Yorkshire Wolds, where they had trained. But here, too, there would be places from which the Germans could stealthily attack—large fields of ripening corn, Norman stone farmhouses surrounded by orchards, and, finally, the Bourguebus Ridge and the high ground to its south, the objective critical to the Second Army's advance toward Falaise and the central Normandy plain.[62]

Spearheaded by 8 Corps, the next large-scale Second Army offensive, Operation Goodwood, began with a massive air attack the morning of July 18. Over two and a half hours, the RAF and US Air Force dropped 7,567 tons of bombs on a frontage of seven thousand yards—the largest-ever concentration of air power in support of a ground operation. Royal Navy warships also contributed to the bombardment. Heavy tanks flipped over, landing in deep craters. Endless, deafening explosions stunned German soldiers. Unable to bear the sounds, shock waves, and ground vibrations, some shot themselves. Older soldiers prayed for the war to end.[63]

With the target areas obscured by dust and smoke, the British could not see that their bombing was far from accurate. The rear of the Bourguebus Ridge had hardly been touched. They were unaware that the commander in chief of Panzer Group West, General Heinrich Eberbach, had formed massive belts of defenses six miles deep, stretching southward and extending over the whole front, including Nebelwerfer positions and a large battery of 88-millimeter flaks.[64]

At first, as Britain's 11 Armoured Brigade led the way down a narrow corridor, the Germans were outnumbered in tanks and infantry. Then, as the brigade crossed a second railway embankment and navigated the ridge, enemy fire came from hedges, farmhouses, wherever Panzer troops could conceal themselves and their weapons. Flaks' shells annihilated 2 Fife and Forfar Yeomanry within minutes. Into the next day, Germany's accurate, long-range weapons effortlessly knocked out British tanks that charged at them like cavalry. Burning crewmen emerged from burning tanks; rolling in agony on the ground, they tried to put out the flames.[65]

One major described the tragic "death ride of the armoured divisions" (four hundred tanks were destroyed) as "monstrous"—a division that had trained rigorously for three years lost two-thirds of its tanks in its second battle. Beyond the devastation wrought in one fell swoop, 8 Corps' troops came up against random attacks in villages around Caen.

In countless "eliminating actions" they fought hand-to-hand, house-by-house, both along the line of advance and in rearward areas.[66]

A few more hamlets were taken, but on July 19 most of the Bourguebus Ridge was still in German hands. The next day, on account of oppressive heat followed by an "almighty downpour"—dust turned to sludge, slit trenches filled with water, tanks sank eighteen inches deep in mud—the operation was called off.[67]

Goodwood's accomplishment: over two days of fierce fighting, the British advanced over seven miles to the south, on a front six miles wide.[68]

Field Marshal von Kluge's post-battle letter to Hitler made another Allied triumph evident: "In the face of the enemy's complete command of the air, there is no way by which we can find a strategy which will counter-balance its actually annihilating effect . . .Whole armoured formations allotted to the counter-attack were caught in bomb-carpets of the greatest intensity, so that they could be got out of the torn-up ground only by prolonged effort . . . The power of endurance of the forces is put to the highest test. In fact it becomes dormant and dies."[69]

Hughes had long insisted on timely and full communication between the army and its medical services. Goodwood affirmed the importance of this practice. Because of the concentration of British forces in the congested bridgehead east of the Orne, the RAMC had only a narrow area in which to operate. Evacuations had to take place against a heavy stream of fighting troops and across two waterways—the River Orne and the Caen Canal. Nothing could impede the forward movement of British forces, so no ambulance could pass back over the bridges unless special permission was granted. The only alternative was to strengthen one of the footbridges so casualties could be carried across it before being transferred to ambulance cars that would drive them to the hospital area surrounding Bayeux. This was achieved, albeit with difficulty.[70]

Quiet moaning permeated the CCS reception area, where casualties were sorted into groups needing either a surgeon or a physician. All types were seen. Exploding German mines mangled limbs. Often, a bullet or shrapnel took part of a face. In these cases, because most of the nerve centers were injured or blown away, the victim was numb. Medics made sure patients were not bleeding profusely and did not lose more tissue, which would be needed later for reconstruction. The tongue was a problem; it had to be sutured to the face bar of specially made headsets to prevent it from dropping down into the throat on the way to the hospital or beachhead. Perforated abdominal wounds were the worst. With severe attendant injuries caused by splintering metal-covered wood bullets, they had to be cleaned and bandaged carefully for the patient to be evacuated. Otherwise, Hughes cautioned against trans-ferring patients with such injuries from one ward to another. "It is amaz-ing the fatal results of moving those recently operated a few yards."[71]

Then there was the matter of disease. Owing to the large number of flies swarming over the battlefield, medical staff saw a high incidence of dysentery and diarrhea. And, in addition to typhoid fever, they treated malaria—not only in the two thousand admissions from formations that came to Normandy from North Africa but also in thirty men who con-tracted the illness in the marshy area around Caen. Enteritis was another common problem. Finally, medical issues attended particular lines of work. For example, crews standing in confined and overheated tanks developed painful swelling and small hemorrhages in their ankles.[72]

Captured German soldiers also occupied beds in the hospitals Hughes appropriated. Though their response to treatment varied, most badly wounded Hitlerjugend behaved similarly. A British nurse de-scribed how one boy of about sixteen tore off the bandage with which she had dressed his serious wound, shouting that he wanted to die for the Führer. Another flung food in her face. She quelled yet another teenage warrior's agitation by threatening to arrange for him a transfu-sion of Jewish blood.[73]

In the main hospital in Bayeux, wounded German prisoners smiled at a British colonel when he greeted them. Then, one morning, they shunned him. A wounded SS officer had been brought in, and they feared he would see them interacting with the enemy. In serious condition, the SS officer needed a blood transfusion. When the procedure was underway, he asked, "Is this English blood?" When told that it was, he yanked out the needle, announcing, "I die for Hitler." He did. The German prisoners became friendly again.[74]

In Hughes's top secret memoranda pertaining to Operation Goodwood, we find not only updates about the strength of enemy resistance and medical protocols but also references reflecting his worldview, colored by the time and place in which he came to manhood. Among twelve hundred prisoners—most from 1 SS (Adolf Hitler) Panzer division—in their cages, Hughes called a particularly frightened captive "a rather terrified liver and white spaniel puppy, quite unable to give his name, rank and number." (He derided cowardice.) And, after a night on which the enemy made a vicious air attack using flares in the bridgehead east of the Orne River, he wrote, "Judging by the craters, missiles varied in size from cricket balls to one sea mine" (a soldier-sportsman's points of comparison).[75]

When, on the morning of June 19, the falling of the flag was preceded by "noise and turmoil rather reminiscent of the Downs on Derby Day," Hughes may have recalled a once-illicit venture. Derby Day at Epsom—the home not only of the famous downs but also of the school he attended—enticed the enforcer of rules to break them. On one sweltering June day, all the boys at Epsom were required to report for roll call every hour. The strict "Derby Day check" ensured that no one would escape to the area's racetrack. But Hughes, then sixteen, was not about to miss the race featuring Signorinetta, the renowned British thoroughbred. The prefect's getaway impressed students who could only imagine witnessing, with thousands of spectators, including royals, the filly's win—one of the greatest events in sports history.[76]

The day Operation Goodwood ended, Hitler, at his Wolfsschanze (Wolf's lair) headquarters near Rastenburg, survived an assassination attempt. Among civil and military leaders implicated in the intricate plot were those motivated by the threat of an Allied breakthrough in Normandy and the Führer's refusal to face reality.[77]

Shortly after, Hughes, in his regular record keeping, calculated the RAMC's reality: by July 26, D+20, nearly all surgical cases had been evacuated to England—38,581 by sea and 7,710 by air.[78]

Ten days after the attempt on Hitler's life, on July 30, 15 Scottish Division and 6 Guards Tank Brigade led 8 Corps in its third and last major operation of the summer: Bluecoat. It was a scorching, clear-sky Sunday, and the infantrymen were permitted to attack in their shirtsleeves. Aiming to control roads to the south, which the Germans would need for their retreat, the battle over mine-filled territory against 9, 10, and 21 Panzer Divisions was preceded by an Allied bombing attack and heavy artillery bombardment. British tanks did well on the steeply hooded slopes of the ridge, and the Germans could not counterattack in time. Ultimately, the enemy committed the last of its reserves; 21 Panzer Division withdrew, having lost one-third of its strength, and von Kluge appealed to the German high command for reinforcements.[79]

Around the time 8 Corps launched Operation Bluecoat, Rachel and Elisabeth were accorded a new lease on life. But they had not easily reached the end of July.

As they had not been tattooed, the sisters' existence was even more provisional than those whose arms the Nazis bothered to ink. But when the camp administration needed to send inmates to labor squads, auxiliary camps, or armaments plants in the Reich's interior, they considered "depot" prisoners. At the end of a mid-July day, Rachel and Elisabeth were among thousands paraded before the SS. An arbiter of life and death sent Elisabeth to the group selected for work. He sent Rachel to a holding pen for those to be killed.[80]

No one could enter or leave the locked-down barracks of the condemned. Elisabeth came to one of its windows. Through a glass pane, the sisters beheld each other's torment. Tears flowed from Rachel's sunken eyes. She would later feel guilty for telling Elisabeth, "You are leaving me to die by myself."

Elisabeth could not let Rachel go to her death alone. She hatched a plan with a girl her age, whose younger sister had also been placed under lockdown. The girl's sister would bring the pail of waste out of the barracks to the latrine, where Elisabeth would meet her. They would trade places; Elisabeth would bring the emptied pail back into the barracks, reuniting with Rachel. (The other sisters would likely be leaving Auschwitz.) The number of isolated prisoners would remain what it was—satisfying the obsessive SS.[81]

The plan worked. Rachel and Elisabeth now shared the same destiny. They huddled together among hundreds of other doomed women and teenagers. For the moment, they were alive—not least because of limits to the crematoria's capacity.

A reprieve: after three days under lockdown, those who had slaved on the road *Kommando* were sent back to work. Two weeks passed. Another selection.

Rachel pinched her cheeks to give them color. Both she and Elisabeth were sent with other temporarily spared prisoners to a barracks with a mud floor. Rachel climbed into a rough wooden cubicle. A *kapo* distributed pieces of bread. Adhering to her policy of saving food (one did not know how hungry one would be tomorrow), Rachel allowed herself only a bite.

A woman and her teenaged daughter sat on the ground amid scurrying rats. The woman's eyes fixed on Rachel's ration. "Won't you give your bread to my girl?" she asked. "She is a growing child." "I too am a growing child," replied Rachel. "And my mother is not here to beg for me." Tucking her bread inside her sack dress, she lay on the hard, filthy boards and slipped into a nightmare—a state kinder than the one in which she existed.

Another selection. A naked selection. Sack dresses and shoes placed off to the side. A long line of defenseless women waiting to be inspected by Dr. Mengele or Dr. Heinz Thilo or a munitions factory supervisor. Anyone who had a blemish or sore anywhere on their body would be sent to the gas.

Approaching the Nazi officer, Rachel concentrated her efforts. She stood high on her toes, adding inches to her five-foot-two frame. She placed her hand over lesions on her right thigh, gotten while pressed against the cubicle's hard surface. Directed to the group fit for labor, she then turned to watch Elisabeth.

A girl covered in sores immediately preceded her sister. Confusion. The Nazi condemned both the girl and Elisabeth. Rachel held her breath as a neighbor from Sighet reached out and with a commanding push directed Elisabeth to sneak back in line. A second chance for Elisabeth.

Defying Nazi dictates, others also made quick and audacious moves—in some cases choosing to die together. During a selection in which Aranka Siegal and her sister were separated, Aranka cried hysterically. A friend of their mother's "fast switched two people" and got Aranka in the line with her sister; they were now both provisionally spared.[82]

After selecting Elisabeth and a few others for labor, the SS reached its quota. A *kapo* disclosed that the rest, sent to a barracks under lockdown, would leave Auschwitz via the crematoria. Rachel did not see the woman who had begged for bread or her daughter.

The larger scheme that saved certain able-bodied inmates: During the summer and fall of 1944, as they faced civilian labor shortages and failed to mobilize foreign workers, Nazi Germany hastily established slave-labor camps inside or near factories. German industries turned to Auschwitz to provide free labor. Hence, friction at the death camp. Those who felt the need to kill more people were in conflict with those who wanted to make sure Jews were being delivered for slave labor. The primary goal for Auschwitz SS men was the annihilation of the largest numbers of "enemies of the state," therefore, extensive gassings. Oswald Pohl and SS-WVHA (SS-Wirtschafts-Verwaltungshauptamt) managers, the command authority for the concentration camps, disagreed, wanting to extend the pool of slaves to include even weak Jews who would produce for a short time. The ultimate authority, Heinrich Himmler, wavered between the two positions. The default option was to send Jews arriving in Birkenau directly to the gas chambers. Though there was great variation, on average around 20 percent of Hungarian arrivals were siphoned off as potential slave laborers. Managers of Gross-Rosen (the largest concentration camp in Lower Silesia) and its numerous relatively small sub-camps built near armaments plants away from industrial centers in the west and center of Germany, and away from the front lines, came to Birkenau to select tens of thousands of slaves.[83]

After retrieving their sack dresses, those selected for work turned them in to be sanitized. Rachel clung to her boots that doubled as her pillow. That night the hopeful lot slept, naked, on the concrete floor of a cavernous hall. Though it was midsummer, it was a cold evening in Poland. That none of them got sick seemed a miracle to Rachel.

The next morning saw a greater miracle. The two hundred fifty women and teenagers, most from the Hungarian provinces, were reissued sack dresses, ushered onto flatcars, and given a ration of bread, margarine, and salami. It was August 1, 1944. They were leaving Auschwitz as their compatriots burned, as a transport of French Jews arrived at the death camp, and one day before the extermination of 2,897 Roma.[84]

Rachel leaned back against the wall of the flatcar and stretched out her legs. She and Elisabeth had tried to stay close to others from Sighet, and she was glad to be in the same wagon as Eszti and Joli Basch and their mother. The Wehrmacht officer escorting them said they were lucky to be leaving Auschwitz alive and not through the chimneys. The weather was mild; he allowed the cars' doors to remain open, but they could not look out. As the train traveled northwest through farmland and into Silesian forests, Rachel inhaled deeply. Fresh air. For so long her nostrils had been filled with the sweetish, sickening smell of burning flesh.[85]

It was late afternoon by the time the prisoners reached Christian-stadt, a village on the River Bober. Uniformed female officers awaited them on the train platform. One, the apparent head, ordered the women and girls to line up alongside the wagons in rows of five. The arrivals amazed their captors with the speed by which they fell into formation. The "honey-tongued" *Aufseherin* (who days later "morphed into a beast") told them they were fortunate—though they would have to work hard, they would find their living conditions satisfactory. They could divide up into rooms as they wished; mothers and daughters or sisters could stay together.[86]

After marching along a paved road through a fragrant pine forest, the prisoners entered a camp bounded by a wire fence and watchtowers. Rows of barracks, with windows that looked out onto the forest, contained attached rooms—each with six to twelve bunk beds, each of which had a straw mattress and blanket. One person to a bed! Rachel and Elisabeth, Eszti and Joli Basch and their mother, and three sisters from the outskirts of Sighet took one room. Rachel claimed a top bunk. Naturally. Rachel always sought the highest possible places—for privacy and vantage point. At home, in Sighet, she would climb up to the attic above her family's shed, where she could view the action below its roof's extended overhang, and where with her sewing kit and scraps given her by the local seamstress she fashioned rag dolls and dresses for them—creations that delighted her younger sisters, Judy and Faige.

Even Yitzhak, her pesky brother who followed her everywhere, knew to respect her privacy in this spot.

✳ ✳ ✳

Christianstadt was one of forty-two women's slave labor camps—SS-run *Frauenarbeitslager*—within Gross-Rosen's complex of more than one hundred sub-camps. It soon filled with women and girls from Theresienstadt, the Lodz ghetto, and Hungary (mainly of Czech, Polish, Hungarian, or Romanian origin), by way of Auschwitz.[87]

For several days, Rachel and Elisabeth investigated their new surroundings. Among pleasant surprises were a nearby washroom with hot showers and a military-style dining room with piped-in music. Compared to Auschwitz, this place seemed like paradise.[88]

Issued a uniform of gray pants and a shirt, Rachel made use of her sack dress from Birkenau. With ripped threads from the sack's bottom, a needle, and the help of an older inmate, she fashioned for herself a belt, a kerchief, and a tie-on bra. She cinched the bottoms of her baggy pants with string so she could hold small objects at her ankles (a trick she devised back home, needing a way to stash walnuts from a neighbor's garden). Rachel also demonstrated for her young friends how turning their tops around could improve their outfits.[89]

German officers assigned the women and girls to various jobs. Initially, many worked in the forest, felling trees, lopping off branches, and dragging stumps. Then, in the swath made, they dug up earth down to a layer of sand and laid narrow-gauge tracks along which sand-filled tipping cars traveled. Those who worked in the quarry would soon bear the torture of the cold; they had but thin clothes and wooden clogs. Many wrapped their feet in newspapers. Rachel worked in the production of special explosives for the Heereswaffenamt, the Wehrmacht's weaponry office. (The SS at Auschwitz had received a special order from Alfred Nobel & Co. for females; small, deft fingers were needed to pack explosives into grenade casings.) Guards kept close watch over the prisoners as they marched six kilometers (3.7 miles) to the large factory complex in or near Nowogrod Bobrzanski, a village east of Christianstadt. It was no small advantage for Rachel to have her boots from home; women wearing the wooden clogs issued at Auschwitz suffered bloody sores.[90]

The work of weapons manufacturing was extremely important to the Reich Ministry of Armaments. Commanders of the Gross-Rosen sub-camps, spread over vast distances, communicated closely with Gross-Rosen headquarters, sending lists of labor details each day, calling in at least once a week, and obeying executive directives from the main camp. Given its distance from headquarters, however, Christianstadt maintained its own organizational system.[91]

Factory workers received a half liter of milk to supplement the camp diet of ersatz coffee, brown bread, and soup—a benefit Rachel immediately appreciated. She also felt grateful to be working indoors.[92]

At the Deutsche Dynamit Aktiengesellschaft munitions factory, consisting of adjacent halls outfitted with long tables and benches, Rachel used a tool to gouge holes in hardened lead that filled copper grenades, into which pins would be inserted. The work required steady exertion. When painful calluses developed on her palms, Rachel resolved to conserve her strength. Behind the backs of two male overseers, she scraped only a small amount of lead out of the grenades. Passing along defective ammunition, she contributed to widespread sabotage. Others, assigned to clean grenades, knocked them against the table when no one was looking—the method was faster, easier, and less dusty than scraping material off the explosive. But when the Germans saw the toxic substance splattered on the table, they yelled. Did the worker want to blow up the whole factory? (A spark was all that was needed; to prevent a chain reaction in case a building blew up, huge mounds of sand were placed alongside the dozens of factory buildings.) The inmates were unafraid. Some urinated into the vats filled with chemicals. Some loosened the material inside the grenades, then added them to the reject pile. There was "a hell of an uproar" when there were too many rejects.[93]

The grenades had been brought to Rachel's group from an adjoining hall where women filled them with the hot gray matter that immediately hardened—and that burned their hands and clothes. The heat, deficient lighting, and foul-smelling vapors in that hall made for oppressive, seizure-inducing conditions. Back in their room, Rachel watched helplessly as Joli Basch, who worked near the noxious vats, foamed at the mouth, involuntarily jerked her limbs, and fell to the floor. In camp jargon, such epileptic-type fits were called "fizzes" on account of the foaming.[94]

Rachel knew that some women found notes in packages of empty grenade shells that arrived from another factory. In the next hall over, where filled grenades were readied for shipment, prisoners tucked secret missives into crates.

Assigned to work that exposed her to both the elements and toxic particles, Elisabeth returned from shifts covered from head to toe in gray dust. Rachel worried. It would take time before she found a way to help her sister.[95]

After Rachel had been working in the factory for two weeks, Dora-neni ("Aunt Dora"), the in-charge thirty-six-year-old who wore a turban and a motherly smile, had a message to relay: the *Aufseherin* needed helpers. Who would assist her?[96]

To come forward was risky. Upon their arrival in Christianstadt, SS officers asked pregnant woman to present themselves. Assured they would be sent to a place with lighter work and better nutrition, the unwitting women boarded a train that returned them to Auschwitz. Disregarding rumors that the youngest among them would also be sent back to the death camp, Rachel volunteered.[97]

As it happened, Luci, a blonde, well-built *Aufseherin*, needed a group of girls to accompany her on a berry-picking expedition. When they reached the woods, Rachel realized that the outing served as a cover for Luci's rendezvous with a male officer. As the five pickers busied themselves looking for blueberries and Luci enjoyed her romantic tryst, rain clouds opened. Standing beneath a tree's leafy canopy, Luci blew her whistle. Buckets in hand, the girls ran to the *Aufseherin*, who led them back to the camp.

In broken German, Rachel told Luci that she could not take her 6:00 p.m. shift in the factory because her uniform was drenched. "How old are you?" asked the Nazi officer. "Sixteen," Rachel lied. Luci instructed her to ask another girl to take her shift. She should stay back in the camp.[98]

Rachel held a successful example for pleading one's case to a potentially dangerous authority figure: her mother's daring exploit during World War I. When Rachel's grandfather was killed, Blima had to stop attending school to tend to her younger siblings and to help Chaya, her mother, who sold poultry. She was just sixteen when she traveled by train to a distant village to purchase freshly killed geese, an illicit venture. Taking precautions on her way back, she hid her filled basket under her large skirt, spread wide over the wooden bench upon which she sat. But when stepping off the train, she was unable to conceal her contraband. An officer apprehended her. At the police station, Blima maintained her composure, explaining to the authorities the circumstances in which her widowed mother tried to eke out a living. Blima beamed with pride when she told Rachel how the police let her go and allowed her to keep the merchandise.

There were times one had to take a chance. A calculated risk.

Three days later Doraneni again relayed a message. The *Aufseherin* needed girls for special work. Remembering Auschwitz, few came forward. Rachel lined up outside the barracks with nine others. Of them, Luci chose five, including Rachel. By the end of August, the young recruits would replace women on the kitchen crew. In a place where women and girls worked under grim or torturous conditions, endured persistent hunger, and suffered terror and abuse, Rachel suddenly found herself occupying one of the most privileged posts of war.[99]

Though Bluecoat officially ended August 10, fierce fighting in Normandy continued for twelve more days. With the British having driven a wedge between the German Seventh Army and Panzer Group West, Hitler—against the advice of his commanders—ordered a counter-attack. While the Allies suffered heavy casualties, the German army was nearly wiped out. Advancing German columns, subjected to waves of Allied bombers, found themselves squeezed between Dempsey's British Second Army from the north, Bradley's US First Army from the west, and Patton's US Third Army from the south. Though thousands trapped in the Falaise pocket managed to escape before the gap closed, a hundred and fifty thousand German soldiers, many of them wounded, were taken prisoner. When at the month's end men of 8 Corps were sent to evaluate German losses, they found ghastly carnage. Tens of thousands of dead lay in the road and fields (between Chambois, Saint-Lambert-sur-Dives, Trun, and Tournai-sur-Dives) in various stages of decomposition. The "Corridor of Death" made for an impassable choke point in the German retreat. Among miles of burned-out tanks and destroyed vehicles were carbonized ambulances filled with wounded men. Animals lying on their backs, kicking their legs in death throes, and moaning cows that had not been milked in weeks suffered alongside bloated horse and cow carcasses. Hughes ruminated on the problem of burying vast numbers of dead. The Allies saw no choice but to use bulldozers to push both human and animal dead into mass graves.[100]

British troops had to take to the fields to progress across the country. Among memories of the unreal scene that would stay with those who witnessed it: the stench of cadavers rotting in the summer sun. Even fighter pilots could smell the foul odor as they flew over the battlefield.[101]

On August 21, Montgomery announced that the German armies in northwest France suffered a decisive defeat: "The destruction of enemy personnel and equipment in and about the so-called 'Normandy pocket' has been terrific, and it is still going on; any enemy units that manage to get away will not be in a fit condition to fight again for months . . . The victory . . . south of the Seine, marks the beginning to the end of German military domination of France . . . The end of the war is in sight; let us finish off the business in record time."[102]

Three days earlier, Field Marshal von Kluge—whom Hitler had dismissed and replaced with Field Marshal Walter Model on August 16—wrote a letter to the Führer. Imploring him to end the war and the "untold suffering of the German people," the despondent commander noted that both he and Rommel foresaw, given the Anglo-Americans' "preponderance of material," the current situation. "We were not listened to. Our appreciations were NOT dictated by pessimism, but from the sober knowledge of the facts." Von Kluge expressed the hope that Field Marshal Model would still "master the situation" but that if he failed to do so, the Führer would show his greatness by putting "an end to a hopeless struggle." One day later, on August 19, Hitler's once-able leader swallowed cyanide.[103]

It now seemed the war would be over within one or two weeks. By the beginning of September, informed opinion on all sides considered that "the greatly superior mobility and strength of the Allies, striking deep into Germany, would bring about the final collapse of the Hitlerite power." Though Rachel still hoped she would see their parents again, in all likelihood she and Elisabeth had become orphans while in Auschwitz. They already would have had no home to return to. Nevertheless, had they been freed in Christianstadt, they would have been spared ineffable trials.[104]

But the successful campaign in Normandy, during which 8 Corps spearheaded every operation and saw more fighting than any other corps, was not, as it turned out, a reliable indicator of when the war would end. Even though the enemy suffered a half-million losses (half in dead or wounded; the remainder as 21 Army Group prisoners). Even though the Fifth and Seventh German Armies had been all but destroyed.[105]

After the Battle of Normandy, the four involved Allied armies (First Canadian, Second British, First US, and Third US) advanced freely through undefended territory. As the Americans liberated Paris and as Allied divisions prepared to cross the Seine and pursue the Germans into Belgium, Hughes dealt with an epidemic: a virulent form of typhoid fever had broken out in a squad of the Guards Armoured Brigade. Thankfully, the unit was on reserve. Sadly, of the eighty cases, nine died. Though food from the cookhouse was suspected, no source of infection was discovered.[106]

FALL 1944
September, October, November

Horsemeat, vegetables, and bread arrived in Christianstadt by the truckload. After cleaning the produce in a washroom, two women carried it in huge bowls to the kitchen. From there, Rachel and a few others prepared meals for the thousand prisoners. Rachel stoked the stove with logs. Under the supervision of Miep, a pleasant woman from Holland, she poured salt and other measured ingredients into a cauldron. Through a large window that opened from the kitchen into the dining room, she served one ladleful of soup to each starved and exhausted laborer—returned from her long shift, waiting in line, presenting the tin that dangled by its handle from her makeshift belt. Each hoped for Rachel's beneficence. Rachel reached in deep for an extra bit of potato or meat for those she knew and for women who seemed exceptionally drawn. At the day's end she climbed into and scrubbed the copper-lined cauldron.[1]

Sometimes Rachel brought meals out to armed guards in the watchtowers outside the gate. She never had an incident as traumatic as Aranka's, who in running from a guard who made advances toward her tripped, fell, and lost a tooth.[2]

Rachel helped Hoffmanová and Roubitscheková—women from Prague who prepared food for the SS, who dined at tables with white tablecloths in a separate room—with cleanup and other chores. (The two Czech women had told the SS they were chefs. They were not. Hoffmanová was a diva; the SS loved listening to her sing operettas as she worked.) Access to the German officers' leftovers enabled Rachel to enjoy spreads on her bread, usually, butter and jam, sometimes, marrow from bones of boiled horsemeat with chopped onions.[3]

By mid-September, Rachel obtained a work transfer for Elisabeth. This she accomplished by pestering Miep, who was friendly with the *Schreiberin*, the Dutch secretary. Could Miep plead on her behalf? Soon, Rachel brought food directly to the *Schreiberin*. She shined her shoes. Worn down or warmed, the office worker changed Elisabeth's assignment from mining or weapons production to cleaning camp barracks and common areas.

For five propitious months, Rachel worked in Christianstadt's kitchen. Ever aware of her good fortune—in August she was scavenging for potato peels in the trash (the Nazis never adequately fed even those they needed to produce for the war effort); evading the wrath of the SS, who whipped women on their trek to the factory; and waking at 4:00 a.m. to stand for *Zeil Appell*—she bore, too, the specter of Auschwitz. Even the "privileged" were "skating on thin ice."[4]

Allied generals hardly had Nazi victims and slave laborers in mind when deciding strategy. They knew about the genocide and could have bombed railway points between Hungary and Auschwitz or the gas chambers in the death camp, disrupting the killing. Their standard line was that they could not divert air support essential to the success of forces engaged in operations, and the best way of helping the enemy's victims was to defeat the Axis. On September 1, General Eisenhower assumed direct control of the ensuing land battle and instituted a "broad front policy," with the British, Canadian, and US armies lined up along a four-hundred-mile stretch from Switzerland to the sea, along the Rhine River. Given the supreme commander's more cautious approach, Field Marshal Montgomery had to abandon his idea of throwing "the whole of the resources of the Allied Armies" into "one full-blooded thrust across the Rhine and into the heart of Germany." He moved forward with an aggressive plan to establish bridgeheads over the Maas and Rhine Rivers and to capture Antwerp, the port city from which the Allies could be further supplied.[5]

Meanwhile, German supreme commander Model rallied his confused and dejected troops with spirit-boosting talk: "We have lost a battle, but I tell you, we will still win this war!" "Despite everything that has happened, do not allow your firm confident faith in Germany's future to be shaken one whit." "This moment . . . should separate the weaklings from the real men." Model enjoined his soldiers not to rely on luck, to hold their heads high in all difficulties, and to be irritated by nothing, especially pessimistic rumors. He told them new troops and new weapons would come, and that "we must gain time for the Führer!"[6]

During the post-Normandy planning period, many British troops enjoyed a well-earned rest. On September 2, 8 Corps Headquarters moved to Morgny, France. It was not far to the forests of Rouen, where Hughes joined a colleague on a French-organized wild boar hunt, a "jolly sight more dangerous than the front line."[7]

Preparing for the advance into Brussels, Hughes added hospitals in the area of Rouen to those in Bayeux, noting the number of beds available and organizing special units, including neurosurgery, maxillofacial surgery, orthopedics, and mobile bacteriological labs. British soldiers— the army's most valuable asset—would have access to the best medical care, normally available to only the advantaged few. The DDMS also instituted "air cushions," casualty clearing stations with surgical facilities situated close to the perimeter of designated airfields. No longer would he be troubled by the unreliable schedule of Royal Air Force aircraft assigned to carry wounded soldiers back to England and the awful scenarios in which cases were returned to already full medical units.[8]

Entering Brussels on September 16 with 8 Corps' Guards Armoured Division, Hughes could hardly believe his eyes: masses of jubilant civilians rode atop each tank. Had it been necessary, "it would have been quite impossible to fight them in a hurry." He was grateful for access to "friendly" civilian hospitals, including a modern city hospital, until recently controlled by the German military, that contained wounded British soldiers who had been captured a few days earlier. Finally, during his brief time in Belgium, Hughes met Thelma Marion Pembroke, a VAD (voluntary aid detachment) with transport duties, who would five years later become his wife.[9]

On September 17, the Allies launched the Battle of Arnhem, code-named Market Garden. Its objective: to thrust northward over sixty miles from the Belgian border along the Grave-Nijmegen-Arnhem axis, seize key bridges over the Maas and Rhine, crash through the enemy's line, and cut off communication between Germany (the Lower Rhine) and Holland (the Dutch frontier). To take advantage of the enemy's disorganization, Market Garden began six days earlier than planned. This scarcely allowed General O'Connor time to bring all his brigades up from Normandy, consult with 30 Corps' leaders (whom he would be supporting), and develop a scheme.[10]

For the next nine days, the British army continually changed direction; not knowing from where the next blow would be coming gave the enemy "no rest." Nevertheless, Panzer troops fought a skillful defensive battle, recovering from heavy losses and reorganizing mauled formations. The "touch of a master hand" was evident—Hitler had swallowed his pride and brought back Field Marshal von Rundstedt as supreme commander of the west. The expert tactician exercised a high degree of discipline and coordination.[11]

Hughes's 8 Corps faced emboldened and determined German soldiers as it tried to reach the River Maas. Bombs and mines exploded under vehicles. Countless canals and rivers, and roadblocks and booby traps, impeded the Allies' advance. Casualties, amounting to nearly twelve thousand in thirteen days, arrived at two hospitals in Brussels on alternate days. Among the slaughtered were members of the Irish Guard, the lead regiment of the Guards Armoured Division. In their effort to link up with paratroopers, General Montgomery ordered them to drive two abreast down a wide road. German 88s "knocked them off . . . like ninepins—two at a time."[12]

Conditions were deteriorating. Some who were being treated in regimental aid posts were caught in cross fire and wounded a second time. In a hotel taken over by a field ambulance, a surgeon without instruments used a sterilized hacksaw to perform an amputation. But even stranger things happened. On September 24, an assistant director of medical services (ADMS) made contact with a German divisional commander, who said he was "very sorry that there should be this fight between our two countries." The German offered the ADMS and his interpreter sandwiches and brandy and allowed them to help them-selves to "priceless stocks of captured morphia."[13]

On that same day, Hughes went to meet the commander of a US Airborne Division that had just come under the command of 8 Corps, to see whether he could be of help. He brought with him Gwyn Evans, his ADMS, who having been "tied to his stool at Army headquarters needed fresh air." They crossed the river at Nijmegen and made their way up the narrow road to Arnhem. The heavy traffic both ways once again reminded Hughes of Epsom on Derby Days.[14]

On their way back, at a point between Uden and Grave, Hughes spotted several gray-clad figures one hundred yards away. At first, he thought they were odd-looking Americans. Suddenly, the windshield on the jeep just ahead shattered. Turning to Gwyn and his driver, Hughes said, "I am afraid we have had it; don't move, I will try and make that ditch on the right, and if you see I have made it follow me."[15]

Darting through trees, not knowing who might turn up next, felt eerie. Hughes returned to the road. He contacted a dispatch rider and sent for help from an armored regiment some miles away. He directed the white-with-fright drivers of all the lorries now at a standstill to line the road and keep up a rapid fire, even when they could not identify a target. The *boche* should feel there was strong opposition, though in fact there was little. Shortly after, three or four British army tanks arrived.[16]

As Hughes stood talking to a commander, a projectile passed under his nose and destroyed the officer's tank. Two days later, he survived a barrage of shellfire that plastered the bridge across the Rhine at Nijmegen, the very moment he was on it. Now he knew he had nine lives.[17]

For his actions along the road to Arnhem, for preventing a surprise attack by 107 Panzer Brigade supported by infantry, including German and Dutch SS troops, Hughes was awarded a second bar to his Distinguished Service Order (DSO).[18]

As DDMS, Hughes would not normally have taken control of an engagement. Nor would he have expected to come out of the last war as one of the most highly decorated RMOs. But when situations arose that called for quick and decisive action, he displayed those habits and dispositions he developed as an adolescent and young man, as an athlete and leader. Private G. H. Swindell, who came to know Hughes in Flanders, wrote that he was "the most courageous doctor I ever served under."[19]

Hughes had earned his first DSO for "conspicuous gallantry and devotion to duty during operations" in early July 1916. In front of Thiepval, a fortress village on the Somme, incessant German shelling and heavy rain had obliterated 1 Wiltshire's trenches; dead, dying, and wounded lay everywhere. The regiment then sheltered in a quarry. Because of its proximity to the front line, casualties had to be evacuated after dark. Seeing stretcher-bearers with their "poor bump of locality" wandering toward enemy lines, Hughes laid down a line of the regiment's dead, along which they could walk and "keep direction."[20]

The next day, he learned that seriously wounded men of another battalion were lying out in no-man's-land (the area between the British and the German trenches). He went over the parapet and crawled under heavy fire to the seven men. He dressed their wounds. He made them as comfortable as possible in shell holes. He lay out in an exposed position for one and a half hours before running back to the trench. At nightfall, he took stretcher-bearers out under a heavy barrage to bring the wounded back to the aid post. Had eyewitnesses survived, and had the commanding officer had more experience (and known how to submit the recommendation), Hughes might have been among the few doctors in the Royal Army Medical Corps to be awarded the supreme British award for "gallantry in the face of the enemy"—the Victoria Cross (VC). (Only 633 VCs were awarded in World War I, and only two bars, both to medical officers. It is estimated that only one in ten survived actions qualifying them for the VC.)[21]

Hughes earned a second medal, a bar to his DSO, for action that again transcended his duties as RMO. On the evening of July 7, 1916, the decimated 1 Wiltshires moved down to the Ovillers / La Boiselle area where they held a difficult stretch of the front line resisting the Prussian Guard, who kept trying to advance out of their trenches to attack. Grouped (wrongly) in a corner of their trench, officers tried throwing Mills grenades. As they were unable to get the necessary range, Hughes, recalling his skill at cricket, had an officer hand him a succession of bombs with their pins out. He kept up rapid fire. Until someone's head got in the way of his forward-moving arm, knocking a live grenade out of his right hand. It fell among bomb-filled boxes. With just seconds to go before explosion, Hughes dove for the grenade and flung it over the parapet.[22]

In October of the following year, in the Givenchy sector east of Bethune, Hughes earned the highest French decoration of valor, the Croix de Guerre avec Palme, for retrieving an officer who was killed while on patrol in no-man's-land. The challenge "was quite exciting," as the Germans went for the body at the same time. Had they succeeded, they would have been able to identify the troops opposite them. Reaching the "very heavy chap" first, Hughes managed to bring him back over rough terrain.[23]

Finally, in March 1918, during the famed Battle of Bapaume, a confused defensive fight with enemy units pushing forward on all sides, Hughes earned the Military Cross, an award for outstanding service and gallantry in the field.[24]

He had just dealt with the aftermath of the most intense bombardment, during which his division's billets took a direct hit, his medical aid post was destroyed, and his faithful corporal and medical orderlies were killed. Moving quickly to dress and evacuate the casualties, Hughes also scrambled to replace lost equipment. When he and others reached the reserve line (behind the front line, where extra medical supplies and food were normally kept), they found it almost completely bare, with but a scrabble of wire. In a shallow trench, in the bitter cold, Hughes and a captain lay in each other's arms to try to get some warmth.[25]

When daylight came, the Germans were in full view. Some of their officers were on horseback, and only a few hundred yards away their forward infantrymen were sheltering behind tombstones in a graveyard. Hughes sprang into action when a runner reported that Captain Tom Hayward had been shot in the arm and the regiment was running out of ammunition. With his orderly and Hayward's runner, Hughes loaded up with firearms and headed for the front line. Upon reaching the wire, he instructed the others to "go through and not . . . present too good a target by remaining immobile." Jogging, he then turned to go through the wire himself. Enemy fire. A bullet from the graveyard pierced his thigh. Because of his movement, it ricocheted off his femur without breaking it. It missed his femoral artery but penetrated the capsule of his hip joint.[26]

Disregarding his own severe injury, Hughes went into the trench to treat Hayward, whose arm wound was slight but who had been badly concussed by another shell. He attended to other casualties. He left the scene of action unwillingly and only when ordered. While lying on a stretcher, Hughes called brigade headquarters to report a concentration of the enemy in the Vaux region.[27]

As it happened, the injury likely saved Hughes's life. On the morning of March 24, Germany artillery shelled 1 Wiltshire's trenches. By late afternoon, the British commanding officer was ordered by phone to retreat. Upon receiving their instructions, two battalions on the right quickly drew back, leaving the left flank—composed of 1

Wiltshires—exposed. As they withdrew, the regiment was practically exterminated by German machine gun fire. Distressed by the calamity, Hughes also felt bereft at having to end his time with the battalion. He had no choice. His hip joint became septic and would take a long time to heal. He spent the next several months recuperating, then enlisted as RMO to the Grenadier Guards, among the oldest and most famous of regiments, which had formed a fourth battalion.[28]

When later lecturing RMOs, Hughes urged them to take an interest in all things military, in tactics and in the handling of their unit at all levels. He had abided by this stance to the extreme. His World War I citations (explanations attending his medals) were thus not "strictly accurate in all cases." His reasoning went like this: "I was serving as Medical Officer to the battalion and as such not permitted to take up arms and so no reference could be made to some of my activities; in justification I can say that at no time . . . did I wear a Red Cross brassard and . . . always wore the badges and buttons of the Wiltshire Regiment and never RAMC insignia."[29]

Now, twenty-six years later, the doctor-combatant earned his place in the annals of the Battle of Arnhem, an operation in which the Allies failed to take the fifth of five bridges, losing the ability to gain a foothold north of the Rhine. But 8 Corps did manage to broaden the base of the Second Army salient and advance nearly fifty miles in six days over treacherous country. Feelings of accomplishment on September 25, the day Market Garden ended, were tempered when hidden enemy "half tracks" killed two commanding officers, survivors of the Normandy fighting. All told, during Market Garden 8 Corps sustained 663 casualties and took more than eleven hundred prisoners. As the Germans retreated, Royal Army engineers worked hard and effectively to replace destroyed bridges.[30]

Exhausted RAMC doctors, who "had saved a lot of lives and limbs" and "seen a lot of tragedies," who had been "short of rations and shorter still of sleep," stayed behind to take care of approximately twelve hundred wounded soldiers who could not be evacuated. And Hughes took on his first civil affairs task: the examination and disinfection of forty thousand civilians evacuated from west of the Maas River, between Nijmegen and Arnhem.[31]

Situated between bloody fighting on two fronts (Christianstadt lies 470 miles east of Arnhem and 380 miles west of the Dukla Pass, the site of a then-fierce battle between the Russians and Germans), Rachel had her own concerns. Among them, how to safely filch bread and potatoes.[32]

Rachel gave stolen food to trusted friends, but her efforts concentrated on Elisabeth. Ever generous, Elisabeth indiscriminately shared what Rachel brought her. When Mindi, the nineteen-year-old (and eldest of three sisters) in their room said that in the event of an inspection she would reveal the source of found "contraband," Rachel worried.[33]

At home, where Elisabeth would sneak wood from their shed for a neighbor, Rachel was forever annoyed by her sister's eagerness to help those outside their struggling family. And when their mother returned from an errand, Elisabeth reported precisely how many pieces of wood she had put on the stove, whereas Rachel could not recall all she had done while Blima was away—from fetching water from the well to washing dishes and diapers. But that was at home. Under Nazi rule, siblings could ill afford to squabble. Though Elisabeth had put Rachel in double jeopardy—it was risky enough bringing her food; now Rachel would be implicated if the SS discovered some in others' straw mattresses—she would continue to do all she could for her sister, for both their sakes.

Rachel could not, however, help Elisabeth through one of her worst ordeals. Afflicted with a toothache, the distressed sixteen-year-old visited Christianstadt's infirmary. The treatment: drilled-out, cement-filled holes in her upper teeth.

With a stuffed apron pocket, twenty-six-year-old Ratza Roth stepped outside Christianstadt's kitchen and distributed carrots and potatoes. When the SS got wind of her largesse, they carved a red X into her scalp and banished her to a water-filled, rat-infested cellar. There she stayed until the Germans realized that no one else had the strength to carry the heavy bowls of vegetables. Rachel cautioned Ratza not to again endanger herself. Undaunted, Ratza swore she would again feed the hungry. She thought Rachel terribly fearful.[34]

Had Rachel been overcome by fear, she would have blended into the masses, not stepped forward, and never had the opportunities afforded by her kitchen coworkers. Roubitscheková and Hoffmanová had with them their daughters, aged fourteen and thirteen, respectively. Wanting to further their girls' education, they gathered the young kitchen and office workers in the evenings for lessons in poetry and literature. While a group of thirteen-year-old girls worked in Christianstadt's ordnance factory, relying on adult prisoners for protection and a bit of food and on the grace of night shift supervisors who might let them rest, Rachel learned that Shakespeare's Hamlet asked, "To be or not to be?" Later, she and the others would perform a skit for SS officers.[35]

On October 8, Rachel celebrated her fifteenth birthday. Awaiting her in her barracks' room at the day's end were her coworkers and friends from Sighet. Hoffmanová had baked a cake decorated with a gingerbread house, a scene from "Hansel and Gretel." When Aufseherin Luci stopped by, Hoffmanová (who prepared confections for the SS) told her that the cake was made with coffee grounds. In fact, she had used real chocolate.

Skilled Polish women had crafted for Rachel a hat, slippers, and pocketbook out of straw from their mattresses. Rachel was sure that her coworkers paid handsomely for these fine gifts. And she could not imagine how the daughters of Hoffmanová and Roubitscheková obtained colorful crepe paper, from which they made her delicate flowers. Overcome with gratitude, buoyed by the affection of friends, Rachel, for the first time since being separated from her parents, felt valued.[36]

Aufseherin Luci also appreciated Rachel. Every other week, the SS officer brought the young, blue-eyed prisoner to her villa outside the camp. Rachel shined Luci's tall boots and scrubbed her wide-planked pine floors to a golden sheen. This she knew how to do. At home, when she tried to stop her siblings from walking on surfaces she had just polished to perfection, her mother admonished her: "Floors are meant to be walked on, and if you are going to complain you may as well not do the job."

✳ ✳ ✳

One day before Rachel's birthday, *Sonderkommando* prisoners at Auschwitz-Birkenau revolted and destroyed Crematorium IV. Shortly after her birthday, Hitler established the Deutscher Volkssturm (People's Storm)—a new militia of men between the ages of sixteen and sixty, the Reich's "last manpower reserves" that would repel the enemy.[37]

And, as the leaves turned brown, Hughes's administrators found time to "sit back a little and take stock of their methods, carry out investigations, and generally profit from their experiences." Men moved from tents into buildings. The Dutch allowed Allied medical units to use their excellent schools. Surgeons in the forward areas returned to hospitals at the base to check on their patients, and study days at forward CCSs focused on problems facing regimental medical officers. Hughes considered such developments enormously helpful. And he was proud of the RAMC's accomplishments.[38]

In Belgium and Holland, venereal disease rates skyrocketed among British troops. Penicillin produced "revolutionary results"—men with gonorrhea were gone from their units for but twenty-four hours, and those with syphilis for only seven to ten days. Special treatment centers attached to each corps carefully documented cases and tested men to ensure they were cured before going on leave.[39]

Another bright spot: the British army did not—in spite of a period of heavy rain and in contrast to US forces—have a major problem with trench foot and frostbite. Hughes attributed the achievement to preinvasion training of combatant officers, who adhered to rigorous preventive measures.[40]

But new problems cropped up for which there were no straight-forward solutions. Three thousand troops contracted diphtheria, then endemic to Holland. Six died. Surgeons also saw an increase in post-operative chest complications. Even the fit suffered from respiratory conditions.[41]

Then, during Operation Constellation—O'Connor's four-phase plan to attack from the small town of Overloon along woods on the outskirts of the Netherlands' "Peel," a large tract of marshland extend-ing from the west bank of the River Maas for about twenty miles on either side of Venlo ("the worst country in the world for armoured fight-ing")—Hughes had his first taste of "really unpleasant conditions."[42]

Upon entering the small town of Venraij, the British army found two large asylums containing approximately three thousand mentally ill women and men. Patients and nuns in the female institution had suffered severe trauma on account of preparatory British bombing and shellfire. Their move to cellars had helped keep them safe, but at the expense of sanitary conditions. Hughes encountered appalling below-ground scenes: dank and dark rooms, with no hygienic facilities, into which hundreds were crowded. With "superhuman effort," nuns, some of whom were injured themselves, kept order for more than a week. Hughes's men evacuated all, including two hundred twenty in strait-jackets, before capturing the town.[43]

The next day, the British liberated the male asylum. Here, the enemy, four hundred yards from the asylum's front entrance, had a clear view of goings-on. Orderlies ushered the patients through another exit, which they did without loss.[44]

The entire venture exacted a "heavy call" on medical personnel and ambulance drivers, who had not expected to deal with this human mis-ery and "tactical encumbrance." Hughes was ashamed to later report that "conditions in the men's asylum were definitely worse," which "has always been my experience in this campaign in assessing the results

achieved by the two sexes in adversity." He noted, too, that the terrible
conditions "were no warning to the future."[45]

So close to clearing the Maas pocket of three determined German
divisions (which lost two thousand first-class infantrymen and whose
defense system—including two outer lines facing northwest and a third
encircling the bastion of Venlo—was crumbling), 8 Corps (whose
strength, with divisions on loan from the US Army, was more than
ninety thousand troops) had to stop in its tracks, a great disappointment for its commander and divisions who had fought so hard, and
so successfully, to wear the enemy down. The "flawless plan" to "fold
up the whole Maas pocket" was "spoiled in the very moment of its triumph" on account of an urgent call from Second Army Headquarters.
The Allies had captured the port of Antwerp, Belgium, in the beginning of September, and now 15 Scottish Division was needed to put it
"in working order" (that is, to clear the area that allowed access to it,
including the estuary of the Scheldt River, of German troops and naval
mines) before the winter set in.[46]

The weather, by mid-October, indeed turned very cold. After a brief,
uneasy period of calm, heavy fighting resumed with an enemy attack in
the village of Meijel, twenty minutes west of Venlo. Though 8 Corps
lost 1,265 men of all ranks by the end of the first week in November,
it was now, with more than a hundred and ten thousand men (having
accomplished its mission, 15 Scottish Division was called back), at its
greatest strength ever. Germany's outnumbered 47 Panzer Corps could
not sustain active opposition in the face of Montgomery and Eisenhower's determination to once and for all eliminate the Maas pocket, a
"thorn in the flesh of Second Army."[47]

But the enemy would not easily be dislodged from its position of
strength. As the Germans withdrew, they laid mines and booby traps
and destroyed every bridge, no matter how small. Britain's 8 and 12
Corps had to cope as well with problems related to "bad weather combined with frightful country." Special roads and tracks laid down by the
Royal Engineers did not help for long against the rising tide of mud and

water; tanks, transport vehicles, and even the "Weasel" (designed for the conditions) became bogged down and stranded.[48]

Exhaustion again plagued the British Second Army. From July to September 8 Corps had seen 8,930 exhaustion cases, amounting to 20 percent of casualties. To Hughes's dismay, the fall saw 1,736 exhaustion cases, 14 percent of all casualties. (The total for the whole campaign would be 13,255, or 15.6 percent of troops.) The DDMS realized the multiple causes: heavy rain and seas of mud followed by weeks of intense cold made for terrible fighting conditions; poor flying conditions meant less air support for ground troops; a lack of sleep and hot meals, long periods "in the line," and the loss of favorite officers sank morale. Then there was the matter of mines. November saw a marked increase in the enemy's use of this "anti-personnel scheme" that caused the destruction of one or both feet, with great disruption of tissue and muscle damage well above the main lesion. Surgeons performed more amputations that month than they had throughout the campaign to date. A complication in some cases was anuria (kidney failure), with a terrible prognosis—patients died despite every treatment. In other cases, severe damage to muscle and trauma produced shock.[49]

Another cause of exhaustion was "inefficient briefings and consequent ignorance of the intention and method of the operation." A staunch advocate of "conferences at all levels so that everyone is in the picture," Hughes had little control over what was or was not ultimately conveyed to troops. Since D-Day, the entire Headquarters staff gathered daily at 9:00 a.m. for a briefing on the progress of the war and to discuss intentions for the day. A morning newssheet, *The White Knight* (General Dempsey's laudatory moniker for 8 Corps), included a short account of the previous day's fighting. In the evening, staff gathered to discuss the day's events; when cold weather arrived, hot tea or cocoa was served at 10:00 p.m., lending a coffee-house-like atmosphere to hearing the news. But such innovations did not help those in the trenches.[50]

Even inaccurate press reports contributed to exhaustion. Troops needed to know that their efforts were followed and understood by their families back home. Many correspondents, who appeared at Headquarters daily, provided accurate coverage of events. But they could not betray secrets and thus could not always relay whole truths to the national presses of Britain and the United States.[51]

Five months later, soldiers' ignorance would have catastrophic consequences.

Five months later, reporters would feel a moral imperative to tell the whole truth.

Gradually, Britain's 8 Corps and 12 Corps surged forward and, by November's end, succeeded in breaching the Germans' second defense line in Holland (though two or three stoutly defended outposts and perimeter defenses along the river's western bank remained in German hands). By this point, Hughes had settled in among the hospitable, albeit hungry, Dutch inhabitants of the small village of Mierloo, three miles west of Helmond, where 8 Corps Headquarters would remain through the bitter winter.[52]

When the cold weather took hold, kitchen workers at Christianstadt had the first pick of clothing that arrived from Auschwitz. Rachel chose a black-and-white herringbone coat. An eight-inch square had been cut out of all the coats' backs, marking their wearers as *Häftlinge* (prisoners). On a crisp day, when Aufseherin Luci took Rachel and four other young kitchen and office workers along on an errand in the town of Christianstadt, an hour by foot from the camp, Rachel realized the impossibility of escaping. With their defaced coats, they could never disappear into the crowd. Shoppers stared at the inmates trailing the SS officer.[53]

WINTER 1944-1945

December, January, February

December 1, 1944. The first night of Hanukkah. Rachel had pilfered items from the kitchen for an improvised menorah. Halved potatoes, with their insides scooped out, served as holders for oil, into which Baschneni ("Auntie Basch"), Joli and Eszti's mother, inserted twisted threads to serve as wicks. During the holiday's eight nights, Baschneni and Doraneni took turns lighting these wicks with the *shammash* (the attendant light)—a tall kitchen match sunk into a potato half. As they led the girls in the barracks in quiet prayer and song, Rachel thought of the victorious Maccabees and prayed for another miracle, a moment soon in which the Jews would prevail.

Standing in the glow of lit threads, Rachel hoped to see her parents again. And Allied leaders five hundred miles due west, in the Netherlands, hoped they would soon "win through." In fact, an air of confidence permeated the Supreme Headquarters Allied Expeditionary Force, now in Versailles, France.[1]

Though Hitler was not yet ready to surrender, 21 Army Group's chief intelligence officer regarded a German offensive unlikely. Evidence showed the Germans resting, refitting, and forming an armored reserve in the Cologne area. These Panzer formations would act when and wherever Allied pressure on Germany's vital areas became too great. Or so the Allies thought. The British army planned to continue to draw into battle enemy formations that stood in the way of its entry into the Ruhr and greater Germany. It planned to attack southeast from Nijmegen through the Reichswald Forest, clear the area between the

Maas and Rhine Rivers, launch an assault on the Rhine, and "storm the fortress" early in the new year.[2]

But all did not go as planned. While the Allies focused on their offensive strategies, the Germans maneuvered with great secrecy. Radio traffic was minimal, and aerial reconnaissance poor; Ultra (a secret project involving code breakers) and other intelligence sources failed to learn that German troops and equipment were being moved under the cover of darkness. On December 16—one day after General Montgomery stated that inadequate manpower, equipment, and resources precluded any German assault, on the actual day Hughes's 8 Corps divisions began moving north in preparation for the Reichswald action—two Panzer divisions with two hundred thousand troops, five hundred tanks, and nineteen hundred guns and mortars crashed through the thinly held US lines in the Ardennes region. The next day, the Allies identified fifteen German divisions involved in the surprise attack. Ultimately, the Americans would commit six hundred and ten thousand men to the Battle of the Bulge. They would suffer eighty-nine thousand casualties, including nineteen thousand killed. Germany's objective in making a twenty-mile-wide and twenty-five-mile-deep breach into the largely undefended, heavily forested area in Belgium and Luxembourg was to split the Allies in two, disrupt communications, and reach the port of Antwerp. The western Allies would then negotiate a peace treaty in Germany's favor, enabling Hitler to fully concentrate on the eastern theater. Or so he thought.[3]

Hughes believed the enemy revealed "the importance of the occasion" in captured Orders of the Day. On December 16, Commander in Chief von Rundstedt wrote, "Soldiers of the Fatherland. The hour has struck. Strong attacking armies are advancing. Everything is at stake. Every man must do his duty and make superhuman efforts for the Fatherland and Führer." Then, a message from Field Marshal Model: "During this month of December we have drawn the sword of revenge in order to fight the great winter battle in the west. We know that all Germany looks on us with pride and expectation. Their hopes were never greater. We shall give the happiest Christmas present to Germans and our Führer Adolf Hitler. Some day there will be the peace of Christmas over Germany again."[4]

Hughes described the "long and flowery ultimatum" delivered to the American commander of 101 US Airborne Division as a "side light . . . couched in the iron hand in the velvet glove style so beloved by the Teutonic mind." The reply epitomized, for the DDMS, the "spirit of the U.S. Forces":

> To the German Commander,
>   NUTS.
>   The American Commander.[5]

✳ ✳ ✳

December 25, 1944. Christmas. The present Model had in mind for the German people and their Führer had not materialized. While British troops enlivened the hard winter by throwing St. Nicholas parties for Dutch children who "had had no fun during the German occupation," German divisions that had swung northwest toward the Maas River seemed to be losing their *Schwerpunkt*—their drive, focus, center of gravity. They moved armor with great caution toward Dinant, on the northern banks of the Maas, where on Christmas day they engaged the British in battle.[6]

On December 26, Britain's 8 and 12 Corps attacked enemy positions. Moving forward, they captured vehicles and intact self-propelled guns (assault guns mounted on tank chassis). Neither the vehicles nor the mobile artillery had any fuel. The "gross miscalculation in the Germans' petrol and supply systems" astounded Hughes. But then he recalled an odd order issued by the commander of a Volks Grenadier Division, dated before the start of the Ardennes attack: "If you are brave, industrious and resourceful you will ride in American vehicles and eat good American food. If however you are stupid, cowardly and lack initiative you will walk cold and hungry all the way to the Channel." Some German commanders had little faith in Hitler's last supreme gamble and doubted it had requisite support.[7]

A few days later, Hughes was impressed by the Luftwaffe's performance. On January 1, the German air force strafed Allied airfields from the Maas through Eindhoven and as far back as Brussels, in strategically timed, well-coordinated attacks. They "scored a spectacular success" in crippling Allied air activity, "an embarrassment to the Ardennes battle."[8]

Had the British army's plan to "storm the fortress" in early January been realized, Rachel's Hanukkah prayers may have been answered. Developments in the east might also have led to imminent liberation. As it was, the new year brought vicissitudes the young girl did not have the luxury to ponder. She focused on immediate tasks and needs.[9]

In Christianstadt, work at the munitions factory stopped. (How could the Germans transport weapons to the front without petrol?) Food deliveries decreased; prisoners grumbled about the lack of bread. (Providing for the Wehrmacht and home front took precedence over feeding expendable laborers.) Explosions, owing to fighting in the area, grew louder, rattling windows and accelerating the readying of bunkers. During *Zeil Appell*, the captives detected worry on the faces of the SS. And they observed Germans on the other side of the fence; horses, buggies, and strollers carried the belongings of a now fearful, defeated people.[10]

Privy to their conversations, Rachel knew that Aufseherin Luci and the other SS officers, who dined in the room off the large kitchen (entered, by permission, through a door in the far-left corner), wished for the war to end then and there—in Christianstadt. Any punishment for war crimes would be mitigated by the relatively decent conditions in the camp.

But their superiors had other ideas. On January 15, Himmler placed SS-Obergruppenführer (Senior Group Leader) Ernst-Heinrich Schmauser in charge of evacuating Auschwitz and the fifteen Gross-Rosen camps in the path of the Red Army. Inmates were to be driven out; not one was to be left alive. Johannes Hassebroek, commander of Gross-Rosen and its sub-camps, conveyed the evacuation order to the SS at Christianstadt, who would be among the first to force their prisoners on a march.[11]

Meanwhile, the successful Vistula-Oder Offensive had brought the Soviet army up to the River Oder and forty miles from Christianstadt. During the third week of January, an air raid alarm sounded. Panicked workers dropped what they were doing and ran to the bunker in the adjacent forest. Before leaving, Rachel grabbed boiled potatoes. Cradling them in her apron, descending the incline into darkness, she made her way from one long corridor to the next, asking whether anyone had seen Elisabeth. Upon finding her sister and their friends in the low-ceilinged maze, Rachel stealthily shared her booty.

Rachel witnessed the SS officers' dismay upon receiving a written alert from Gross-Rosen headquarters. The hazy directive included a sketch of the evacuation path through the Sudetenland and the Protectorate of Bohemia and Moravia and an explicit charge—anyone who could not keep up was to be shot.[12]

Rachel went to the storeroom and chose for herself blue and gray wool sweaters, gloves, and a hat. She picked warm clothing and decent walking shoes for Elisabeth. She still had her brown leather ankle boots from home. Preparing for the unknown, she sewed her two sweaters together and deep pockets on the inside of her coat, compartments that would hold two loaves of bread, a tattered kitchen towel, and her pocketknife.

A group of women from Budapest arrived in Christianstadt wearing civilian clothes. The end of January also saw the arrival of prisoners transferred from the Neusaltz women's camp, dressed in pants made from blankets. Evacuees from the Grünberg women's camp arrived in flimsy dresses. Forbidden from speaking to the newcomers, the kitchen workers fed them, extending rations as far as they were able.[13]

✡ ✡ ✡

By January's end, the Soviet army had completed its massive offensive in the east, crushing Germany's defense line in Poland and liberating Auschwitz; the British had crossed the Maas River and were moving toward Germany's Rhineland; and the Americans had defeated Hitler's army in the Ardennes, clearing areas west of the Rhine River. Hitler held to his maniacal plans while distrust and resignation fomented among his generals. Chaos reigned.

The opposite was true of the British army's medical services. Hughes's meticulous planning and organizational skills—evidenced in his detailed lists of supplies based on calculated needs; charts indicating the order of evacuation, with maximum efficiency even in trying conditions; and secret memoranda outlining procedures for heads of tactically located medical units—ensured straightforward and orderly processes and soldiers' confidence that medical attention was near. Even in poor climatic conditions, such as the extreme cold of mid-January, when 8 and 12 Corps, after hard fighting, cleared villages and hamlets in the Roer Triangle of enemy troops and advanced the front line into Germany, only twenty-five medical cases were reported in one division, and no man in battle suffered exposure to the elements.[14]

Excellent prospects for survival, even in the forward areas, even for the wounded, bolstered British soldiers' morale. The refrain "Thank God we've got such a medical service" reflected the fact that death resulting from wounds was less than 2.5 percent and that the impact of hemorrhage, sepsis, and shock—the most serious problems of battlefield casualties—fell to the lowest ever levels in the winter of 1944–45. Air evacuation saved lives. Ample blood supplies, improved surgical techniques, and the mass use of penicillin and sulfonamides dramatically helped the personnel situation; because soldiers' flesh wounds closed within three to five days, they could return to the front line in approximately six weeks.[15]

This evacuation scheme, sketched by Hughes, outlines the journey of a wounded soldier from the regimental aid post (RAP) to the advanced dressing station (ADS) to the main dressing station (MDS) to the casualty clearing station (CCS) to the general hospital. Note distances from the front line indicated on the left. On the opposite page are Hughes's notes (specifying rations), for a 10 Corps conference.

The Museum of Military Medicine.

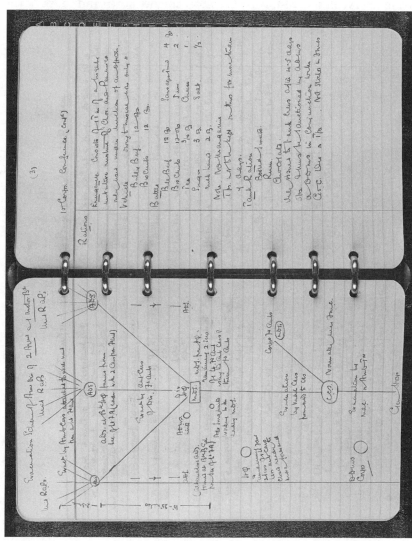

The German army's medical services, inferior from the start, were deteriorating. Unable and unwilling to devote resources and efforts to modern or even adequate medical care for their soldiers, their divisions saw low survivability. Chances of wounded troops returning to battle were weak; generals disciplined through fear.[16]

The situation contributed to Germany's failed Ardennes offensive. With a hundred and twenty thousand men lost, Hitler no longer had a strong reserve in the west. Allied reinforcements north and south of the area blocked access to key roads. Improved weather enabled air attacks on German forces and supply lines. Germany lay open and unbarred. The British army began to clear the area east of Nijmegen, to prepare for the crossing of the Rhine River.[17]

Hitler's acolytes now concentrated on the war against the defense-less. They would march more than one hundred and fifty thousand prisoners out of Auschwitz, Stutthof, several Sachsenhausen satellite camps, and Gross-Rosen, the second-largest concentration camp, with 76,728 prisoners, including twenty-five thousand women in its satellite camps. The operations, "side effects of the general anarchy" spreading throughout Germany, were to complete the extermination process.[18]

On February 1, Rachel and her coworkers distributed a last ration of bread. The next day, the SS chased Christianstadt's inmates out of the barracks, shouting for them to take their blankets and personal belongings. (Most had a spoon and an empty food tin. Those who were "rich" also had a comb, a piece of clay-like soap, and a wooden toothbrush.) Roll call. Right face. Armed Wehrmacht officers surrounded the two thousand prisoners, in rows of five, as they walked through the camp's gate and proceeded west. Rachel, Elisabeth, and the three sisters from Sighet with whom they had shared quarters (including the redoubtable Mindi) formed one row. A few rows ahead of them marched Helen and Esther Mermelstein, blankets over their shoulders, makeshift rucksacks on their backs, rags wrapped around their clog-clad feet.

Christianstadt's evacuees were given nothing to eat for the first few days. Then, a pattern developed. Every day, the officers rode ahead on

horses to find a barn that could accommodate them for the night. Terrified farmers gave up their beds and drew baths for the guards and
provided the exhausted throng with turnip soup or potatoes or what
they fed animals. Anything tasted delicious to those who ate snow and
licked salt off roads. The farmers also brought out pails of water; Rachel
washed as best she could.[19]

Where were they being taken? A hopeful answer to the endlessly
discussed question: if they reached the western front, the Americans
might liberate them. In any event, they could not move at a fast pace.
Many were wearing worn-down clogs tied to their feet with a piece
of string or a rag. Blustery winds and frigid temperatures intensified
their suffering. The Wehrmacht shot those who sat down because they
were cold and starved and could not take another step. Rachel saw that
the mother of two teenagers could not keep up; a guard shot her in the
head. At one stop, a girl about her age dared to step out of a barn in
search of bread. A Nazi put an end to the teen's hunger; her sister buried her in the snow with her own hands.[20]

Rachel's friend Aranka felt so tired, hungry, and cold. She wanted to
die like those on the side of the road, so her blood would warm her. Her
sister prodded her on. She put one foot in front of the other, buoyed,
at times, by the thought of returning home to be with her mother and
little siblings. Rachel harbored the same hope that one day she would
again see her family.[21]

Ten days into the march, Rachel was plagued by an effect of the good
nutrition she had enjoyed in Christianstadt: her period. In corners of
stinking, overcrowded barns, she wiped herself with straw. She cried.
She ripped her dishtowel in two and rigged up alternating pieces between her legs until her menstrual flow blessedly stopped.

One bitter cold day, as the prisoners marched uphill, several women
who could not go on sat by the side of the road. Gunshots. The murdered remained where they keeled over. Rachel looked down into the
valley below but saw little. She heard bells ringing. The sound grew
louder as the worn hostages neared the top of the hill and a church

came into view. As they trudged to the right of the church, a funeral procession approached from a different direction. Dozens of black-cloaked mourners accompanied a wooden casket atop a horse-drawn cart. Rachel's blood boiled. "Are we not also human?" Those around her heard her muffled cries. "How is it that one person is being buried with dignity when we are shot and left to die on the road?"

In mid-February the marchers stopped in Pirna, ten miles south of Dresden. The British and the Americans had in the previous days dropped twenty-six hundred tons of explosives and incendiary bombs on the German city, a cultural and transportation hub of more than six hundred and fifty thousand residents. Firestorms leveled buildings and claimed tens of thousands of lives. The marchers had heard the deafening explosions and now saw their aftereffects: stunned adults and their weeping children fleeing their destroyed homes.[22]

At this point, Rachel was two hundred fifty miles southeast of the concentration camp where she and other battered inmates would ultimately be deposited. Glyn Hughes, moving from the southwest into Germany, was even nearer to that inconceivable place. But it would take him and 8 Corps' 11 Armoured Division one month longer to get there.

First, Britain's 21 Army Group would have to fight its way through the difficult terrain of the Reichswald Forest. Its units would have to find accommodations in the confined space between the Maas and Rhine Rivers that were large enough for a buildup of bridging mate-rial and ammunition. They would have to select a medical area with hospitals, bearing in mind air, rail, and road facilities. Questions con-sumed Hughes. What medical units could fit into the forward areas, and what commitments could the army make to the rear? What was the state of the buildings that were available for medical units between the rivers? What possibility existed for extra accommodations for "crisis expansion"? What was the optimal timing for moving medical installations forward? And, not least, what was the Order of Battle and estimated number of casualties?[23]

Every day, Hughes asked to see air photos, which he carefully examined and on which he found large installations. He requested that priority for these be given to medical services. It appeared that the Venraij area (five miles west of the Maas River) fulfilled many requirements. It was forward of the deplorable roads running back to Helmond, near the proposed airstrip, and it had three suitable (though in need of repair) buildings with room for twelve hundred beds and crisis expansion up to two thousand. Venraij could be the site of one field dressing station for the "minor sick," advanced depot medical stores, a blood bank, and an ambulance car company. Hughes studied train timetables and possibilities of air evacuation from the general hospital and assessed the likelihood of increasing medical units' holding capacities in the event the bridges over the Maas were destroyed by enemy air attack. He appointed a medical officer to coordinate the evacuation of casualties, organize a conference for involved personnel, notify rear medical units of casualties to be received, and study methods of evacuation from hospitals. And to report to him before and during the ensuing battle.[24]

Operation Veritable, the clearing of the Reichswald Forest and the area between the Maas and Rhine Rivers, mounted by the First Canadian Army, began on February 8. Hughes regarded the massive buildup of men (including three British corps, part of an American airborne corps, troops required for maintenance) and supplies (ammunition, petrol, vast quantities of bridging material) within twelve days an incredible feat. He was struck by the fact that whereas from the Seine to the Albert Canal only two equipment bridges had to be built, this operation required the building of more than two hundred bridges, stretching from the Rhine to the Elbe. Given the great destruction and congestion, it would be difficult to find adequate accommodation for medical units sufficiently far forward. The daily air photographs would tell him whether medical installations he planned for were still standing.[25]

With the heaviest artillery barrage of the campaign, the Canadians and British 30 Corps fought a complex battle—the Reichswald had few roads; the Germans had released the area's sluices, flooding and rendering impassable areas north and south of the forest. They were nevertheless able to break through Germany's thick series of fortifications along its border: the Siegfried Line. Allied forces reached the Rhine by February 13. But poor weather and stubborn German resistance made clearance of the area to the north difficult; the enemy would not withdraw across the river for weeks. Finally, on March 11, the operation ended.[26]

The battle cost Germany seventy thousand men and its foothold in the Netherlands. The British sustained fifteen thousand casualties, and, once again, Hughes saw many "exhaustion" cases—the consequence of a bitter and protracted struggle against 1 German Parachute Army.[27]

It was during this time that Hughes's talents and abilities gained him a promotion. From January 20 to February 3, he had filled in as DDMS Second Army while Brigadier R. W. Galloway, who held that post, was on leave. On February 12, he received a posting order; the next day he left for Second Army headquarters to officially assume the role of deputy director of medical services of the British Second Army. He would now be responsible for the welfare of more than a hundred and fifty thousand men. He would serve as liaison between the commanders and six assistant directors of medical services, as well as other medical personnel reporting to him.[28]

Hughes threw himself into planning for the Rhine assault and the entry into the northern plains of Germany. From the medical point of view, the advance would differ materially from the advance into Belgium. Now every division of all three corps would be engaged, and there would be few reserve medical units available. There would be no extra transport and spare ambulance convoys to call upon. There would be increased resistance by Germans, now fighting in their own country; Hughes expected greater numbers of casualties. Further, he and his men would be unable to rely on help from friendly civilian hospitals; they would instead face an added complication—all captured military and civilian hospitals would need screening and supervision.[29]

There would be populations beyond the military with whom the RAMC would be concerned. Many segments of the civilian population would likely require medical treatment. Allied prisoners of war, displaced persons, slave laborers, concentration camp inmates, and enemy prisoners would certainly need medical care.[30]

Hughes studied all fathomable problems. Only later would he realize that he had underestimated the need for army medical services. And feel grateful that at least one important decision had been resolved ahead of time: to prevent the flooding west of millions of hungry slave workers and escapees who might spread infection and disease into the western countries, which would also complicate feeding problems in Holland and to a lesser extent in Belgium and France, barrier zones would be established at certain water obstacles. Everyone who approached the Rhine, the Dortmund Ems Canal, the Weser, and the Elbe would be held at vast camps, where inspection and disinfection would be thoroughly carried out. At the campaign's end, they would be sorted and concentrated by nationality to facilitate their departure.[31]

Other commitments would be dealt with as they were met. But no one, as Hughes later explained, "could possibly envisage the appalling conditions and intolerable cruelty that this so-called enlightened nation was capable of inflicting on all and sundry."[32]

Seventeen miles south of Pirna, Rachel and the other marchers reached Zinnwald/Cinovec, a mountain village on the border of Germany and Czechoslovakia. On this high land, where the wind howled and blew ice-cold mist, their guards drove them into the large auditorium of a summer resort. Rachel and Elisabeth crossed its parquet floor and climbed onto an elevated stage. Rachel placed her remaining loaf beneath her head for safekeeping and fell into a sound sleep. With dawn came heartbreak—her bread had been stolen.

Zinnwald also marked the start of a new trouble. As the building into which the marchers had been herded was heated, it "had the effect of a hothouse," causing an outbreak of lice. Rachel had had lice once before, when she was eight or nine years old. Her mother would not allow her in their apartment without first washing her hair with kerosene and raking her scalp with a fine-tooth comb. Now Rachel had no way of getting rid of the parasites.[33]

The auditorium's locked doors opened. Shouts for everyone to line up outside. Waiting in line for tea, Rachel saw icicles jutting off women's chins. The second the tea dripped, it froze.

Descending Cinovec's slopes entailed sliding down ice. Women toppled and collided, sustaining bruises and sprains. Carefully navigating the perilous terrain, Rachel and Elisabeth managed to avoid injury.

Trudging through villages and towns through snow, sleet, and, as February melted into March, days as sunny as springtime, Rachel saw how those who had no one to encourage—or who could urge them on—gave up the fight. Rachel and Elisabeth, so different in temperament and proclivities, supported and survived for each other.

Fields, if there was even a chance of reaching them, were often frozen. Some daring girls tried to reach farmers' doors, where they could beg for bread. A Wehrmacht officer caught Esther Mermelstein darting from a farmhouse. He grabbed her arm. "Do you know what is going to happen to you now?" he asked. "You are going to kill me," she said. He let her go.

One day, shortly before dusk, Rachel determined that she could make it undetected to a farmer's kitchen door. What stopped her in her tracks was not a guard but a German shepherd with an angry bark.

Back in Sighet, her mother had fortified Rachel against certain threatening situations. In 1942 and 1943, when she delivered poultry to customers in distant neighborhoods and had to make her way back in the dark, violating the Hungarian-imposed curfew, she would hurry past the cemetery where a dead person might rise from its grave and grab her. Blima softened this plausible scenario by explaining that one of the dead was a mother who cared so much for her children that after she died she came back each night while the children slept to clean their home, wash their clothes, and prepare food for them. Another was a drunkard who rose from his grave when he heard a wagon carrying barrels of wine go by. He scared off the driver so he could have the drink he craved. (Even the dead are able to satisfy their needs.)

Blima also taught Rachel a mantra for placating menacing dogs. Standing perfectly still, she now recited the Yiddish words:

Hunt, hunt, di biszt Eszau's hunt. Ech bin Jakov's kind. Ven di wilst mech kimen baysn wilt komen mine fater Jakov und veln dech zureissen.

Dog, dog, you are Esau's dog. I am Jacob's child and if you dare to bite me, my father Jacob will come and tear you apart.

She then walked past the immobilized animal and up to the farmer's door, where her audacity was rewarded with a piece of bread.

Rachel had yet another way of reaching those who might spare food. Tall and pretty Mindi attracted the attention of a Wehrmacht officer. He allowed her and her younger sisters to go freely to farmers' kitchens. Whereas the other starved marchers waited in line for barely anything, the favored sisters might receive boiled potatoes or warm stew. Rachel followed them, pretending to be their sister. She shared what she got with Elisabeth.

Mindi told Rachel to stop tagging along. "If you come, there will be less for us," she said. Rachel told her that she was sorry, but that she and her sister were hungry too. "I will stop when the officer tells me to stop," she said.

The nineteen-year-old told Rachel that even her father would forgive her for having relations with the Wehrmacht officer. She was saving her sisters.

✴ ✴ ✴

After crossing into Bohemia, some of the Czech prisoners recognized familiar landscapes. On the main street of one town, women near Rachel pointed to the windows of their own apartments. Rachel thought they would not dare to run for their homes. If caught, they would be killed.

City dwellers, like residents of villages and towns, gawked at the "parade of witches" traipsing through their streets. No one tried to give them food or help them in any way. Soon, Rachel gazed in awe at what she beheld: buildings with large glass windows in Karlsbad and colonnades and historic edifices in Marienbad. The clear sky allowed the sun to brighten these famous spa towns.[34]

Consumed with trying to survive, neither Rachel nor anyone around her knew that the Allies had just recently launched their postponed attack on the Reichswald Forest. Nor could they imagine what was about to happen.

SPRING 1945
March, April, May

Rachel and the other captives had no idea where they were being taken. The Wehrmacht themselves received confused directives. Under consideration, after reaching Czechoslovakia, was depositing the marchers at a concentration camp in the area (Theresienstadt, to the east, or Flossenbürg, in Bavaria, on the Czech border). Then came orders to move them deep into Germany, as far as possible from approaching Allied forces. And so, after Marienbad, the forlorn were marched northwest, toward the train station in Cheb, on the Eger River. It was there that on March 9, after covering two hundred and fifty miles on foot, Rachel was forced into a crammed boxcar. Knees pulled to her chest, she sat among dozens of women and girls in lonely, communal wretchedness. For six stifling days and five bitter cold nights, the locked cars moved or were shunted aside for passing military trains or repair of bombarded lines. At railway stations, some pushed their tins through the barbed-wire grids covering the small windows, begging passersby to fill them with water. Afraid to come close, most ignored them. Occasionally, a guard took the tins and brought water back. And bread. He might also allow someone to empty the car's pail of waste.[1]

Rachel missed being on the road where she could at least try to wash and organize a bit of food. White lice were now getting fat off her blood. Though she and Elisabeth continually picked them out of each other's hair and clothes, the vermin proliferated. She regretted sewing her two sweaters together; the double garment made for a fertile breeding ground.

On March 15, the boxcars arrived at their destination. Rachel and Elisabeth were among four thousand of forty thousand prisoners evacuated from Gross-Rosen and its sub-camps to reach the concentration camp near the town of Bergen and the tiny village of Belsen, fifteen miles north of historic Celle, on Germany's Lüneberg Heath.[2]

Around this time Anne Frank, who had arrived in Bergen-Belsen several months earlier, succumbed, as did her sister Margot, to typhus.[3]

And the British Second Army, after a month-long "slogging match" during which it finally cleared the Reichswald Forest, was preparing for Operation Plunder, the crossing of the mighty Rhine River, Germany's last natural defense. The army produced a massive, actual smoke screen to hide supplies, road construction, and the transport of twenty-six royal landing craft. Hughes briefed medical and ancillary commanders on how, precisely, the assault crossing was to be fought and how medical plans were to be carried out.[4]

One month later he would be laying down the law in a place he could not as yet imagine.

Rachel had landed in that place. Built for 4,000, Bergen-Belsen held 41,520, having swelled from 15,000 a few months earlier. It would grow to 53,000 in the next four weeks. Meanwhile, the Germans did nothing to provide for the thousands of ravaged internees. No medical services. No habitable housing. No sanitation. No disposal of the dead, whose numbers increased with devastating speed.[5]

Rachel would quickly learn that in this place it was impossible to clean oneself of mud and dirt, to get rid of the lice that burrowed everywhere. And that one could not escape the unbearable stench of decaying bodies, lying everywhere. Or the vision of people gone mad with hunger; all day long they shambled, carrying their little tins in case they happened upon some food. She would learn that when *kapos* turned up with cans of dishwater-like soup, only those inmates strong enough to fetch it had some. Many would push and step on the weak and sick; those who rushed the line could be beaten to death. Rachel would learn the macabre routine: each morning open trucks would come through the women's camp to collect corpses—stripped of their clothes and anything else on them—that inmates had removed from the barracks and piled up outside. The stiff bodies were dumped in corners of the camp.[6]

And Rachel would see the effects of typhus (brought into the camp with a February transport)—excruciating headaches, delirium, and diarrhea—in her friends. And she would eventually fall prey herself to a virulent disease.

On the night of her arrival, greeters, emaciated men in striped pajamas, led Rachel and those from her transport to an immense barrack, the size of many houses. Lining the walls on both sides were three tiers of wooden shelves. As always, Rachel climbed up to the top. Elisabeth followed. Rachel took off her boots and placed them under her head. She said her prayers. It took a long while, but in this hellish place, in her lice-infested clothes, she fell asleep.[7]

After midnight, Rachel woke to the sounds of a crash and screams and a jolt that flung her across the aisle and into the crowded bottom row on the opposite side. The shelf on which she had been sleeping had collapsed, crushing those beneath it. Barking *kapos* silenced the cries and moans of the injured.

Rachel sat upright the rest of the night. Her boots had flown out from under her and she would have to wait for daybreak to search for them. Apart from needing them to walk, they were all she had from home. She had to find them.

In the dim light, she made out figures across the aisle, trapped under wood. She reflected on the cause of the collapse. The structure had not withstood the weight or movement of a latecomer to the top shelf: Mindi, returning from a meeting with the Wehrmacht officer who gave her food.

At dawn, after a determined search, Rachel found her boots. *Kapos* moved the group of about eight hundred to a bare hut, an open room built for one hundred. Rachel, Elisabeth, and others from their hometown sat near the doorway. Rachel staked out a spot next to the wall, against which she could rest her aching back. Elisabeth guarded her place while she walked around.

A high wire fence separated the men's and women's camps. The appalling scene beyond the wire shook Rachel. There were hundreds of the kind who greeted them. She could count their protruding ribs. She could make out the teeth in the jaws of these skin-and-bone *Muselmänner* (exhausted inmates who appeared apathetic and near death). They all looked the same. If her young father were among them, she would not recognize him.

She witnessed an over-the-fence exchange: a man with a tin cup and a woman with a morsel of bread traded their commodities. A *kapo* stormed over. Raising and lowering his wood baton, he repeatedly struck the emaciated soul savoring his last bite. The man's lifeless body jumped like a ball in response to each blow. Rachel's heart beat wildly. She had seen people being kicked or shot for the slightest infraction or for no reason at all. But never before had she seen one person beat another to death.

She scavenged about the kitchen for potato peels. She canvassed the area for anything she might find. After a few days, she came upon her father's cousin, Rachel Hecht. They were glad to find each other, but Rachel was sad to see that her twenty-five-year-old relative, who had adored Moshe (she had carried Rachel's father's photo, pretending he was her boyfriend), was in bad shape.

On Saturday afternoons in Sighet, Rachel and Elisabeth would visit Rachel Hecht, who sang to them until the sun set and havdalah (the ritual separating the holy day from the rest of the week) marked the Sabbath's end. Rachel especially loved hearing "Papirosen," the song about an orphaned boy who sold cigarettes and matches so he could buy food for his hungry little sister.

When Rachel went to see her father's cousin again, she was gone. No one could say what happened to her.

✯ ✯ ✯

Thirsty and starved, Rachel felt her energy ebb. Time slowed in waiting for redemption from she knew not where. After her first week of
eternities, the British Second Army launched the great northern assault
on the Rhine. Under its command: 12 Corps, 30 Corps, and US 16
Corps (making up the initial assault), then 2 Canadian Corps, and 8
Corps. Their orders: to take Wesel and then Emmerich, further west.
The area between these German towns east of the Rhine, two hundred
miles west of Bergen-Belsen, was approximately five to ten miles wide,
flat, with water meadows on both sides of the river. The night of March
23 saw a massive opening bombardment: four thousand guns fired for
four hours while British bombers attacked Wesel. The next morning,
the Allied corps engaged in separate, highly coordinated operations.
They established five bridgeheads across the river. For the first time ever
in an assault, airborne formations (parachutes and gliders) followed
ground forces.[8]

The enemy's main strength, its 1 Parachute Army, was composed of
well-trained, fanatical troops. Other of its forces were weak, in some
cases little more than small battle groups short on armor and munitions. Nevertheless, the Germans were able to wreak havoc. In retreating
over the Rhine, they demolished its bridges. They destroyed the banks
of the Ruhr (east of the Rhine), causing a deluge over the wide landing
area, deserted farmland rising to woodland. Britain's 15 Scottish Division, landing between Wesel and Rees, ran into German machine-gun
nests. And the enemy generally fought hard—not only because they felt
a surge in defending their own country but also because they desperately needed the high ridge running from the Rhine to Osnabrück, part
of a very narrow front extending eighty-five miles, in order to extricate
their forces from Holland.[9]

Von Rundstedt's Orders of the Day included a message to Germany's
"soldiers of the west": "My brave fighters . . . The coming battles will be

hard but we must give our very last. Your steadfastness will break the great assault of the enemy. With unwavering confidence we shall flock round our Füehrer [*sic*] to save our people and our Reich from a dreadful fate."[10]

Now that "Fortress Germany" had been penetrated, Hughes faced new medical challenges. At first, British commandos who captured Wesel had to pick up the wounded and carry them forward. Then, innovative Buffalo and DUKW (amphibious vehicles), along with jeep ambulances, enabled the evacuation of casualties back over the Rhine to Nijmegen casualty clearing stations.[11]

As the Second Army advanced into Germany, medical units and stores had to keep pace with movements over large distances. This problem was solved by an allotment to medical services of its own transport company. With a centralized system, a definite schedule, and the use of air and rail transport, the RAMC was able to efficiently attend to vast numbers of casualties. The move of several general hospitals from Belgium to Germany also helped the situation. And, for the screening and supervision of overrun German installations, Hughes had each infantry division give up one of its two field dressing stations. The British would treat those the German army abandoned: thousands of Allied prisoners of war, displaced persons, and other sick or wounded.[12]

During this period, the medical corps saw exemplary performance on the part of Lieutenant Colonel Mervin W. Gonin's 11 Light Field Ambulance, a unit working in the most forward areas—chasing tanks, evacuating the wounded to advanced dressing stations, administering emergency medical treatment to casualties—which had not had more than two consecutive days of rest since helping to clear the Roer Triangle, in January, and then the muddy, bloody battles of Cleve and Goch, in February. At the Rhine it evacuated seventeen hundred casualties in fifty-six hours. Never, in the history of warfare, had such a feat been accomplished. Unbeknownst to Gonin or anyone else, his unit would soon assume an even more remarkable role.[13]

Not all went well. When heavy German shelling caused Osnabrück's airfield and CCS air cushion, as well as the nearby two-hundred-bed general hospital, to go down for a week, casualties nearly one hundred miles forward had to travel two hundred miles back to the medical base west of the Rhine. Evacuation over crowded highways proved a "severe test."[14]

Hughes undertook an exploratory tour. He found an enormous number of small hospitals in converted schools and other buildings. He had public health concerns: many, overcrowded and in poor condition, were hotbeds of infection. It would be up to well-organized British medical units to treat and contain communicable diseases.[15]

Certain discoveries confounded the brigadier. A factory near Hamburg had an adequate stock of drugs and medical appliances for four to six months; in other places, he saw a shortage of anesthetics, dressings, morphine, plaster, and insulin. Although the German military had decent, lavishly packaged medical supplies, these never made their way to the civilian population, whose health-care workers constantly asked British medical services for needed items. Searching for and collecting medical stores from *Wehrkreis* (military districts) proved difficult; fearing Allied bombs, the Germans had dispersed what they had.[16]

The dearth of artificial limbs was obvious. Hughes saw hundreds of men on crutches. Was this because factories had been shelled? Or did it reflect callous indifference toward no longer useful combatants?[17]

Hughes's tour took him through cities, towns, and rural areas surrounding the hell he was about to uncover. He only now realized the magnitude of the chaos in the soon-to-be-defeated nation. Millions of displaced persons (DPs), hungry and possibly diseased, poured westward on highways. Some had been slave laborers; some, prisoners of war; others, both men and women, had simply walked out of concentration camps. Many were trying to get away from the advancing Red Army. Though the vast majority traveled on foot, countless hordes rode in horse-drawn vehicles, on bicycles, in baby carriages, on tractors, and even, in one instance, on a steamroller. Some plundered vehicles sported national flags—how these were obtained, he "could not think." By April 7, just two weeks after the start of Operation Plunder, the British Second Army had accommodated more than twenty-five thousand DPs.[18]

One day, the brigadier benefited from the fact that so many were always in view. Driving along an unfamiliar road for a "fast run" in a staff car (rather than his usual jeep), he bypassed a blown bridge, only to come to another that had sunk into a small stream. Though its incline was very steep, it seemed passable. On the way up he "bellied" and got stuck. In that minute, along that stretch of road, five hundred now-free POWs saw what happened. Twenty shouting and laughing Russians rushed over and lifted Hughes "bodily on the top." Had they not acted, he "would have been done."[19]

Owing to the bombing preparatory to the Allied assault, the few towns Hughes encountered west of the Rhine, such as Cleve and Goch, had been completely destroyed. Now he saw that the same was true of towns in the bridgehead and beyond. Wesel, Bochold, and all the towns of any size throughout the Ruhr region were practically uninhabitable. From the air, they appeared to be standing, but, on close inspection from the ground, they were mere shells, flattened, gutted by fire. Münster, near the famous marshaling yards of Hamm, was "the worst of the biggest." Towns farther afield, such as Brunswick, Hanover, Bremen, and Kiel, were also severely damaged.[20]

Hughes observed an amazing phenomenon: within a few hours of an assault, during which a town seemed deserted, civilians appeared in droves. Their salvation had been the first-rate cellars beneath their homes, however small. Even the suburban villa he occupied at Rhine Army Headquarters had a solid five-room cellar.[21]

Of the large towns, Hamburg had in the summer of 1943 suffered the heaviest casualties—a hundred and twenty thousand over so short a period. During intense Allied bombings at the end of July (Operation

Gomorrah), when high winds sucked flames and heat from fires into shelters and hideouts, the city registered more than forty thousand dead.[22]

Everywhere, Hughes took stock of how German civilians were dressed, what stores (food, including bottled fruits and vegetables; material goods, such as leather, silk, and rubber) were available to them and whether they looked well or wan. Except for the Ruhr towns and cities that "had taken the hardest and latest knocks," where some appeared undernourished, the condition of the Germans was excellent. Children in rural villages and small towns appeared fat, healthy, and well dressed, and women and girls, even those working in fields, wore silk stockings. Their clothes bested those of the English, and they had items—hairbrushes, combs, and metalware—that were in short supply across the Channel.[23]

The brigadier regarded the Germans as sullen but obedient. Many feared reprisals and looting by ex–slave laborers and troops. He found that local attitudes reflected the depth of Nazism in the area. Senior police officials, especially those who were ardent Nazis, had disappeared.[24]

By April 4, the British had come upon the first stalag (POW) and oflag (officer) prison camps. Every few days they discovered others. In some, hygienic conditions were satisfactory. But Hughes and his men also saw evidence of the maltreatment of prisoners, the worst being a severely overcrowded camp containing twelve hundred infirm Russians, including five hundred serious cases of tuberculosis. In another camp, built for one thousand, they found 2,170 Italians, including 1,794 officers. Such commitments taxed medical resources. But they would be "nothing compared with the future."[25]

While Germany continued its futile fight, in some corner of Bergen-Belsen moribund Jews observed Passover in whatever way they could. But the holiday came and went with Rachel too sick to notice. Had she been aware, she might have remembered what happened last spring, in Sighet, when she was sitting around the seder table with her family. Their inebriated neighbor had predicted that the war would be over in one year. His foretelling would prove more accurate than that of military generals.[26]

Rachel and Elisabeth could now stretch out their legs. With the dead removed, there was more room. Day and night, they and other of Belsen's prisoners heard the "chant of the dying." Moaning. Begging for water. Praying for mercy.[27]

The second week of April brought a high point in horror. No more flat cars came around to take away the corpses. The distribution of food and water ceased. Those too weak to move relieved themselves where they sat or stood. Dead and dying now lay everywhere, inside and outside the barracks. Rachel leaned against the wall and cried.

Fania Fénelon (who had survived Auschwitz by playing the violin in an orchestra comprising selected musician inmates) thought she "must be losing her reason." Walking over the cold and muddy ground in search of a place where she could stretch out, she came to a pile of corpses. She climbed to the top and slept, even as "an arm or leg slackened to take its final position." David Grynberg spotted a nice white blanket on someone who died. When he picked it up, swarms of lice fell off—the blanket, it turned out, was black. Ernest Levy saw a man atop a truck piled with dead and dying suddenly sit up. He said, "My name is Dr. Weiss. I am a physician from Budapest. I'm not dead, I'm just weak." He then lay back down.[28]

Knowing the end was near, anticipating the arrival of Allied troops, the SS endeavored to tidy the camp. Since January, the camp's two incinerators for corpses could not cope with the numbers of dead. The SS arranged bodies into piles interlaced with wood; doused with petrol, these became funeral pyres. After the local population complained about the smell, that plan was abandoned. The SS then had prisoners dig a large burial pit at the end of the camp. But in the last weeks it was too much to try to move the overwhelming numbers of dead; each day, several hundred were piled up in areas to the rear of the huts. Finally, the SS *Rapportführer* (report leader) said, "We shall organize a procession." On April 11, guards forced inmates who could walk to drag bodies to burial pits at the end of the camp's main road—a dirt track running from east to west. Branko Lustig later recalled how those who brought a corpse to the pits received a piece of bread. But not if a hand had fallen off, for then the corpse was incomplete.[29]

Some were given string to tie to the arms or legs of the dead. Rachel and Elisabeth had nothing but their bare hands. Bent forward, arms stretched out behind her, Rachel hauled corpses and, once or twice, someone who was still breathing. Elisabeth, beside her, also dragged those who had survived so much, who could no longer endure, over stones and through pools of mud. "Look," Rachel said. "This woman's mouth and eyes are wide open." "Because she wanted badly to live," Elisabeth explained. "We all want to live," said Rachel. "But I don't think we will."

The slow-moving slaves kept dropping. After several days, the SS ended the cleanup. Stripped bodies now remained where they breathed their last. Those suffering from typhus and dysentery expired in the huts. The starved shuffled outdoors until they collapsed. Feverish, parched, Rachel retreated to her spot against the wall. She watched helplessly as Agi—who had lived on the outskirts of Sighet—called to her dead brother. She cradled tall, round-faced Eszti Basch, also delirious.[30]

Four years earlier, when they were eleven, Rachel, Eszti, and their friend Raize strode through their town and past fields of grazing cows, then hiked up Solovan Hill. Looking down from its tower into the valley, they beheld Sighet's landmarks and hikers picnicking. They drew cold water from a spout that reached down deep, sat on grass and ate their lunch, and played rummy. When the sun dipped, they chose not to return via the trail—it seemed more fun to descend the mountain's steep side. Only when they began running did they realize the danger. Fast in motion, they were headed straight for the Iza River. Eszti grabbed onto a tree. Raize fell and held herself in a sitting position. Rachel also fell but kept rolling. She came to a stop against Raize's back, narrowly missing the fast-flowing water at the mountain's base.

As they grew, there were more adventures. Rachel, ever shy, admired self-assured Eszti, who would include her when she hung out with boys at her father's soda factory. Now, Eszti was slipping away in her arms. Spirited Raize would die of the tuberculosis she had contracted in Bergen-Belsen before she turned seventeen.

Rumors abounded. Helen Mermelstein believed what *kapos* told them—the camp was mined and they would all be blown up. Abel Herzberg, who had seen Bergen-Belsen's terrible evolution over fifteen months, heard that Hanover and Bremen had been taken, that liberation was imminent. Given the Germans' proclivity to take their prisoners with them, he wondered whether survivors would be evacuated. Rachel heard they were about to receive a last ration—bread laced with crushed glass.[31]

What Rachel heard was true. The SS had brought bread baked with glass to a section of the camp. Everyone had to have a piece. Mendel Flaster felt the crunch between his teeth. He saw people die by the thousands. The poisoned ration "cut the *kishkes* [intestines]."[32]

Hitler would have been pleased. But Reichsführer Heinrich Himmler, the senior Nazi official responsible for the Final Solution, now had something else in mind. Two months earlier, while Rachel was on the death march and Hughes was preparing for the Rhine assault, Hillel Storch, a representative of the World Jewish Congress in Sweden, met with Felix Kersten, Himmler's personal masseur. Storch implored Kersten—the only one able to palliate the high-ranking Nazi's debilitating stomach pains, the only person Himmler considered a friend—to convince his patient to countermand Hitler's order to bomb Bergen-Belsen and other concentration camps. Kersten took up the charge. He persuaded Himmler that it was imprudent, for political reasons, to kill all the remaining inmates. The *Reichsführer* ordered the handing over of certain concentration camps, intact, in an orderly fashion, to the advancing Allied armies.[33]

On April 12, Hela Blumenthal, who worked in Bergen-Belsen's kitchen, saw an SS officer at his desk, his head buried in his hands. She saw him, with other SS, take barrels of documents down the main road. Other internees saw SS officers digging long trenches, in which they then burned volumes of incriminating records.[34]

On April 12, America's president, Franklin Delano Roosevelt, died of a cerebral hemorrhage. Some inmates who were aware thought the loss of the Allied leader spelled doom.[35]

Also on April 12, Lieutenant Colonel Hans Schmidt and two other German officers appeared at the front line in Celle, waving a white flag. British troops thought they wanted to surrender. No. They were sent by their commanding officer to deliver an important message. Blindfolded and escorted to 8 Corps headquarters in Schwarmstedt (twenty miles west of Celle), they there told Lieutenant General Brian Horrocks that they were not far from a civilian detention camp called Bergen-Belsen. Sanitation in the camp had completely failed, and owing to Allied air raids there was food for only six more days. Fifteen hundred detainees had typhus. Were a battle to be fought in the area (the camp was directly across 11 Armoured Division's line of advance), prisoners would escape and spread disease. "Responsibility for the camp was international in the interests of health."[36]

Horrocks saw sense to this "most unusual proposal." The British army could not have contagious individuals roaming the countryside. He sent his second in command and a captain back with the German officers to work out military details. Blindfolded, they traveled for two hours to meet General Walter Barenthin, commander of Germany's 1 Parachute Army. Upon reaching an agreement, both parties signed a document setting out the terms and then returned to their respective headquarters. Soon after, Horrocks instructed Second Army DDMS Glyn Hughes to form a party and investigate Bergen-Belsen, the only concentration camp formally turned over to the Allies.[37]

After truce negotiations for the handover of the Bergen-Belsen concentration camp concluded, German officers were blindfolded and led through British lines at Winsen. To contain the outbreak of typhus, a forty-eight-square-kilometer area around the camp was placed out of bounds to combatant units on both sides (except those engaged in relief efforts at the camp).
© *Imperial War Museum (BU 3624).*

Given fierce resistance at the Aller River and fighting along the entire Second Army front, Hughes could barely manage the additional burden of fifteen hundred typhus cases. But he thought an allocation of one casualty clearing station, one light field ambulance, and two field hygiene sections—the only units available, as they were "on wheels, waiting for the next advance"—would suffice. He also decided to open a two-hundred-bed general hospital in Celle, where about twenty hospitals contained German wounded and Allied POW cases, as soon as possible.[38]

Hughes learned the details of the negotiated truce: No troops were to be deployed within the camp perimeter, and no artillery fire was to be directed into or out of the designated zone surrounding the camp. Apart from eighty SS officers required for administration, who were to be disarmed and taken prisoner, most would leave the camp before the British arrived. Approximately eight hundred Wehrmacht officers would remain to prevent contagious individuals from escaping; when

British forces took over, they would be conducted back to German lines. Hungarian guards would be at the disposal of the British.[39]

The truce seemed not to matter. In exchange for the delay it caused the British army, the Germans had offered to surrender intact the bridge at Winsen over the Aller River. Instead they blew it up. And they continued to fight, delaying the British army's progress over the woodland.[40]

Finally, on April 15, a warm and misty Sunday, Hughes and his reconnaissance party—including twenty-four-year-old supply and transport captain Major Richard Williams, a member of the Royal Engineers and an officer from the military government—went forward with a white flag, a map, and instructions to find the camp. Fifteen miles up the Bergen Road from Celle they arrived at the designated location. Dense woods lined both sides of the road. There were no signs. After turning in to a small clearing on the left, they rounded a bend. Thirty yards ahead stood a red-, black-, and white-striped sentry box. A disinterested Hungarian soldier lifted a bar pole, behind which loomed a tall barbed-wire fence reinforced with timber and a double gate. Outside a two-story building stood fully armed SS and German army personnel. The massive SS Haubsturmführer (SS Captain) Josef Kramer and the blonde Aufseherin Irma Grese came forward to meet the brigadier.[41]

Hughes ordered Kramer to provide two German escorts for each of the men on his reconnaissance team. He sent Williams to check on food and water supplies, the engineer to ascertain the availability of electricity and water, and the military specialist to determine the method of administration and head count. He would explore the medical conditions and facilities. He ordered his men to report back to him in one hour. As they had no information about the internees, they were to refer to them as "displaced persons."[42]

What did the reconnaissance team find? Not a blade of grass. Copious amounts of barbed wire. No water (the supply had been cut). No electricity (it was down). Hundreds of displaced persons, their pleading eyes sunken in gray faces. Hundreds holding onto barbed-wire fences for support or lying where they had fallen. The place was suffused with a "heavy acrid haze," owing to "skeletal humans" burning soaked and infected materials from their huts. Out of five cookhouses, four were completely bare; one contained five pounds of rotten turnips.[43]

Williams thought the quietness oppressive. The terrible stench evoked for him the aftermath of the large-scale battle of the Falaise Gap in August 1944—the carnage, desolation, and putrefaction. He felt vulnerable and was horrified when his German escorts shot two inmates who tried to approach him.[44]

Hughes ordered Williams to return to 8 Corps headquarters to demand of Colonel Walter Blackie food and water, "as quick as possible, if not sooner."[45]

Having arrived at 3:07 p.m., Hughes and his party were not the first British military men to enter Bergen-Belsen. Earlier that day came those unaware of the truce. Twenty-four-year-old John Randall, a member of the Special Air Service, a secret parachute commando service involved in forward reconnaissance, entered the gates of the camp "hidden in a wood" on one of his final stops. He and the driver of his jeep, and the driver and occupant of the jeep that followed, were horrified by the sights and the smell. Feeling repelled by people on the verge of dying clamoring over his jeep, Randall tried to hide his shock. He sickened when Kramer and Grese gave him "a conducted tour as if the camp were a garden." Later that day came Bergen-Belsen's official liberators: 63 Anti-tank Regiment, Royal Artillery, commanded by Lieutenant Colonel Taylor, and the 249 Oxfordshire Yeomanry Battery, commanded by Major Barnett. By the time Hughes arrived, Colonel Taylor had interviewed Oberst (Commandant) Karl Harries regarding the numbers of Wehrmacht, SS, and Hungarian troops in Bergen-Belsen; Harries told him that Kramer was solely responsible for and in complete charge of the camp. The SS leader, Kramer, was also interrogated. He was immediately ordered to stop the shooting inside the camp and told that he would be held personally responsible for any man killed. He was placed under close arrest; the next day all the SS personnel were rounded up and confined.[46]

Harries would not live long. When Hitler learned that he ceded territory to the enemy without resistance, he summoned him to Berlin and had him tried for treason and executed.[47]

Steeling himself, Hughes assessed the situation. Camp One, containing about twenty-eight thousand women and twelve thousand men, was one of three separate areas at Bergen-Belsen. Roughly triangular in shape—two miles at the bottom and a mile and a half on each side—its entrance included an administrative area with offices, guards' accommodations, and prison cells. Fifteen-foot fences wired with electrical lights surrounded the camp's perimeter. Hungarian guards manned forty-foot watchtowers spaced at two-hundred-yard intervals.[48]

More than ten thousand corpses lay on the ground between barracks, amid the living in the huts, and in enormous piles. Hughes judged one pile of corpses in the main women's camp to be seventy to eighty yards long and many feet in height. He learned that seventeen thousand had died the previous month. An enormous grave pit was open and half filled.[49]

At 6:00 p.m., Hughes joined Lieutenant Colonel Taylor in interrogating Kramer. Interrupting them, a runner reported a shooting by SS guards at the western end of the men's camp. Taking Kramer with them, Hughes and Taylor headed for the crime scene: a stack of straw-covered potato plants thirty yards east of the crematorium gate.[50]

Three or four SS guards had their automatic weapons trained on foragers. As Hughes approached, he heard and saw the SS firing and prisoners dropping. Taylor ordered the SS to stop, making clear that "any further case . . . would result in one SS guard being shot for every internee killed." Blood ran down the face of a man on the ground; other casualties had collapsed on the ground or straw. Hughes called for stretchers. He directed the wounded to be removed for medical attention and the dead, for burial. Recalcitrant, Kramer complied only

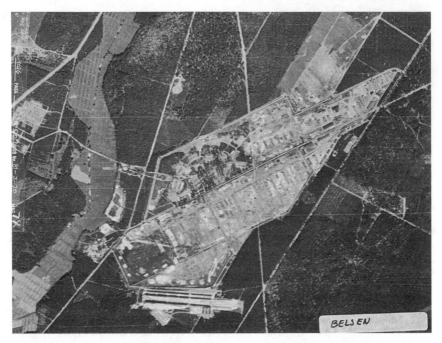

Aerial reconnaissance photo of Bergen-Belsen. A main street and a path parallel to and above it diagonally divide the camp. Between the street and the
path are two cookhouses. At the far left, between the street and the path, is the
crematorium, and next to it is the potato patch. The area at the top left is the
large women's camp. The bottom, from left to right, shows burial pits, a sizable
women's camp, and a large men's camp. The SS compound, near the camp
entrance, is at the top right. *Belsen Uncovered*, by Derrick Sington, contains
the liberators' drawn map indicating these locations.
*United States Holocaust Memorial Museum, courtesy of Dino Brugioni (National
Archives, College Park, public domain).*

when Captain Derrick Sington pushed a revolver into his back. Carrying away one of the dead, he "showed the utmost reluctance to comply
with the order."[51]

The concentration camp exceeded in horror anything Hughes had
ever seen. Tough soldiers and officers confronting the "never-imagined
depth of human depravity" vomited, cursed, and cried. Some froze,
like statues, for twenty minutes. Charged with compiling a historical
record, Sergeants Harry Oakes and William Lawrie, cameramen of the

army's Film and Photographic Unit, also arrived that first day. Feeling untrained to portray sickness and death on such a vast scale, they could not, initially, do their job. When they did, Aranka and her sister Iboya stood in front of the camera and next to piles of corpses, hoping their father would see the footage and recognize them.[52]

The weak animal-like cries of "many only just able to realize that there might still exist a ray of hope for them" moved Hughes to the core. He understood why, in this place, normal standards had disappeared; self-preservation was the only instinct left. Daunted, assaulted, he sank into despair. He was an expert at evacuating casualties. He could organize personnel and communications, medical and surgical teams, and hospitals. He had overseen burials and controlled chaos during rescue missions. But in this hell, where to begin?[53]

Hughes calculated that he would be unable to save ten thousand of the twenty-eight thousand requiring immediate hospitalization. (His estimate would prove quite accurate. Approximately thirteen thousand died in the aftermath of the liberation: ten thousand before they could be evacuated, three thousand in the hospital.) He set the first night's priorities: obtain food, water, and more troops.[54]

Darkness fell. Hughes summoned Dr. Fritz Klein, the camp's doctor, to the nearby Panzer training school. Earlier, Hermina Krantz, a twenty-five-year-old Slovakian woman who cared for orphaned children in a protected hut, had grabbed Klein by the jacket and threw a stone in his face. Hughes now ordered the Nazi to produce by the next morning answers to specific questions about Bergen-Belsen's medical facilities, medicaments, and the inmates' medical state.[55]

Left in charge of Bergen-Belsen camp were thirty-five soldiers of 11 Armoured Division and trigger-happy Hungarian guards—who the next day killed seventy-two Jews and eleven others who tried to scavenge potato peels from around a staff kitchen.[56]

Hughes and his assistant director of hygiene also stayed all night. The next morning they returned to 8 Corps Headquarters, reporting on the appalling conditions they found.[57]

(below)

On the afternoon of April 16, Hughes and Taylor, riding in green jeeps, led a convoy of army vehicles—including tanks, armored cars, and motorcycles—slowly down the dirt road bisecting Camp One. Beginning just inside the wired gate and ending at the distant crematorium, they passed water tanks, a gallows, and cookhouses, one near mounds of potatoes. They observed first hundreds, then thousands, of ecstatic, and in some cases hysterical, skeletal figures staggering toward them. And many who hardly bothered to look up.[58]

From a speaker atop the loud hailer car following the jeeps, Sington blared an announcement, first in German, then in French: "The Germans have nothing more to do with this camp. The camp is now under control of the British Army. Food and medical aid are being rushed up immediately. Obey our orders and instructions. By so doing you will help us and it is the best way by which you can help yourselves."[59]

While the stronger survivors rallied at the miraculous sight, most Camp One inmates barely registered what was happening. Helen Mermelstein suddenly heard shooting and the sounds of trucks entering the camp. Renate Lasker sensed the confusion and excitement; the repetition of the proclamation helped her absorb what was taking place. Situated up front, twenty-one-year-old Maria Tenenbaum observed the soldiers' shock and horror. "We almost tore [them] apart," she said. Chaja Szlosberg sat numbly on a bench in front of her barracks, holding her shaking knees. An SS officer had just thrown her to the ground, and jumped on and kicked her, for stealing three potatoes from the German kitchen's garbage cans.[60]

Some screamed, "We are free, we are free, the English are here!"

Rachel neither saw the tanks nor heard the announcements.

At the road's end, as the army vehicles turned around, Harold LeDruillenec, bedraggled and cloaked in a gray blanket, approached the liberators. The schoolmaster from Jersey (the largest of the Channel Islands, the only part of the UK that was occupied by the Nazis) told an attentive Hughes his story: In June 1944, the Germans had arrested him and his sister for helping to shelter an escaped Russian

POW. Two weeks after the Normandy landings, the Nazis tried and convicted him and sent him to a prison near Reims. From there he was sent to the Neuengamme concentration camp, then to slave labor at an armaments plant at the naval port of Wilhelmsharen, and finally, on April 5, to Bergen-Belsen, where over the next four days he consumed what amounted to one pint of soup. After that, nothing. (He had calculated he would meet his end on April 14.) Sleep had been impossible in the severely overcrowded barracks, with its wet and fouled floor. Like other internees, LeDruillenec had spent four days, from dawn to dusk, dragging corpses to a mass grave. There "seemed no end to the number of bodies." Guards beat those who tried to dodge the work by hiding in the huts.[61]

Hughes and Taylor left their vehicles and surveyed the camp on foot. Men and women in striped pajamas or any rags they had managed to cadge, many without shoes, walked slowly and aimlessly, their hollowed faces expressionless. At the sight of a group around a concrete pit with a few inches of dirty water, trying to fill tins tied to the ends of long sticks, Hughes's eyes welled with tears.[62]

Accompanying the military leaders were aides who, in efforts to protect them from the highly contagious typhus, kept inmates rushing to touch or kiss their hands ten feet away. While trying to calm the masses, the aides asked for those with knowledge of English to come forward. Translators were needed to communicate with at least eight thousand Hungarian, Polish, Romanian, Czech, and German Jews; two thousand Russian women; and several thousand Yugoslavian, Polish, French, and Russian resisters.[63]

Darting out of a barracks, a distraught woman stopped the first British soldier she saw. He could not understand her. Running on she "came face to face with a tall, impressive-looking soldier." Clutching his sleeve with her bloody, filthy hands, she asked if he understood French. Hughes nodded. She pulled him toward her block. There he saw why

Dr. Gisella Perl was frantic. With her bare hands she had just helped a woman give birth; the baby was safe, but the mother was in danger—blood gushed from her typhus-infected body. Hughes immediately ordered water and disinfectant. He wept.[64]

That evening, Hughes called a meeting of officers to receive reports on what was found. What was needed, he said, was *a plan*. He instructed the men, most in their late teens or early twenties—trained combatants who had fought the enemy for the past ten months—on how to deal with the human disaster. Their major priority, he said, was to save as many lives as possible. He outlined immediate tasks: provision of food and water, burial of the dead, evacuation of the camp, hospitalization of the sick, rehabilitation of the fit. He assigned these to various officers.[65]

Needing to maintain order until help arrived, the British left the Hungarian guards in control of the camp. From watchtowers, they shot at inmates who tried to get to potatoes stored under the earth. Rachel ran to a mound, dug out four spuds, and dashed away. Trying for the same, Iboya, with whom Rachel had worked in Christianstadt, got shot. So did the youngest of the three sisters from Sighet; dodging bullets, her sisters dragged her from the fire zone.[66]

With planks and splinters torn off barracks, Rachel and Elisabeth built a fire on the ground. As they watched their potatoes bake, a skeletal woman crawled up from behind them, stuck her bony hand into the fire, and snatched one of them. Spooked, Elisabeth lost her appetite. Rachel had risked her life for the potatoes, and now Elisabeth refused to eat.

Hughes made urgent demands on the British Second Army. In the ensuing days and weeks, he would bring to Belsen medical units, military government detachments, and garrison troops. He would call for help from UNRRA (United Nations Relief and Rehabilitation Administration), Red Cross sections, experts in typhus control and feeding the starved, and other groups. He would press German nurses and doctors into service. The emergency assemblage would be woefully inadequate

Women preparing a "meal" within a few days of the liberation. No one paid attention to the corpses in the background—a usual sight.
United States Holocaust Memorial Museum (National Archives, College Park, MD).

in numbers. Had he ten times the personnel, he might have been able to stem the death rate of roughly five hundred people each day, a tragic statistic that continued for weeks.[67]

The first medical units to arrive in response to Hughes's appeal appeared on April 17. Among these was 32 Casualty Clearing Station, a mobile front-line hospital with nine doctors, eight army nurses, one hundred men, and medical equipment to treat two hundred wounded. Hughes appointed its lieutenant colonel, James Johnston, Bergen-Belsen's senior medical officer.[68]

Hughes had promised Lieutenant Colonel Gonin of 11 Light Field Ambulance a reprieve from the battlefield. After months of intense and dangerous work, his unit was to spend seven days supervising overrun German hospitals. After just four days, Hughes sent Gonin a "special request": his men were needed immediately in Bergen-Belsen, a concentration camp where typhus had broken out.[69]

After surveying the camp, Gonin brought Hughes to a "hospital" he discovered in a section of Bergen-Belsen that formerly housed Russian prisoners of war. Among three spacious barracks equipped with beds was a ward for a hundred and fifty children. There, Dr. Hadassah Bimko had worked "miracles of care" without medicine but with storytelling and compassion. Hughes marveled at the high standards of hygiene the Polish dentist had managed to maintain. As they left her hut, Gonin saw Hughes, a man with three war medals for bravery, "crying like a child."[70]

Communicating in French, Dr. Bimko guided Hughes around the camp. Together they walked into a hut crowded with the dead and near dead, "a sea of crying, screaming bones." What had been in plain view was ghastly, but it was not until this moment that Hughes grasped the enormity of both the crime and the work ahead. Living skeletons shared bunks and the floor with the dead. They used the dead as pillows and mattresses and to warm their bodies. They had little to nothing in the way of straw or blankets. They wore filthy clothing or none at all. Every face bore signs of misery. Hughes sobbed. He vowed that, despite the army's critical need for medical services, he would save as many of Belsen's sick as possible. He asked Bimko to serve as an administrator at the hospital that was in the process of being readied, to work alongside British medical personnel. She immediately set to recruiting doctors and nurses from among survivors.[71]

Ten months later, Hughes would try to convey what he saw to members of a medical society who would be "incapable of appreciating" the horror:

Imagine at the time dry weather and a fairly strong wind opening the door of one of these huts and being met by a gust of fetid air and a stench incapable of description. [Imagine] a hut [in which] all [were] suffering from starvation, diarrhaea [sic], and unable to get out. The floor thick in filth of all descriptions and [people] lying in this . . . One had to step over the dead to move about . . . One hundred percent were lousy and . . . practically everyone who had not had typhus previously in such endemic areas as Poland or had only just arrived at the camp had contracted it in Belsen. Most of the inhabitants were in the final stages of starvation and too weak to stir or perhaps only able to move a few yards from where they lay. It was quite impossible to say whether any individual was suffering from starvation, tubercle, typhus, or a combination of all three.[72]

On the morning of April 17, Rabbi Leslie Hardman traveled from regimental headquarters in Celle to Bergen-Belsen. He had been told by his colonel to "keep a stiff upper lip." And that in Belsen he would "find a lot of [his] people." Affronted, he thought, "My people? Anyone's people—everyone's people. These once human beings were now reduced to hideous apparitions bearing no resemblance to man." When he went into one of the worst women's huts, he thought that those lying on the floor, in dirt and in their own excrement, were middle-aged or old. The majority were in their twenties. Hughes entered, had the hut measured, and counted twenty women in thirty-five square feet—four in each bunk, four below the bottom bunk, and others packed tightly all around. The space would have barely sufficed for one British soldier in the most crowded conditions. When Hardman later appealed to Hughes, who "listened . . . gravely and sympathetically," to get the dying to a hospital, he had to accept what could be offered at the time: a former SS dispensary. He furnished it with a paltry twelve beds, each for two people.[73]

On the afternoon of that same day, after a "puffer boy" at the camp gate sprayed Richard Dimbleby with DDT (anti-louse powder), Hughes warned the BBC news correspondent, "I hope you have a strong stomach, you're going to see something horrible!" While proceeding by jeep into the compound, the reporter spoke of his responsibility to "get all the details." When their slow-moving vehicle swerved around a man who fell in front of it, Hughes leaned out twice to look at him, the second time pronouncing the man dead. Incredulous, Dimbleby asked, "Dead? He can't be dead just like that." Hughes enlightened the newcomer: "There are ten thousand people dying here, and ten thousand dead."[74]

Pulling the toppled man by the heels, someone dragged him over to a pile of unburied bodies by the side of the road. No one but Hughes and Dimbleby noticed.[75]

Following Hughes on foot, the dazed correspondent stepped over bodies in and outside of dark huts. In one hut, they heard a "voice that rose above the gentle undulating moaning." A girl who had almost no hair, fingers like brown pencils, two holes for eyes, and a face that resembled yellow parchment, stretched out her "stick of an arm." She repeated the words "English" and "medicine." She did not have the strength to cry. Hughes guessed she was twenty. They both knew she would be dead in thirty minutes.[76]

In giving his account, Dimbleby emphasized the humanity of the liberated prisoners, explaining that there were in Bergen-Belsen musicians, authors, chemists, and lawyers; there were respectable citizens who had—owing to the depredations and lack of privacy—long stopped caring about normal conventions. Naked women washed themselves with cups of water taken from British army water trucks. People squatted while they searched themselves and each other for lice. Victims of dysentery leaned against huts, straining helplessly. Dimbleby described how British soldiers and medical men were moved to "cold fury." He wished that everyone fighting in the war could have come with him through the barbed-wire fence into the inner compound of the camp, to see the "swirling cloud of . . . the dust of thousands of slow-moving people, laden in itself with the typhus germ." He wished they could experience the "sickly and thick . . . smell of death and decay, of corruption and filth." Of the many terrible sights he had seen in the past five years, nothing approached the "dreadful interior" of the hut he entered in Belsen. During two hours of reporting, he broke down five times. Doubting the truthfulness of his account, the BBC in London demanded confirmation from other sources. The correspondent threatened to resign.[77]

Conditions at Bergen-Belsen shocked each newcomer. Sergeant Norman Turgel of 53 Field Security Section of the British Intelligence Corps found himself paralyzed on the third day after the liberation. A doctor stuck pins in his legs; he felt nothing and could not get out of bed for twenty-four hours. George Rodgers of 5 Army Film and Photographic Unit felt so uncomfortable and voyeuristic that he vowed never again to take wartime photographs. Private E. Fisher of 32 Casualty Clearing Station pinched himself. He could not believe what his eyes saw: a "scene more like a Hollywood-produced representation of a concentration camp than the real thing." He hoped that none of the women he helped would look in the mirror for a month.[78]

All rescue operations take time. Hughes managed the process as quickly as he was able. Headquarters immediately ordered the Royal Army Service Corps (RASC) to send as many water bowsers (mobile tanks) as possible. These were emptied and refilled over and again from dawn to dusk for several days, until the civilian fire service in Celle brought in portable pumps and drew water from a stream at the camp's edge. When the army's engineering unit arrived and repaired the water mains the SS had damaged before leaving Bergen-Belsen, the problem of obtaining water was resolved. Soldiers at six distribution stations helped weak inmates and prevented mobbing.[79]

Next, food. The RASC sent trucks, boilers, and several cooks, who prepared a watered-down stew from the contents of compo packs (army rations): tinned beef, tinned pork, bacon, and sausage. Some cheese and hard biscuits were also distributed. The rich fare caused lethal cramping. Wanting so much to help, British Tommies also gave those with shrunken stomachs and shriveled intestines what they could

not tolerate. When they saw the effects of their generosity—and ignorance—they ran around to the blocks screaming, "Don't eat!" It was
too late. More than two thousand died on account of their first meal.[80]

Distressed by the calamitous initial feedings, Hughes tried to control
the two-meal a day menu. He brought in experts on famine relief. He
worked up diets according to varying degrees of emaciation, allowing
for increased caloric intake as people gained strength. To start, those in
the worst condition were to be served a daily diet of two liters of skim
milk, two ounces of sugar, one-sixteenth of an ounce of salt, three vitamin tablets, and one liter of water given in small amounts, frequently.[81]

Five cookhouses, staffed mainly by relatively fit former female inmates, became operative. Owing to the tendency among prisoners to
hoard, the army brought in food for only one meal at a time. When
fresh milk was obtained, men from 32 Casualty Clearing Station
opened a "milk bar" and supervised feeding.[82]

On April 18, 314 Mobile Laundry and Bath Unit set up outdoor
showers. Pipes extended to showerheads positioned above those who
had been unable to wash for so long. Reveling in the sensation, Rachel
soaped herself and stood under the water as long as she could.[83]

Around the time the showers came, so did strange entertainers:
men in plaid kilts, members of a Scottish regiment. They played bag-
pipes. They tried to teach survivors the hokey pokey. How odd, Rachel
thought. She had never seen men wearing skirts.[84]

Somewhat revitalized, Rachel explored. The cookhouse had nothing.
A few barracks away, she came upon a storeroom. Through one of its
windows, she could see clothes piled two-thirds of the way to the ceiling. She climbed in. Two other girls, busy in their respective corners of
the huge room, paid her no attention.

Sitting atop a heap, wielding the pocketknife she had kept on her
since Christianstadt, Rachel spent hours opening seams, lapels, and
hems. She accumulated a stash of valuables: gold rings, a gold pen, US
dollars, other foreign currency. The pockets of her tweed coat filled,

Outdoor showers at Bergen-Belsen. Any sense of modesty was long gone.
© *Imperial War Museum (BU 4237).*

she felt rich. She decided to keep the storeroom a secret; she would not even tell Elisabeth. She planned to return the next day.

The 11 Armoured Division left Belsen to do battle with the remaining pockets of German resistance. Traveling 238 miles in twenty-four hours, a far larger party of soldiers arrived on April 18, including troops of 113 Light Anti-aircraft Battalion of the Royal Artillery (RA). One of the biggest problems they faced was how to feed surviving inmates. RA carpenters and anyone who knew anything about building undertook the vast job of adapting and erecting cookhouses. Initially, they served an uncontrolled diet from dustbin-type food containers. To ameliorate the difficulties of feeding thousands, including those too sick to move

and who had no one to bring food to them, they pitched "a dump of tentage." Those able to walk could move into the tents, relieving the overcrowding in the huts.[85]

Rachel, Elisabeth, and the three sisters from Sighet with whom they had formed a row on the march moved into a tent. Mindi set up a rotation—each night a different girl was responsible for closing the tent's flap door. On the fourth night, a driving rain soaked the ground. It was Rachel's turn to pull down the flap. Achy and weak, she could not get up. Elisabeth volunteered to do it for her. Mindi said no. If Rachel was unable to perform her duty, she did not belong in the tent.

Rachel crawled back to the hut. Someone was now sitting in her spot against the wall. She tried to reclaim it. Incensed, the spot's occupant and those around her kicked and pummeled Rachel until their energy was spent. She had made it through the entire war without anyone laying a hand on her, and now, after the liberation, her own people beat her to a bloody pulp. She was sure she would never again walk upright. Her last thought before losing consciousness: we are no longer human.

In fulfilling his vow to save as many lives as possible, Hughes made a heart-wrenching decision. The doctor in him wanted to give each sick and starved person the care he or she needed. As a military leader short on help and time, however, he knew that "thorough diagnosis and elaborate treatment" of individual patients would make it impossible to provide elementary care to greater numbers. The best chance to save the most was to place "those who had a reasonable chance of survival under conditions in which their own tendency to recover could be aided by simple nursing and suitable feeding, and in which further infection could be prevented." His highly focused plan involved placing inmates into one of three categories: those likely to survive, those likely to die, and those for whom immediate care would mean the difference between life and death. The medical officers going into the huts would have to make a quick determination: Would the individual stand a

Part of Bergen-Belsen became a "tent city." Note the proximity of the tents to the huts, which contained those too ill to move.
The Museum of Military Medicine.

Those who were strong enough to fetch food crowded together on Bergen-Belsen's main street. In the background is a large pile of victims' shoes.
United States Holocaust Memorial Museum, courtesy of Hadassah Bimko Rosensaft.

better chance of surviving if evacuated to receive rudimentary care? Rescue efforts sprang from this principle.[86]

Camp One was so infested with disease that the idea of setting up medical facilities there was instantly dismissed. A large, typhus-free military barracks area a mile and a half away "saved the day." Called Camp Two, it had been used by the Germans as a training ground for twenty thousand soldiers, mainly Panzer troops. Comprising dozens of two-story dormitories with beds and bedding, dining halls, and lecture rooms, it also included a two-hundred-bed hospital and medical supplies. The former encampment now housed fifteen to seventeen thousand male prisoners, recent arrivals who suffered varying degrees of malnutrition (many were starved beyond recognition; dysentery was rife among them). These men would be transferred to other accommodations while the sixty-six stone and cement barracks around a square were cleaned and converted into a hospital for nearly seventy-four hundred patients.[87]

Adjoining the promising barracks area was a well-equipped military hospital with five hundred beds. Its large officers' dining room, the *Rundhaus* (roundhouse), could be outfitted with an additional two hundred beds. Also nearby were modern accommodations housing eight hundred German and two thousand Hungarian soldiers. These would constitute Camp Three, where fit survivors would stay until they could be repatriated.[88]

At the first of regular evening conferences, beginning at 9:00 p.m. after grueling workdays, Hughes and his men settled on a drill: 32 Casualty Clearing Station would clean and equip the hospital complex for fourteen thousand and—with the help of internee doctors and nurses—care for the ill survivors; 10 Garrison Detachment and the 113 Light Anti-aircraft Regiment would set up improvised feeding stations and bury the dead; 30 Field Hygiene Section would contain and combat the typhus epidemic; 11 Light Field Ambulance would supply medical equipment, transport the sick to the hospital area, and remove those who had died there.[89]

A reconnaissance of the area uncovered a large warehouse near Camp Two containing stores of electrical equipment, beds and bedding, furniture, and scouring powder. A central dump in nearby Celle contained two thousand tons of medical equipment (including drugs and dressings) captured from the Germans. Further combing the region, Captain "Frosty" Winterbottom of the RAMC and others of the Second Army amassed cupboards, bedpans, crockery, and toiletries. They were able to equip seven thousand beds and organize thousands of sets of clothing and footwear for the liberated as well as a hair salon, and plumbers and carpenters for the hospital. They were able to found workshops for seamstresses (who mass-produced the "standard Belsen nighties" for the sick) and repairmen (who fixed radios and bicycles). They rounded up all the civilian German nurses and doctors they could find and brought them to work at the hospital.[90]

Gonin later recounted how his own lorries brought more than two hundred fifty tons of medical equipment to the hospital area. He had told his transport sergeant to "for God's sake get them." Each evening, nurses would run to incoming lorries to collect needed items. Demand always exceeded supply.[91]

Hughes faced another excruciating decision. With the impending heat of summer came the threat of cholera—he saw no alternative but to bury the dead in mass graves as quickly as possible. On April 18, the work began. Rabbi Hardman arrived just as a large, open-jawed bulldozer ate out a pit for five thousand bodies. He beseeched the DDMS. "Is it not possible to show some reverence to the dead?" Hughes promised the rabbi that he would have him sent for when the work was done; he could come back to the site and say prayers.[92]

Hughes would later explain that it was impossible to separate the bodies by nationality and the situation was like a natural disaster in which the dead are buried together. Displaying empathetic imagination, he said the victims would not have wished to be separated.[93]

At first, thirty-five 11 Armoured Division soldiers forced forty black-uniformed SS men and women who had remained at the camp to perform the burial work. They made them pick up bodies with their bare hands, load them onto flatbed lorries, and then place them in huge and deep graves. One SS officer threw a head separated from the trunk of a body on the trailer, with no sign of remorse or discomfort. But the survivors displayed emotion. They stood around and jeered. The SS were given meager rations and allowed breaks in which they could lie face down at the bottom of a burial pit. Though surrounded by tanks, two SS men tried to escape. They were shot and buried alongside the camp's prisoners.[94]

The corpses could not be handled safely without blankets, and these could not be spared. On two occasions, bulldozers pushed them into the pits. Army chaplains Hardman and Levy held brief services at the side of each filled pit. Notice boards indicated the approximate number of people interred. (The number of dead buried after the British arrived was approximately twenty-three thousand.) The rabbis also held private services at the distant perimeter of the camp for those who could identify a family member or friend who had died.[95]

Deeply disturbed by the way in which emaciated bodies had been cast anonymously, "helter skelter" into the pits, Rabbi Levy believed their "place of disposal set the seal . . . on the denial of their humanity by the Nazis." He tried to identify the living, to record survivors' names and countries of origin. In doing so he joined Rabbi Hardman, who, owing to around-the-clock efforts to minister to survivors, was near a breakdown. Many would die as soon as they gave the rabbis their names. Rabbi Levy asked Hughes to request the authorities make special appointments of chaplains and relief groups. "The Man of Belsen" was "ready to help in every way."[96]

Moving thousands of sick and dying from Camp One to the hospital complex would entail several steps. First, squads of fifteen stretcher-bearers and one medical officer from 11 Light Field Ambulance, all in protective gear, would go hut by hut, removing those the medical officer identified as having a chance of survival. They would strip the individuals, wrap them in blankets, and take them on stretchers to "contaminated ambulances." These vehicles would bring them to a cavalry stable—a long building near Camp Two dubbed the "human laundry." Each survivor would be placed on one of sixty wooden tables. Two German nurses would be assigned to a table. Under the direction of 32 Casualty Clearing Station officers, they would wash, shave, and dust Hitler's victims with DDT. Wrapped in fresh blankets, survivors would then be moved in "clean" ambulances to the makeshift hospital wards. That was the plan.[97]

On April 22, seven days after the liberation, a ward in the hospital barracks was finally ready to receive the first patients. At 7:30 a.m., ambulances were set to move off. At 7:25 a.m., Gonin received word that Wehrmacht soldiers had cut the electricity coming from Celle. The tragic consequence of this act of sabotage was that the pump bringing water to the hospital failed. The evacuation would have to be delayed. Gonin knew that many Camp One survivors pinned their hopes on this day; they would give up the fight were there no evidence of imminent medical treatment. He "went to the poor expedient" of having ambulances drive around the camp. He later wrote, "We did not lift a patient but word went round the camp that the ambulances had come. No one knew that they left, as they arrived, empty."[98]

On April 23 or 24, stretcher-bearers entered the hut in which Rachel lay unconscious. Judging her as someone who had a chance of recovery, a medical officer marked her forehead with a red cross. She was lifted onto a stretcher and transported to a washing station. There, a German nurse sponged her with soap and water, dusted her with anti-louse powder, and wrapped her in a blanket. Rachel roused long enough to realize that the treasures she had collected in the storeroom had been taken from her. Distraught, she again lost consciousness.[99]

When medics entered Helen Mermelstein's hut, she begged them to take her sister, Esther. Only later did she beg to be taken as well. Eszti Basch likewise pleaded for a medic to take her very sick sister Joli, who

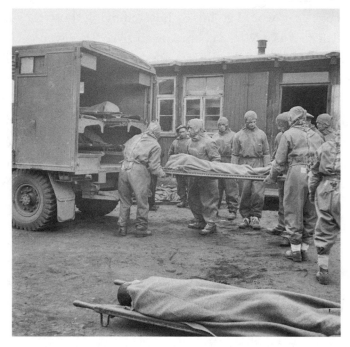

Men of 11 Light Field Ambulance, RAMC, wearing protective clothing, evacuating a sick inmate from a hut in Camp One (the "Horror Camp").
© *Imperial War Museum (BU 5458).*

would have been left to die, to the hospital. (Eszti would die three months later, "her lungs too damaged to sustain her." Baschneni, Joli and Ezsti's mother, died on the day of the liberation.) One unmarked girl pressed her forehead against her sister's so the inked cross would rub off on her and she would be taken as well.[100]

The triage system left some for dead who might have been saved. And brought some to the hospital who, under the circumstances, had little chance.

Molly Silva Jones, one of four Red Cross nurses to arrive in Bergen-Belsen from Holland on April 20, noted how "living corpses" processed through the human laundry came to a hospital with no pillows, very few bedpans, no washing bowls, few towels, and not enough cups. Most patients suffered from acute diarrhea and defecated and urinated where

The "human laundry." The British officer on the right was supervising the work of German nurses, who bathed and disinfected the sick before they were taken in clean blankets to the nearby hospital complex.
United States Holocaust Memorial Museum, courtesy of Madalae Fraser.

they lay. They could not grasp that someone would come if they called. One week after her arrival, close supervision was still near impossible—two trained nursing sisters (one English and one Swiss) were assigned to every six hundred patients. At night, there was no supervision at all.[101]

When Rachel came to, she found herself in a room with twelve beds, six each against opposite walls. Brown paper (the substitute for mackintosh sheeting) covered the palliasses (straw mattresses). To reach the pail in the corner, she with great difficulty moved off her bed, then staggered between beds upon which she leaned for support.

At first, she could not touch the food on her bedside table. The others in her ward also ignored their trays. They died. Every morning, men removed eleven corpses from the room. Every afternoon, they brought in eleven nearly dead to fill the empty beds. One week. Two weeks. Three weeks. Each day saw the demise of those with whom Rachel shared quarters. Only she, occupying the twelfth bed, remained.[102]

During moments of clarity, Rachel contemplated the reality of her longed-for liberation. Throughout the war she had focused all her energies on trying to survive. She hoped she would see her parents again. But what she had heard, smelled, and seen with her own eyes in Auschwitz and in Bergen-Belsen told her that, of their family, only she and Elisabeth survived. If she died, Elisabeth would be alone. And, she thought, it would be tragic, after all her struggles, to die now. She was only fifteen.

Her father's parting words came back to Rachel. He had confidence she would make it. If only to fulfill Moshe's expectations of her, she had to muster the will to live.

✳ ✳ ✳

In the aftermath of the liberation, Hughes measured progress by unusual milestones: When were the mass burials completed? When did the death rate begin to drop? By when was typhus eradicated? On what date was the last deathly ill patient evacuated to the hospital? Leading one of the most innovative relief efforts in history, he raced against time.

While the Second Army's task was in process, on April 25, he brought six *Bürgermeisters* (mayors) from the surrounding area to Bergen-Belsen "to witness what their countrymen had perpetrated on innocent people." As the mute men moved around the camp, loudspeakers blared an indictment: what they were seeing, which was not half as bad as what the British found ten days earlier, "provides the final condemnation of the Nazi party and complete justification for any measures the Allied nations may take to extirpate the Party." The Germans would never be able to say, "It never happened."[103]

Hughes had impressed upon the British Second Army that "the dictates of humanity required quick action." Long, hard workdays would eventually involve more than thirty-seven units of the British Second Army, as well as units from other Allied armies, volunteer organizations, and physicians from France, Belgium, Poland, Switzerland, and Czechoslovakia. (By June 9, 1945, UNRRA had sent 205 teams, each

As British Army officers led *Bürgermeisters* of towns in the region around
Bergen-Belsen, SS guards loaded a lorry with dead bodies.
United States Holocaust Memorial Museum, courtesy of Hadassah Bimko Rosensaft.

with a doctor and a nurse, to Belsen.) Evening meetings would last past
midnight. At 11:00 p.m., the women (who with but two or three excep-
tions were not allowed into the Horror Camp) would be dismissed, and
gin, brandy, and champagne would appear. In the words of a member
of 32 Casualty Clearing Station, "If we were not to drink we would go
stark staring mad. We are doctors and are supposed to heal, but this task
is hopeless. They die on us as soon as we touch them."[104]

   With a glass of whiskey in hand, Hughes would weigh in on seem-
ingly insurmountable difficulties. (Gonin thought the brigadier had the
"gift of turning up just when things were going wrong" and "never failed
to put them right.") When they ran out of blankets to wrap around inmates stripped of their lice-infested clothing, it seemed that evacuation
from the Horror Camp might be delayed. Upon hearing this, Hughes
asked, "What is the population of Celle?" He directed Gonin to go to

the town's *Bürgermeister* and say that the DDMS ordered each civilian
to hand in one blanket by midday tomorrow. By the following night,
the army had eighteen hundred blankets.[105]

The extreme situation called for resourcefulness, improvisation, ex-
perimentation, and patience. There was the initial truculence of German nurses assigned to work in the human laundry; after confronting
ravaged inmates, they toiled tearfully and without rest, washing and
delousing an average of seven hundred each day. On April 27, the electricity was again sabotaged, shutting down water in the hospital area;
the Royal Air Force brought in a German water cart while engineers
restored the supply. And, upon seeing their immense distress, a prominent pathologist attached to 32 Casualty Clearing Station, who had
come to conduct scientific research, put his instruments aside, pulled
on overalls, and shook hands with every patient who went through
a human laundry cleansing station—the first kindly gesture made to
many in years.[106]

There was the matter of food—satisfying inmates who demanded
it; trying to control those who, when assigned to distribute it, favored
their compatriots; managing the effects of hoarding (mattresses and
blankets held mangled scraps of bread and butter); and getting nutrition into those too weak to lift a cup to their lips.[107]

Fortunately, most patients were able to take food and water if fed to
them in appropriate forms. When tried, intravenous therapy required
caution; even small amounts of fluids given by slow drip "overloaded"
the severely dehydrated. In May, diet experts brought in Bengal famine
mixture, a sweet gruel that had been effective in India but that disgusted
those with European palates.[108]

Different from anything they had ever experienced, the hospital-
center felt to the relief workers like "another planet," one in which
conventional ideas of tidiness, cleanliness, and morality did not apply.
It required "the greatest mental effort . . . to maintain the right attitude."
Nurses supervising the care of as many as five hundred patients needed
not only technical skills but also abundant human kindness. They

encountered so many whose health had been completely destroyed, who lay mute, helpless, dying. They encountered patients whose psychological state was difficult to understand. Some who were strong enough crept out at night to go on "pilfering expeditions." One nurse found two live chickens under a patient's pillow. Another found half of a calf under a bed.[109]

Desperate for help, the British brought in German doctors and nurses from the original Panzer barracks hospital, as well as from their POW camps. Many aware patients protested; some became hysterical. They could not bear being treated by a German.[110]

As the one hundred men of 32 Casualty Clearing Station, along with other doctors, nurses, and volunteers, struggled to attend to the hospitalized, men of 11 Light Field Ambulance strove to keep inmates still in Camp One alive. For several weeks, survivors in both places died in great numbers. Finally, in mid-May, the daily death rate fell to fewer than one hundred. Hughes attributed this to the advent of extra helpers: the arrival of additional medical units (available now that the war was over) and, more particularly, a group of British medical students.[111]

Ninety-seven students from London hospitals had volunteered to go to Holland to assist the Red Cross in famine relief work. Hughes appealed for them to come to Bergen-Belsen instead. Their primary assignment would be to see to the proper distribution of appropriate food to those inmates remaining in Camp One.[112]

On May 2, the day of their departure, the students learned of the change in their destination. After a long plane trip, they found themselves at the *Panzertruppen Shule*, in rooms formerly occupied by SS guards, one mile from the concentration camp. On Thursday morning, May 3, after a briefing by UNRRA dietician Dr. Arnold Meiklejohn, they entered the dust-laden bleakness. Everything was gray or brown but for the huts, once painted red, now a shade of pink. Two medical students were assigned to each hut. (By this point, seventy-three hundred sick had been taken to the hospital area, eight thousand "fit" had been evacuated to German "married quarters," and five thousand still remained in the Horror Camp huts.) Supplied with large amounts of glucose vitamin and predigested milk protein mixture (which only some of the starved could tolerate) and powdered milk, they also had at their disposal drugs such as chalk, nicotinic acid, charcoal, and the German Tannalbin for diarrhea and other ailments.[113]

Wearing high boots, they stepped onto floors "carpeted . . . with a thick glutinous mass of weeks old excreta" and over to deathly ill inmates, for whom half an aspirin lifted spirits and instilled hope. The scene in the worst huts was "a mixture of post-mortem room, a sewer, sweat, and foul pus." All of the inmates were smeared with feces. Those with diarrhea could not get out of bed. As a result, urine and feces dribbled through the wooden boards of the top two bunks onto the lowest one, which was where the weaker patients were found.[114]

Medical students saw how inmates, whose age ranged from fifteen to thirty, ate small pieces of bread they kept next to them, regardless of what these had been lying in. At least three-quarters of them had hacking coughs, all had bites and severe scabies on their bodies, and some had bedsores the size of small saucers.[115]

No task was beneath the soon-to-be doctors. They stuffed straw mattresses, hosed down huts with creosol, and set up little self-contained hospitals. They became expert in treating the diseases of the camp: diarrhea, typhus, severe malnutrition, sores, boils, and gangrene.[116]

Mornings began with "corpse rounds"—the dead were picked out and removed with the help of Hungarian soldiers. Evenings involved conferences with Dr. Johnston, the senior medical officer in charge of the hospital, and DDMS Hughes, their "most cheering and inspiring guest in the mess."[117]

On May 9, Dr. Johnston shared what he and his men found upon entering the camp. He detailed the evacuation policy: those who could clamber up two steps onto a lorry with assistance from a Tommy were considered "fit" and taken to Camp Three. The scheme broke down. The "fit" were "going down like flies" and had to be evacuated to hospital beds in Camp Two.[118]

On May 11, Hughes gave an after-dinner account of the handover of the camp. He said, "When conditions got completely out of hand . . . the Germans decided to pass on the baby to us." The SS, and German and Hungarian guards, "behaved like sheep." Several hundred SS had left. He could not imagine why Kramer had stayed.[119]

On May 19, one month and four days after the liberation, the last person was evacuated from Camp One. Now each medical student would attend to fifty to sixty patients in the hospital area, which by this point had a minor operating theater and radiography equipment. They could properly examine patients, make diagnoses, provide more appropriate drugs and treatment, and send patients to the X-ray department.[120]

One week later, they briefed their replacements: one hundred and fifty Belgian medical students. When one of the new arrivals asked where the temperature charts were, he learned they would not even have thermometers.[121]

On May 27, the British students took a group photo with Brigadier Hughes on the steps in front of the roundhouse. Paying tribute to their efforts, carried out at a time "when conditions in the horror camp were still indescribable," Hughes said they "performed magnificently," working long hours "with zeal and enthusiasm," never sparing themselves, and undoubtedly saving some of "the worst cases that had to wait to the last."[122]

The group returned home to London, never to forget the "hardest and most worthwhile month's work" of their lives. Hughes then had to answer to Britain's Ministry of Health, deans of several of the London medical schools, and the students' alarmed parents. Despite having been regularly sprayed with DDT, four of the medical students contracted typhus. Two became seriously ill, and one nearly died. Hughes refuted criticisms of Dr. Meiklejohn. He made clear that louse-proof clothing would have been relatively useless and that no student returned to London in a "lousy state." He acknowledged two mistakes: the students had not been properly immunized, and the deans and parents had not been warned of the possible danger.[123]

Some of the ninety-seven British medical students who came to Bergen-Belsen
to aid in the relief efforts, in front of the *Rundhaus*. Brigadier Glyn Hughes
(FRONT ROW, CENTER).
© *Imperial War Museum (HU 59868).*

✥ ✥ ✥

Camp Three, the newly prepared transit and rehabilitation camp in
the former Wehrmacht barracks, housed twenty-five thousand men,
women, and children who, though suffering from malnutrition and
varying degrees of emaciation, were considered "fit." Alone among
these DPs, Elisabeth worried. Where had Rachel been taken? She went
from place to place searching for her. Finally, after three weeks, in the
still-chaotic atmosphere, she found her deathly ill younger sister.[124]

Rachel had no appetite. Thinking she might find something to help
her, Elisabeth ventured into the countryside. One day, she hurried to
the hospital ward with fresh scallions. For the next several days, as soon
as Rachel woke, she began munching on the tubular leaves. Her appetite thus stimulated, she finished what was on her tray. Soon, she stum-
bled over to others' night tables and ate off the trays of the dead or those
too sick to touch their food.

She tried to prop herself up in bed. She looked forward to Elisabeth's visits and to her stories about the British Tommies, who propositioned attractive teenagers with a few English words: "Promenade, chocolate; bed, cigarettes."

A Russian orderly who came into the room offered her tea. *Pit' chai?* sounded like the Hungarian word for vagina. With an embarrassed smile, Rachel shook her head no.

An aide came over when she saw Rachel sitting up. "Don't you feel lucky that you survived?" she asked. "How lucky am I?" Rachel replied. "I lost my parents and almost all my family. I lost my home and my friends. On top of it all, I lost my health." Rachel also lost the ability to make a single decision. She had no home to return to, no one waiting for her, and barely the strength to get out of bed.

One day, Rachel made her way over to the window. As she looked out onto the street, Szilvi Moldovan happened by. "What are you doing in there?" her old schoolmate asked. "That place is for the dying!"[125]

✠ ✠ ✠

One week after Rachel was placed in a room for the dying, Hitler—after learning that Hermann Göring and Himmler deserted him, that Benito Mussolini had been captured and killed by Italian partisans, and that Soviet ground forces were approaching his Führerbunker—committed suicide. Rachel was unaware. Nor did she know the larger picture of which liberation was a part.

Germany's unconditional surrender spawned a period of even harder work for the British Second Army. The 1.5 million returned, dispirited German troops, initially obedient, soon became assertive in asking for help. Fear of Russians intensified; thousands were fleeing from the Russian zone to that of the British. Demands on British medical services increased.[126]

In the midst of the capitulation, on May 8, came V-E (Victory in Europe) Day. While Field Marshal Montgomery lauded the RAMC's outstanding service, while the Hughes family in England celebrated, in

Bergen-Belsen, the momentous day went unmarked. So long as a single victim remained in the concentration camp, Hughes would not allow the Union Jack to be hoisted. Finally, on May 19, with the last hut emptied, the British Liberation Army completed the great task begun when it landed on the beaches of Normandy almost a year earlier. There would be a ceremony to mark the moment and memorialize the victims of Nazi Germany's bestial creed.[127]

On May 21, a wooden platform with a flagstaff was erected thirty yards from Hut 44 in the smaller women's camp. On one side of the hut hung a large poster of a swastika; on the other, a gigantic iron cross. Both these symbols of National Socialism and militarism, along with an effigy of Hitler that hung between them, would soon burn.

Hours before the ceremony's start, three hundred DPs came down from the area of the former Panzer training school. At the ready stood three Bren gun carriers equipped with flame-throwers. One of these accidentally sent a jet of fire over the hut. The carriers' crew rushed over to extinguish the flame.[128]

At 6:00 p.m., British troops marched down and formed a line behind the platform. Other troops, "the Guard of Honour" for the people who died in Belsen, drew up in front of the platform. Hughes and three officers mounted the platform, as did Colonel H. W. Bird, the new commander of Camp One, who announced that the last remaining hut in Belsen was about to be torched. Hughes gave the order. Army photographers captured images of the hut and the effigy of Hitler ablaze, and the brigadier conferring with fellow officers against a background of smoke. A hoisted Union Jack now flew over the dramatic scene.[129]

Lieutenant Colonel Johnston, who with so few resources had set up and run the hospital, joined Hughes at the ceremony. It was the Scottish doctor's last appointment with the DDMS at the concentration camp. During his month of intense work, the beloved Johnston ("Johnny")—small physically, large in sympathy—established that all internees, even those amiss in their behavior, were to be treated with no harshness. The brigadier granted permission for his unit, 32 Casualty Clearing Station, to be relieved.[130]

Brigadier Glyn Hughes (THIRD FROM THE RIGHT) gives the order to set fire to one of the last remaining huts in the smaller women's camp. Lieutenant Colonel James Johnston, senior medical officer at Belsen (FAR RIGHT).
United States Holocaust Memorial Museum, courtesy of Hadassah Bimko Rosensaft.

Glyn Hughes confers with other officers after a crowd of survivors, British soldiers, and those there to help in the relief efforts watched the ceremonial burning of Hut 44.
United States Holocaust Memorial Museum, courtesy of Hadassah Bimko Rosensaft.

✳ ✳ ✳

It had seemed a miracle to the rescuers that an emaciated person who could barely move a muscle would weeks later begin to look human again, regaining the ability to stand, walk, and display her true personality. Once the former skeletons shed their dirty prison garb and obtained German garments from the newly established clothing center, called "Harrods," they carried themselves differently. The revolutionary effect of the emergency work was seen too in survivors who no longer appeared apathetic or frightened, who smiled at and began talking to their aides, asking questions about world events while confronting their losses and uncertain futures.[131]

The phenomenon touched a place deep within Hughes. He had brought Major R. J. Phillips, an army psychiatrist, to Belsen on several occasions to assess the effects of such trauma on people's minds. On the psychiatrist's third visit, he saw signs of improvement, but, even so, when entering a sick ward he thought it resembled that of a mental institution. Six weeks after the liberation, Hughes made his own assessment. Though still weak, many patients seemed "of good morale." How perfect their recovery would be would depend on their "basic personalities, intellect, and upbringing." He knew that "a large proportion" would again become "reasonable citizens."[132]

On May 24, just days after the burning of the last hut, the DPs organized an international cabaret featuring folk dances and songs. At a dance in a square between blocks, British soldiers and men from the Canadian air force swung recovering girls, dressed in their new finery, on their arms. Belsen survivors, now numbering thirty thousand (including thirteen thousand in the hospital and roughly three thousand convalescents in another area), were beginning to organize themselves into what would become a thriving DP community.[133]

It would not be long before Hughes would attend the first wedding in the Belsen DP camp, to which he received a special invitation. A charming Lithuanian girl and a Polish man stood under a gold-and-red chuppah (canopy) held up by four other survivors. Among the one hundred guests in the former Wehrmacht officers' mess were the rabbi, other British officers, British Red Cross volunteers, and survivors of various nationalities. After a feast, the guests danced to a military band.[134]

Many such occasions would follow. Eager to form families, the survivors would marry at a staggering rate, averaging six weddings a day in the Belsen DP camp for the rest of the year. But the first wedding was symbolic, and twenty years later when he met the couple and "their bonny children" on one of his visits to Israel, Hughes would recall this "brightest interlude."[135]

Actors would perform professional dramatic productions on the stage that once served the Gestapo. In the Kazet (for KZ, *Konzentrationslager*, or concentration camp) Theatre, survivors would see depictions of familiar traumas. A child actor sobbing, "Mother, I'm hungry," or an actress reciting, "Everything that I once knew is gone, burned, mutilated," would bring catharsis to audiences of thousands. Many would weep throughout performances.[136]

Other entertainment would be brought into the camp. On a beautiful, midsummer Friday, survivors sitting on grass would hear violinist Yehudi Menuhin play pieces by Bach, Mendelssohn, and Debussy.[137]

Soon after entering Bergen-Belsen, Hughes realized that the vast majority of its inmates were Jewish. British senior government officials, holding onto old stereotypes, believing the Jews tended to exaggerate their suffering, chose not to disclose this fact. Their narrative of the liberation focused on the defeat of the evil regime and the uncovering of the horrors it inflicted, driving home the purpose of Britain's involvement in the war—fought on behalf of humanity and not one particular group. References to Jews were edited out of journalist Dimbleby's early reports. (One of two recordings he made at the time of the liberation, referring explicitly to the Jewishness of the victims, was not used.) The inmates were to be categorized by their nationalities only; the British aimed for them to be repatriated to their countries of origin.[138]

A minority of Jewish survivors who came from western European countries did return home. But most survivors, from Poland and other eastern European countries, had no homes to which to return; their families and friends had been murdered in Auschwitz and other death and labor camps. Continuing to visit the DP camp and hospital long past the date his formal duties in Bergen-Belsen ended (he subsequently assumed the post of vice director of medical services of the British Army of the Rhine), Hughes would marvel at the emergence of strong leaders from among those who had arrived in Bergen-Belsen just days before the liberation. These young people had in their prewar lives experienced unity and a sense of purpose as members of various Zionist youth organizations. They spoke Hebrew, knew Hebrew songs, and were full of hope. They would help their fellow survivors and mourners see themselves not only as the *she'erit hapletah*, the "surviving remnant," but also as individuals who could aspire to a normal life. They would undertake the provision of food, clothing, schools, jobs, and health services at the camp. They would create a community that offered strength and support, enabling survivors "to reconstruct their sufferings into a coherent and meaningful narrative" by inspiring those from religiously and politically diverse prewar backgrounds to embrace a common, immediate goal.[139]

Josef Rosensaft, a small, wiry thirty-four-year-old who had been a member of the Poale Zion movement, who had endured Auschwitz and harsh labor at Dora-Mittelbau, and who became the DPs' self-appointed (and later democratically elected) leader, listened to his fellow survivors' wishes and tried to meet their needs. He immediately organized a provisional committee. Within weeks, the committee irritated British authorities by advocating for survivors who wanted to make their lives in the Jewish homeland. Given Britain's control over Palestine—a strategic colonial position in the Near East and a vital route to India and its oil supplies—its officials feared complications. They refused to allow Jewish self-government with respect to the Zionist cause. They refused to allow delegations from other parts of Germany or abroad to visit Belsen. They refused to improve the harsh living conditions in the DP camp, ignored the spiritual needs of Jewish survivors, and denied requests for the meeting of a general Jewish congress.[140]

While praising British medical saviors, Rosensaft disregarded British authorities. Soon, he would hold conferences that promoted a united front against the occupiers' strict rules and charge a subcommittee with preparing a Jewish congress in Germany. Soon, soldiers of the Palestine-based Jewish Brigade, in uniforms with a Star of David insignia, would appear. They would involve survivors in cultural activities, schools, and pioneer training programs—all means of telling the story of the *yishuv*, towns and villages in Palestine where Jews lived with pride.[141]

Impressed by the "ball of fire" who advocated on behalf of his fellow survivors, Hughes would attend events that Rosensaft, Rafael Olewski (a former member of the Zionist party in Poland), and other young leaders organized, including the First Congress of Liberated Jews in Germany. Slated to meet on September 26 and 27, the historic gathering would coincide with the Belsen trial in Lüneburg, which would naturally attract journalists and reporters.[142]

Noting Hughes's compassion and gentleness in dealing with patients, Rabbi Levy knew that many hundreds "felt they owed their lives to his devotion and concern." These survivors decided to honor the brigadier. Before the summer's end, they would name the thirteen-thousand-bed complex in the Bergen-Hohne area (less than one mile from the concentration camp) the Glyn Hughes Hospital. Nearly three years later, in February 1948, the DP community would celebrate the birth of the thousandth baby in the hospital. That the Second Army had saved a remnant of the Jewish people from annihilation was a source of pride for Hughes. He considered the recovery of survivors and the formation of a self-governing community in Bergen-Belsen a "glorious moment in Jewish history."[143]

SEASONS AFTER
Healing and Redemption

O f coming back to the world of the living, one survivor said, "Show us the sun, but slowly." Elisabeth had seen some sun and was eager to share the experience with Rachel. At the beginning of June, she brought her sister to Belsen's DP camp. Rachel appreciated the improved food. Though weak, she went to hear *shlichim* (emissaries) from Palestine, who taught Hebrew songs and gave inspiring lectures. She participated in an organized activity—gluing miniature Israeli flags to small sticks.

Elisabeth insisted they take walks around the camp. Rachel noticed how healthy survivors, most in their twenties and thirties, were searching for relatives, trying to look presentable (altering their clothes, for example), pairing off, and making plans. She and Elisabeth had no plans.

The Swedish Red Cross came to Bergen-Belsen. Doctors screened survivors, the sickest of whom could go to Sweden to recuperate. Diagnosed with tuberculosis, Rachel and Elisabeth were among the thousands who qualified.[1]

On June 19, the day survivors left Bergen-Belsen, German soldiers, under British supervision, brought the weak on stretchers to waiting ambulances and, at the train station, carried them onto sleeper cars. Others of the survivors boarded the trains' second-class cars. German orderlies brought everyone coffee and milk. British soldiers distributed chocolate and crackers. A decent supper followed.[2]

Bound for a new situation, grateful for any kindness shown them, the sick and stateless slept through the night as the train transported them over the devastated countryside. At 8:00 a.m. the next day, they arrived at Lübeck's huge underground station. Upon disembarking they saw German soldiers standing at attention, ready to carry the sick up a flight of stairs to waiting ambulances. Swedes in uniform welcomed and escorted them all to the beautiful city of gothic buildings. There, each person underwent a medical examination, registered, and received a number—a protocol somewhat reminiscent of Auschwitz.[3]

On the afternoon of July 10—after weeks of enjoying good food, entertainment by Swedish soldiers, and the gardens near Lübeck's harbor—Rachel boarded the *Crown Princess Ingrid*, a small vessel that traveled slowly and only by day; though the war had ended, the North Sea still contained mines. Separated from Elisabeth, who left Germany's shores on a different boat, she clung to two other girls her age. Nestled beneath the stairwell and away from the overcrowded upper and lower decks, they dissuaded those who asked to share their space. "We have a communicable disease," they said.[4]

After docking in Lund, the newcomers were met by nurses who, concerned that they might be bringing typhoid to Sweden, had them exchange the garb they had on for new clothes. Made to go through a hot steam bath and then an icy shower, Rachel thought they were being tested: Could their frail bodies endure the assault?

Buses transported the group to a quarantined school in Malmö, on Sweden's southern coast. Rachel claimed a top bunk in the auditorium filled with beds. At a long table in the gymnasium-turned-dining-hall, she sat each morning before a bowl of lumpy oatmeal, lingonberry preserves, and cream. She ate only the preserves and cream. Other meals included boiled fish and potatoes. Rachel often took bread back to her bunk. She could not yet trust that there would be food tomorrow.[5]

After several weeks, the sick were sent from Malmö to various locations for medical treatment. Rachel and thirty-five other girls traveled north to Katrineholm, where a converted school housed nurses, doctors, and a medical laboratory. Finally, Rachel could contact Elisabeth, who had been sent to a hospital in Karlstad. They shouted into the telephone, having never before used such a device.[6]

Once again, the refugees were kept separate from the Swedish population. Curious about the arrivals from distant lands, locals came to the chain link fence surrounding the hospital yard. Some tried to speak with the girls. Some invited girls to their homes, for which permission was usually granted.

Sitting on the embankment of a narrow moat, Rachel communicated in broken German with a tall blond boy on the other side of the fence. During his afternoon visits, the sixteen-year-old asked where she came from and about what she had experienced. Having seen newsreels depicting the liberation of concentration camps, he wanted to know, "Was it really that bad?" Rachel told him that it was worse than he could imagine. The boy invited Rachel to his home. Too shy to accept, she felt jealous when another girl went and came back with clothes and other items.

The boy brought Rachel small gifts. One day, he threw a carved-wood nutcracker over the fence. Rachel could place a walnut in the toothless mouth of an old man's head and with a clamp of his jaw produce an edible kernel. (Her first postwar present, it would stay with her all the days of her life.)

On one unseasonably warm day shortly before her sixteenth birthday, Rachel, running to the fence and cavorting about the hospital yard, became hot and sweaty. She went inside and splashed herself with cold water. That evening, she spiked a high fever. Dr. Leffler, a large-framed, bow-legged woman with short, straight hair and a habit of scratching her behind (perhaps, Rachel thought, to amuse the girls), placed compresses on Rachel's forehead and gave her medicine. She stayed by her bedside all night and all the next day, even though she had other patients to attend. As Rachel's delirium abated, she registered the tenderness in Dr. Leffler's lovely blue eyes.

Bedridden for two weeks with pneumonia, Rachel felt deprived of the chance to see the town of Katrinehölm. Girls who explored the area told her about the nice homes and shops and movie theater, about how very clean Sweden was.

When she recovered, Rachel was taken to the hospital's basement clinic, where a doctor tried to perform "collapse therapy" (artificial pneumothorax) on her. The procedure entailed inserting a long needle into her back, between her ribs, and into the pleural space surrounding her lungs; pumped-in air would collapse the damaged organ and give it a chance to heal. Rachel was hopeful. She knew two girls who benefited from the treatment. But the terrible pain she suffered was for naught—broad adhesions overlying her lung sacs made the area impossible to penetrate.

While Swedish doctors tried to help Rachel, the Belsen trial was underway in Lüneburg, Germany. The afternoon after Hadassah Bimko's testimony, Glyn Hughes led members of the court on a guided tour of Bergen-Belsen. Thousands of former inmates lined the road to cheer them. The crowd hissed at Kramer and Klein, who, handcuffed together, walked under military guard.[7]

Though Camp One was destroyed, court members gained a sense of its general layout and the two-kilometer (1.25 mile) distance between "Belsen proper," hidden among pines and surrounded by barbed wire, and Camp Two, at the edge of the Wehrmacht barracks and Panzer school. In addition to showing the locations of the mass graves, Hughes pointed out buildings near Camp Two, erected shortly before the war's end, where conditions, though awful, were not nearly as extreme as those in Camp One.[8]

Four days later, while the Belsen trial was still in session, Hughes again visited Bergen-Belsen—this time to attend a forbidden event. The British could not stop Josef Rosensaft and his committee from inviting political figures from abroad as well as representatives from forty-three displaced persons camps to the First Congress of Liberated Jews. Two hundred and ten delegates representing forty thousand Jewish survivors managed to find transportation to—and accommodations near—Bergen-Belsen, the largest of Germany's DP camps.[9]

ABOVE: The earliest extant photo of Rachel (THIRD ROW, THIRD FROM THE LEFT, WEARING A DARK JACKET) taken five or six months after the liberation. Not yet sixteen, she is among other teenaged survivors who were sent to a makeshift hospital in Katrinehölm, Sweden, for medical treatment. Dr. Leffler (BOTTOM ROW, SECOND FROM RIGHT).

LEFT: Rachel is still bruised in this photograph, so one can imagine how she appeared right after having been beaten in Bergen-Belsen.

On the first day of the congress, Glyn Hughes joined reporters, visiting dignitaries, and thousands of survivors at the roundhouse. Two huge blue-and-white flags and an enormous yellow star hung over the platform. A wide banner, emblazoned with the words "Open the Gates of Palestine," hung from above. Mournful voices blended in the singing of "Hatikvah" (The hope). A group of young survivors wearing blue and white then led a march to Camp One, where heart-rending sobs punctuated prayers intoned at the edge of a mass grave.[10]

Consecrating a temporary memorial near one of the immense graves, Rabbi Zvi Helfgott and Rabbi Leslie Hardman were joined by

a thirteen-year-old orphan who recited the kaddish (memorial prayer).
Muriel Knox Doherty, a British Red Cross nurse, stood on a section of
elevated ground near Hughes. Before the ceremony began, she asked
the brigadier to point out the perimeter of the camp, an area measuring
four-fifths by two-fifths of a mile, in which fifty thousand living and
unburied dead had been concentrated. She thought she could pick out
among the thousands of weeping men and women those who had been
in the Horror Camp—owing to illness and starvation, their hair was
fine and sparse.[11]

Back at the roundhouse, Rosensaft, Rafael Olewski, and others of the
seventeen-member committee appealed to the conscience of the world
to open the gates of Palestine to the survivors. Rosensaft implored the
British to "make our liberty final and true." Calling for the establish-
ment of a Jewish state, he spoke for the displaced in expressing "sorrow
and indignation" that almost six months after liberation survivors still
found themselves in guarded camps.[12]

Rosensaft welcomed representatives of British and American Jewish
organizations. According all factions a hearing, he allowed unpopular
presentations from communists and those advocating a return to their
previous countries. Most of the speeches—in German and Yiddish,
with a few in English and Hungarian—drove home the same points:
Jews in Europe suffered a history of persecution; the present conditions
in the DP camp were poor and needed improvement; and the Jews
had the right to determine their own destiny in their own way in their
own country, to guard their children and coming generations against a
repetition of the cataclysm that had befallen them.[13]

To British officials, the survivors and their supporters appeared un-
grateful. One commentator believed that "the bitter and dirty political
battle between the British and the DPs restored the natural anti-Semitism
of British officialdom." Against this fraught backdrop, Rosensaft extended a special welcome to Brigadier Glyn Hughes, who, owing to his
tireless work on their behalf, was the adopted "father of the Jewish survivors of Belsen."[14]

The congress may not have been the only event at which Hughes would hear political figures fuel survivors' hopes. In the middle of the trial, on October 25, David Ben Gurion, the Zionist leader who would become the first prime minister of Israel, visited Bergen-Belsen. Applause resounded through the tent-theater in response to his impassioned speech on the importance of a homeland; the lack of one made the Jews prey to slaughterers. Again, the "Hatikvah," the anthem that at the moment served as the *she'erit hapletah*'s (surviving remnant's) prayer for aliyah (ascent to the Holy Land), washed over the receptive DPs.[15]

Back in Lüneburg, lawyers for the defense displayed gross insensitivity to witnesses who had been subjected to a long period of cruelty and violence. They pointed out discrepancies in depositions, written statements, and oral testimonies, failing to grasp that in a prison camp without calendars it was impossible to be sure of a particular date or to know whether perpetrators included those presently in custody. Defense attorneys T. C. M. Winwood and L. S. W. Cranfield argued "that it was very likely that many incidents of a trivial nature had been telescoped together to produce one of a grave nature" and called on the court "to be very careful . . . not to confuse fact with fantasy."[16]

Those testifying relayed raw, often absurd, manifestations of evil. Helene Klein of Ternow, Poland, accused former Auschwitz commander Franz Hoessler of selecting her for the gas chamber, of telling her that at nineteen years old she had "lived enough." She said that Irma Grese made sport of the women in Belsen, exhausting them by making them fall down, get up, run, and trot.[17]

One of the witnesses for the prosecution, Anita Lasker-Walfisch, concluded that the trial was a "huge farce." After being interrogated, she explained how she

came face to face with British justice, under which you are innocent unless proven guilty . . . a commendable principle, but . . .

difficult to apply or even adapt to the sorts of crimes that were being dealt with in Lüneburg . . . Questions like: ". . . did you ever see any of these people kill anybody?" If you answered "Yes," the next question would be: "Which day of the week was this, and what time exactly?" Naturally you had to answer "I don't know." You were under oath, but in the camp you had neither a watch nor a calendar, nor would [you] have been the slightest bit interested whether it was Monday or Tuesday.[18]

In his affidavit, defendant Dr. Klein admitted to committing heinous crimes. He said he told Josef Kramer that, had he been in the shoes of an English officer-liberator, he would have taken the both of them and "put them against the wall and shot them." Among other of the trial's absurdities: the denial of the fact that Jews as a distinct people had been singled out and marked for extermination. Belsen's victims were repeatedly referred to as "Allied nationals."[19]

An outraged public declared the trial "an insult to those who had died at Belsen, and to those who liberated it." *Pravda* journalist Trainin denounced the "gentlemanly behavior toward prisoners" by Major Winwood. Arkady Perventzeff, *Izvestia*'s special correspondent in Berlin, called for an immediate end to the trial. He argued that the indictment's formula centered on "bad treatment of prisoners which caused the death of many people," an understatement that failed to link events at Bergen-Belsen to the calculated destruction of millions. Moscow radio commentator S. Victoroif said that the court and the defense "justified the butchery practiced" in Belsen and Auschwitz and that "fascists everywhere have been encouraged" by the trial.[20]

On November 17, five senior British officers rendered their sentences. Fourteen of the SS defendants were acquitted; thirty-one were found guilty. Six found guilty on one count (crimes at Belsen) and five found guilty on both counts (crimes at Auschwitz and Belsen) were sentenced to death. British policewomen marched Irma Grese, Elisabeth

SEASONS AFTER: HEALING AND REDEMPTION

Volkenrath, and Juana Bormann before the raised dais of the tribunal. Tribunal president Major General Horatio P. M. Berney-Ficklin announced that "Number Nine, Grese," was accorded the sentence of "death by being hanged." Volkenrath and Bormann received the same sentence. The three were led out to a pickup room to await transport back to their Lüneburg cells. Grese initially received the verdict with composure; back in her cell, she broke into sobs. On December 13, in a jail in the town of Hamelin, executioner Albert Pierrepoint hanged the eight men and three women.[21]

No effort was made to track down and put on trial the scores of Nazi guards who left Bergen-Belsen on April 13 as part of the ceasefire agreement.[22]

After the trial, Hughes marked the end of his service in Germany with a farewell party at British Army headquarters in the spa town of Bad Oeynhausen. He presented Hadassah Bimko with a certificate of recognition for her work and offered to help her find a position in Britain. He was not, however, able to exert influence on his own behalf.[23]

Hughes was about to assume a temporary position as the commanding officer and inspector of training at the RAMC in Aldershot (the postwar center for the medical corps). Aspiring to an army career, he had applied for a permanent post. An official wrote with disappointing news:

My dear Glyn Hughes,

Your application for a regular Commission was submitted by me to the Director of Personal Services and the Military Secretary who, as you are aware, are the authorities on the policy of the Army in such matters.

I have now heard from both of them and I regret to say they advise that it is impracticable to proceed with granting of a regular Commission to you. I am informed that other and similar cases to yours have been considered and in no case has a commission been granted; indeed the whole question was considered when the grant of regular Commissions to "middle piece" officers was before a Committee and the policy has definitely been laid down. Any departure from that policy would create a precedent which cannot be admitted.

I am sorry about it, but I am sure you will understand, and I know it will make no difference to your keenness in your new appointment.[24]

Hughes had been made a Commander of the Order of the British Empire. He received a citation for Legion of Merit from the White House; President Harry Truman wrote that the services he rendered in combatting and controlling sources of disease and in directing many medical units in the field "materially contributed to the success of the Allied forces in Europe." He was also one of only eighteen RAMC officers to win a second bar to a Distinguished Service Order. The natural progression for someone with such an outstanding military career would have been to advance to a regular commission at the rank of, perhaps, major general. Was Hughes too old? Was his application denied on account of the army's postwar paring down of personnel? Or, as British medical students who served in Bergen-Belsen wondered, was he barred because he "went by his own rules"?[25]

Hughes knew of comparable cases in which commissions were in fact granted. Upon his return to England, he wrote a letter to a general asking his views on the matter and expressing the feeling that "now that they have had all they want out of me I shall be quietly put on the shelf having lost rank and not much else to show for it." His "keenness for [his] new job unabated," he would have wished for "some security of tenure."[26]

In late October 1945—before the end of the Belsen trial and the start of the Nuremberg trials (during which Rachel, listening to radio news coverage, realized the impossibility of justice)—a number of survivors from Katrinehölm were sent to Arvika, a tuberculosis sanitarium in snowy northwest Sweden. Soon after their arrival, two female orderlies invited Rachel and another girl to their room. They seemed affectionate, and the forlorn girls initially welcomed the attention. But when one of the orderlies tried to touch Rachel's breasts, she recoiled. She knew nothing of homosexuality. She had, however, picked up enough Swedish to understand what the molester said as she patted her on the head: "You stupid little girl." When Rachel later told an older survivor what happened, the woman assured her that she was not stupid and that she was beautiful. It had been so long since she heard such kind words.

Having nutritious food, warm clothing, and plenty of rest and fresh air, Rachel began to feel better. By May 1946, one year after the liberation, her health had improved to the point that she could leave the sanitarium for a convalescent home. At the next stop in her uncharted journey—Vikarbyn, 168 miles northeast of Arvika—her obstinacy led to regret. She had a falling-out with a girl she wanted to befriend, who stopped speaking to her after they vied for the top bunk and Rachel refused to yield.

✡ ✡ ✡

Back in September, two months after the refugees had arrived in Sweden, the country's foreign commission issued an order for the youngest among them to be offered some schooling. Eli Getreau, a caretaker of Jewish women's refugee camps, was charged with registering those under eighteen, mostly girls, for ten internat (international) schools in various locations. He became head of one of the schools, near the village of By-Kyrkby (pronounced Be-Chirkby), which opened in October. Elisabeth was among its first students.

In her letters to Rachel, Elisabeth enthused about the school in Sweden's historic Dalarna region. Finally, in September 1946, Rachel was able to join her there. Because most of the students had begun their studies at least six months earlier, Rachel and her friend Sári, also a new arrival from Arvika via Vikarbyn, worked hard to catch up. Instead of attending group meetings and events, they spent evenings poring over lessons.[27]

By-Kyrkby's students hailed from diverse prewar backgrounds. They were the children of tailors or teachers or rabbis. They came from cities or small towns or rural areas. Most were from Czechoslovakia, Hungary, Poland, and Romania, but there were also a Greek and an Italian among them.[28]

All had lived under the constant threat of death. Most had arrived in Sweden after the war weighing about eighty pounds, and most had tuberculosis and had been or would be hospitalized. They carried with them the trauma of their recent past. One girl had sorted the clothes of her friends who had been forced, naked, into the gas chamber. One saw a Nazi break her brother's bones with a baton. Another had been beaten on the head and thought she would forever be blind.[29]

Painful associations intruded regularly. Walking by chimneys reminded the girls of the crematoria at Auschwitz. When passing chickens in the road, one girl broke down crying—the small animals reminded her of her family's farm. Birthdays of murdered family members were sorrowful occasions. Tension attended mail time; rarely was there news of a relative having survived.[30]

By the time Rachel arrived in By-Kyrkby, most of its fifty-five girls had adjusted to the initially shocking milieu—in this school, teachers were called by their first names, students chose the subjects they wished to learn and whether or not to study or participate in activities, and policies were decided democratically at meetings. (How to rotate available rugs among bedrooms engendered deliberation as serious as that of a United Nations session.) Suspicious and bitter teenagers had softened in response to compassionate teachers who, also refugees, understood what they had witnessed and endured. They forged closed friendships, took responsibility for their own learning, and began to trust that the world had something more than terrible things in store for them. They staged plays, threw parties, and celebrated holidays.[31]

Rachel felt intimidated by talented and gregarious classmates. She would not recite poems or raise her hand in class. When she did attend meetings, she refrained from voting on issues or weighing in on current events. She watched from a distance as girls—in eager anticipation of their evening's entertainment—encircled and danced around the automobile that brought movie reels. When a few teenaged boys arrived in By-Kyrkby, Rachel would not compete for their attention. (But when a boy with big brown eyes asked her to dance at a party, she was elated.)

By-Kyrkby's teachers asked Rachel why she looked so sad and invited her to come talk with them. They exposed her to awe-inspiring subjects. Rachel absorbed Alika's lively lessons on the stories of operas. Valli taught Hebrew and Jewish history. (Both women, in their thirties, had been teachers before the war.) Eli Getreau, the handsome headmaster with whom many of the girls were infatuated, devoted Saturday afternoons to discussions of classical composers' styles and compositions. When he played Dvořák's *New World Symphony* on the gramophone, Rachel closed her eyes and imagined the drama of creation.[32]

As the students, almost all orphaned, would soon be on their own, their teachers tried to fortify them. When asked for advice, they turned questions back to the girls, saying, What do you think? What would you say? Alika stressed that she could but give them a taste; they should try to live near a city where they would have access to culture. Valli told them they should strive to improve themselves and meet life with hope and not fear.

Eli Getreau made arrangements for those nearing the age of eighteen to leave By-Kyrkby. In February 1947, Rachel and four other girls were sent to work at a marmalade factory. Having never before had to make decisions concerning her keep, Rachel suddenly had to worry about food and housing. But it was exciting to earn money and cooperate with others; the girls shared an apartment and divided chores.

Rachel rose at 5:00 a.m., walked forty minutes in the cold, and spent the day retrieving oranges from a barrel of warm water, cutting them into quarters, and moving them along an assembly line. She ate as much

as she could. When the manager learned she had tuberculosis and therefore should not be handling food, he transferred her to the upstairs
office, where she stuffed envelopes and filled small containers with bak-
ing powder. Though glad to be productive, she happily returned to By-
Kyrkby when the placement ended. Back just in time to celebrate the
Jewish holiday of Purim, she dressed in her favorite costume—baggy
pants, a jacket and tie, and a mustache.

Eli Getreau found a new placement for Rachel and several other
girls. In late March they arrived in Söderby Sjukhus (South Village Hospital), a large tuberculosis sanitarium in Uttran. Here Rachel roomed
with well-read Olga, who regaled her with fantastic stories, such as that
of the queen of Sheba, who watched her figure by wrapping a snake
around her waist and who traveled from Ethiopia to Jerusalem to meet
the wisest of men, King Solomon. The roommates became fast friends.

In Söderby Sjukhus, Rachel rotated among various departments, including the X-ray department (where it was quite the challenge to fit
long Swedish names on tiny films) and the laboratory (where she performed tests on bodily fluids, hankered to use the microscope, and
decided to someday study to become a laboratory technician). She
watered potted geraniums on windowsills lining long, sunlit corridors.
Rachel's assignments were better than those of most other girls, who
had to make beds and empty bedpans. But one of her posts induced
stress.

Twice a week, Rachel assisted surgeons in the operating room. She
helped them on with their coats and gloves, and sterilized their instruments. She sewed metal pieces into gauze pads so they could be found
by X-ray if accidentally left in a patient.

On her first day, Rachel stood beside a surgeon who cut into his patient with an electric knife. The smell of the man's seared flesh evoked
that of burning bodies in Auschwitz. Rachel fainted. Someone wheeled
her out on a gurney. Upon regaining consciousness, she went right
back into the operating room. After Bergen-Belsen, she told herself,
she could be strong.

But there were limits to her strength. Seeing a bedridden patient able to walk after a successful thoracoplasty (surgery involving the removal of rib bones and parts of lungs) was heartening. But the lopsided posture of those missing ribs gave Rachel nightmares. She herself might need the disfiguring operation.

Rachel had chest X-rays every three months. In February 1948, nearly three years after the liberation, her films showed numerous white areas. For two weeks, the hospital's medical staff withheld the bad news— they needed her in the operating room. Finally, her doctor sent her to a convalescent home in Visby, on the holiday island of Gotland. There she met a young man who engaged her in conversation about the war. The horrible events, he argued, had been foretold in the Hebrew Bible. The text even contained passages predicting cannibalism. Embarrassed by her ignorance, Rachel stayed up late studying the holy book.

When Rachel did not get well after six months, she came back to Söderby Sjukhus as a tuberculosis patient. A year earlier, during Rachel's last weeks at By-Kyrkby, Elisabeth underwent extensive dental treatment. After adjusting to dentures, she came to work at Söderby Sjukhus. The sisters' joy at being together gave way to disappointment when Rachel was sent away to convalesce. Now that Rachel was back, Elisabeth could visit her every day.

Once Rachel got well, Elisabeth decided it was time for them to move closer to the big city. They took jobs at L. M. Ericsson, an electrical meter company a half hour from Stockholm. The factory provided barrack-style housing. Rachel shared a tiny room with Elisabeth and a kitchen, laundry, and storage room with ten others. She hated that her belongings kept disappearing. She and Elisabeth bided their time. It was the summer of 1948; they hoped to follow their By-Kyrkby friends who emigrated to the newly proclaimed state of Israel.[33]

Unlike Elisabeth, who tolerated the tedious winding of wire finer than a strand of hair around spools, Rachel became frustrated because the filament kept breaking. She told the L. M. Ericsson foreman she wanted a different job. He assigned her to an assembly table with eight men. Soldering wires to parts, gluing glass covers onto meters, Rachel produced her quota of eight meters per hour in twenty minutes. But when she complained that she was earning less than a third of what men performing the same job were being paid, the foreman told her that men had expenses related to dating or supporting a family and therefore needed more money than women. She would have to continue to live on pasta and potatoes, to scrimp and save to buy a few pieces of decent clothing.

The assembly-line worker closest in age to Rachel told her that he was a great admirer of Hitler, whose portrait hung in his apartment. She brought her wart remover pen with her to work the next day. "Give me your hand," she commanded playfully. He did. She painted two large *X*s on it. The marks turned black and could not be washed off. Her thoughtless workmate thereafter treated her nicely.

After moving to improved lodgings—a coworker's attic—Rachel and Elisabeth had to take a bus to the factory. But their situation would be temporary. They had submitted applications to emigrate to Israel and needed only medical clearance.

The doctor who examined Rachel told her she was not strong enough; Israel needed healthy young people. She emitted a heavy sigh. "You look," he said, "as though you are carrying the weight of the world on your shoulders." His prescription: see Marx brothers movies. Following her doctor's orders, Rachel relearned how to laugh. And a scene in a Molière play helped her to overcome her shyness: when the protagonist told a lamp how lovely it was, it lit up. When trying to make conversation, she could give a compliment.

In her spare time, Rachel took classes, attended lectures at Stockholm's Mosaiska Församlingen (Jewish Center), played bridge (she and her partner won first prize in a hundred-person tournament), and, as often as she could, bought inexpensive tickets to the opera and Royal Dramatic Theatre. Occasionally, she attended matinee dances. One partner, a German, asked how she knew his native language. She told him she had been in concentration camps. "You must want to kill me right here on the dance floor," he said. She told him she was not a murderer but also not afraid of going to jail. Rachel thought that a Swedish prison would not be so bad.

Other social gatherings included weddings of those within the survivor community. At one such event, the rabbi praised the groom, a Swedish man from a prominent Jewish family, for marrying a poor, sick orphan (who, Rachel knew, lost her physician father and the rest of her family in the war). Infuriated by the patronizing comment, Rachel was at the same time reminded of her own status. On two occasions, boys who had been sweet to her had chosen to marry others. The better catches were a girl whose parents were rich and a nurse. Who was she? At times Rachel felt like a nobody.

When Elisabeth married Mike Pelta, an industrious and caring survivor from Poland, Rachel moved into the three-bedroom apartment the newlyweds shared with their odd photographer landlord. It felt luxurious to now have a balcony, a kitchen, and a bathroom.

April 1950. When someone at the Mosaiska Församlingen told Rachel about a family that needed help preparing and serving the Passover meals, she jumped at the opportunity. It had been six years since she had celebrated the holiday in a Jewish home. It had been six years since she was with her family in Sighet.

The Schnabels welcomed Rachel. (She later learned that they favored attractive young women; with her neatly styled hair and tasteful dress—a purchase for which she had long saved—she cut a fine figure.) Grandpa Schnabel explained that a whole onion could be used in making chicken-vegetable soup—its skin gives the soup a nice color and flavor. Grandma Schnabel and her daughter, Berta, in her thirties, showed Rachel how to make Passover noodles with eggs and a small amount of potato flour.

Rachel and two other female survivors were guests at the seder table bedecked with a damask tablecloth, matching plates of fine china, silver flatware, and crystal goblets. Rachel noted, too, the room's impressive furnishings—a china cabinet, a sofa with two end tables, and an oriental rug.

Grandpa Schnabel conducted the seder. Berta's eight-year-old son, Herbert, asked the four questions. Rachel and Berta served the delicious pot roast and potato pancakes with applesauce. Everyone drank the customary four cups of wine. When it came time to clean up, Berta's brother Max, a handsome, balding doctor with warm, brown eyes, taught Rachel that it was more hygienic to wash dishes in very hot water and let them air dry than to dry them with a towel.

The second night of the holiday went as well as the first.

Having been promised a present, Herbert behaved well enough during the seders. He seemed to like Rachel, who made an effort to engage him. But soon Rachel would discover what had been temporarily controlled: within the boy rumbled emotions that could in an instant erupt into a violent rage.

One year earlier Herbert had been in New York with his father and mother. After divorcing her miserly husband, Berta brought the boy back with her to Sweden, where her father, a diamond dealer, set her up with a jewelry store. Managing Lyckoringen (Lucky Ring) required business travel. On the evenings she was in town, Berta tried to meet up with friends or go on dates. Unhappy with the changes in his life, Herbert discharged his fury on a series of governesses, throwing at them— at the slightest provocation—rocks or pots or anything he could get his hands on. No one would stay with him.

By the time Rachel met Herbert, he had been expelled from several schools. Berta explained the situation when, after Passover, she asked Rachel to babysit. Rachel loved children and thought she could handle the challenge.

Taking two trolleys to get to Berta's apartment on the outskirts of Stockholm, Rachel anticipated a fine time with Herbert. But, as soon as his mother left, he began kicking her. When she told her sister and brother-in-law about the dangerous boy, they said, "What do you need this for?" Rachel nevertheless went back when Berta called. She liked the family and had coped with much worse.

What turned things around was as effective as it was unplanned.

One evening, after Berta left the house, Herbert began throwing books at Rachel. He jumped on her and pinched her. To protect herself, she ran into the bathroom and locked the door. Herbert flipped the light switch outside the bathroom. Rachel feigned loud and bitter crying. She professed her fear of the dark. Herbert turned the light back on. He asked her to please come out; he promised he would not hurt her anymore.

Over the next few months, Herbert occasionally lapsed into his former wild behavior. During an outing at the beach, he bit Rachel's arm. She bit him back. Berta took them both for tetanus shots.

In late December, Rachel quit her job at L. M. Ericsson and began working for the Schnabels full time. She served not only as Herbert's caregiver but also as his companion; she went with him to hockey and soccer games, to see westerns and on ski trips. Grateful for her breakthrough with Herbert, the Schnabels took Rachel with them to fine restaurants and on resort vacations, where she was served breakfast in bed. Never had she been so well treated.

Berta named Rachel, and not any of her own three brothers, Herbert's guardian in the event something should happen to her. Though honored to be considered part of the family, Rachel felt lonely. She had stopped taking classes and going to matinee dances and did not see much of friends. When Max came to dinner and stayed on to talk, she enjoyed the company of another young adult. He told her he had been in New York and came back to Sweden during the war, crossing the ocean at great peril (the Germans torpedoed ships). His parents had wanted him to stay in the United States, but the country's medical schools accepted few Jews.

Max took Rachel for a ride in his new Volvo, demonstrating the car's cutting-edge features. He told her that he was looking to marry an unspoiled girl. She listened with great interest to all he shared but felt

Herbert and Rachel, 1951.

uncomfortable when he asked about her. How and when did she come
to Sweden? Rachel gave vague answers.

Berta feared germs. (Herbert had to wash his hands every time he
came in from playing outdoors.) Had her employer known the truth
about Rachel—who while cooking for Herbert tasted his food—she
would have panicked.

Having to hide her health history weighed on Rachel. Within a year
of working for the Schnabels, her X-rays showed that she had again
suffered a relapse. Beside herself, Rachel confided in her friend Miriam
from By-Kyrkby. How could she tell her generous and anxious employer
that she had an infectious disease? Despite Miriam's assurances, she
could not face the Schnabels. She told them in a letter how sad and
upset she was that she was not cured of tuberculosis and that she prayed
they were all well.

The entire Schnabel family, save Max—who had his suspicions but knew that if Rachel were contagious she would not have been allowed out in public—went for TB tests. Relieved that none of them tested positive, Rachel hoped that she would one day be able to resume a normal life.

Back at Söderby Sjukhus, the sanitarium in Uttran, Rachel wrote Miriam, telling her that she did not need any special treatment and hoped to be out within three months. Her recovery would take much longer than expected. And she would receive special treatment.

Some Belsen survivors regained their health in a short time. Some died within weeks or months of the war's end. And some, like Rachel, suffered debilitating setbacks for years.

While Rachel realized the benefits of socialized medicine in Sweden, Glyn Hughes helped to build the most comprehensive system of social insurance ever formulated—the British National Health Service. As senior medical officer of London's Southeast Metropolitan Regional Health Service, Hughes—the only general practitioner appointed to a high post—began by sizing up medical resources and staff throughout Kent, East Sussex, and his quarter of London.[34]

Though patients appreciated the National Health Service's domiciliary consultant services and having access to specialists, Hughes worried that "certain undesirable features" were creeping into the new program. The training of nurses was ill conceived, and the appointment of senior officers rushed. Financial problems resulted from "inattention to economy from the beginning." Alas, he acknowledged, "there are few bouncing babies who get away without teething troubles."[35]

A change that disturbed Hughes was the sidelining of the trusted family doctor who, according to new rules, would have to report to senior management before performing even minor procedures. He predicted that within fifteen years general practitioner hospitals (and GP units within upgraded hospitals) would disappear, regional hospitals would no longer have outpatient facilities, and people would have to travel a long way to obtain the care "they now receive on their doorstep." He recommended "a cottage hospital within a hospital" where medical students could be trained and allocating fifty beds per hospital to general practitioners. When he founded—with a band of local family doctors—the South-East London General Practitioner Centre in 1957, Hughes was finally able to afford GPs responsibilities that elevated their stature in the eyes of their patients, as well as their morale. They would have diagnostic and treatment facilities; special equipment for examinations and procedures; and consultant advice from a radiologist, pathologist, and social worker.[36]

Hughes had divorced Armorel in 1947. By the time he assumed the directorship of the General Practitioners Centre in 1957, he had been married to Thelma for eight years. Considerably younger than he was, Thelma possessed a refinement and grace that made Hughes proud to have her by his side. The formidable Mrs. Hughes tried to protect her busy husband from overextending himself, but this was near impossible.[37]

In addition to his professional role, Hughes was a founding member and for twelve years honorary treasurer of the council of the Royal College of General Practitioners. He also served for twenty years as president of the Casualties Union, an organization that trained "top level first aiders" from around the world to think not only of treating people's injuries but also of attending to their emotional state. Proficiency in approaching casualties with sympathy could be gained through (shockingly realistic) simulation exercises—at annual competitions actors feigning illness and injury gave those who ministered to them constructive criticism. Were they treated as human beings? Were they given explanations and reassurance?[38]

And then there was Hughes's involvement in the world of sport. In early 1959, Rex Alston, a leading sports commentator for BBC radio, asked him to keep free the evening of Monday, March 9. The reason made perfect sense: because of his experience as a rugby club administrator, he and Alston—together with John Tallent (a former athlete slated to be the next Rugby Union president) and Anthony Craxton and Peter Dimmock (television executives and sports broadcasters)—would discuss the possibility of more televised broadcasts of Rugby Union games.[39]

On the designated Monday, while Hughes and the others were having drinks at Broadcasting House, Peter Dimmock called to say he was delayed; he would send a car for the men so they could join him for dinner. Hughes entered the vehicle unaware of what the others knew— it was heading straight to a television studio. After the driver pulled the car into an alleyway and onto a dock, Eamonn Andrews, host of *This Is Your Life*, approached from the rear. The ruse continued as Rex Alston introduced both John Tallent and Brigadier Glyn Hughes, president of the world-famous Barbarians rugby club. Full lighting then turned on the scene. Andrews asked whether their rugby discussion could wait. He then announced, "Brigadier Hugh Llewelyn Glyn Hughes—this is your life!"

Stunned, Hughes had to quickly adjust to the fact that eleven million people were now watching him on the popular television program. Normally cheerful and at times playful (at committee meetings he was known to extend a ruler with smelling salts on its end to the nose of a dozing colleague), Hughes's shy and self-effacing side was now in view. Feeling trapped, he listened courteously as individuals from his past gave moving testimonies—of his spirit at Epsom College, his bravery during both world wars, his warmth and skills as a physician, and his sensitivity as a liberator of Bergen-Belsen. He was known for remembering and calling people by name, for without hesitation putting others first, and for commanding respect. At the program's end, he stood and watched the Wiltshire Regiment band play familiar songs from its base in Devizen.[40]

Hughes would have foregone *This Is Your Life* in a heartbeat. But he would not have wanted to miss a Blackheath or Barbarians rugby match. Or the opportunity to play golf at the West Hill Club. Or the chance to consult with medical administrators in Nigeria on its health-care system, or give a lecture in Ireland on evacuation in the event of a nuclear bomb. Nor would he want to miss gatherings of Jewish survivors of Bergen-Belsen.[41]

Hughes regarded each survivor of Bergen-Belsen as one he personally saved. Unable to prevent thousands from dying as no person should, he embraced an opportunity that came fifteen years after the liberation—he would prescribe humane treatment for those in their final days.[42]

Over thirteen months, under the auspices of the Calouste Gulben-kian Foundation, Hughes conducted a survey into the provision of care for the dying throughout the United Kingdom. In addition to con-structing widely circulated questionnaires, he personally visited three hundred hospitals, private and public nursing homes, and professionals involved in treating the chronically ill and elderly. He discovered that many facilities were inadequate and antiquated and that, even in places with the best of intentions, such as homes run by religious and volun-tary organizations, a shortage of money and nursing staff contributed to substandard conditions. In his report, *Peace at the Last: A Survey of Terminal Care in the United Kingdom*, he argued that the terminally ill need to feel a "sense of security, that they are not alone, that there is someone to care for them and something to be done for them."[43]

Hughes's motives for undertaking the project would have been un-derstood by Dr. Elisabeth Kübler-Ross, who after visiting liberated con-centration camps in war-ravaged Europe wrote *On Death and Dying: What the Dying Have to Teach Doctors, Nurses, Clergy and Their Own Families*. Had she not seen Majdanek (one of the six death camps in Poland), she would not have campaigned for hospices throughout America, furthering the work of Cicely Saunders, founder of the first hospice, St Christopher's in England.[44]

An early supporter of Dr. Saunders's work, Hughes shared her vision for meeting the physical and psychological needs of the dying. In her review of Hughes's *Peace at the Last*, the inspired Saunders discussed the brigadier's recommendations, including not only the coordination of individual and voluntary efforts, and new laws requiring enforceable standards in nursing homes, but also provisions that make dying at home—among one's own people and possessions—possible. In lieu of this optimal situation, Hughes advised that the terminally ill should spend their last days in a "homely atmosphere combined with modern hospital surroundings and procedures."[45]

Hughes would not extend his compassion for those who suffered to himself. When he was in the hospital for a prostate operation, he called the registrar and asked for an ambulance to take him to a rugby game. Unwilling to accept that he was not in "top form," he privately groused about his arthritic knees. Once, when hit by a bus while hailing a taxi, he suffered several broken ribs and did not let on to his friends that he was in agony.[46]

Hughes's schedule in the days leading up to his death affirms his indomitability. He had had a second serious operation about which his friends knew little. Soon after, on November 10, 1973, he enjoyed the Royal College of General Practitioners annual meeting and twenty-first anniversary celebration. One week later, he attended the Casualties Union Council meeting. Four days after that he attended a symposium on altitude training sponsored by the British Orthopaedic Association and the British Association of Sport and Medicine, on whose executive committee he, an "elder statesman," served. On November 24, he went up to Murrayfield to watch an international rugby match. Scotland XV played Argentina. He spoke at the after-game dinner honoring the teams. He dozed over his plate, then stayed up late chatting with friends. He turned in for the night at Edinburgh's North British Hotel. Usually the first man down for breakfast, he did not appear. Found stretched out on the bed in his dinner coat, the brigadier had died before having had a chance to undress.[47]

Hughes had asked Rabbi Isaac Levy, the former chaplain for the British Army of the Rhine, to say a prayer for the Belsen martyrs at his funeral—a final expression of his bond with the Jewish people, an extension of the altruism inculcated in him at Epsom College, developed while he served on World War I's bloody battlefields, and sustained during his life as a medical doctor. "The ideals for which you work," Hughes wrote to members of the Casualties Union in 1954, "[are] to disseminate the knowledge you have gained for the benefit of humanity and to devote all your efforts without thought of personal benefit. What better goal can we aim at?"

After Levy's prayer at the thanksgiving for Hughes's life at St. Marylebone Parish Church, on January 9, 1974, Judge Carl Aarvold spoke of the brigadier's distinctive, confident walk; his underlying enjoyment in all he did that defied misfortune; his infectious laughter. He said that "great and generous Hughie, full of knowledge, full of truth . . . showed us Man as perhaps Man was designed to be. Not always good, not always right, not always wise, but always loyal, always direct, always courageous, always powerful for fair play and decency, always incapable of being devious or underhanded."

Aarvold also said that Hughes would have instantly refuted any reference to his generosity of spirit.

✧ ✧ ✧

Following her brief stay in Söderby Sjukhus, Rachel was sent to a converted mansion (a rest home) in Tammsvik, thirty miles west of Stockholm. Abutting mirrorlike Lake Mälaren, surrounded by a peaceful forest, the setting—which included a great orchard and vegetable garden—could not have been more conducive to healing. And it was here that Rachel received the prayed-for cure: 150 mg/kg of PAS, para-amino salicylic acid, in two daily doses, for six months. The antimicrobial treatment, discovered by the Swedish chemist Jörgen Lehmann, was the second antibiotic after streptomycin found to be effective in treating acute exudative TB. Introduced into clinical use in 1948, it was by the early 1950s standard treatment. Years later, when Rachel saw chocolate sprinkles, she thought they resembled the oral medicine given her in a half-shot-glass-sized dose.[48]

Determined to make the most of her time, Rachel enrolled in correspondence courses in English, typing, and business. She wove baskets and afghans. Adolf Gold, the only other Jewish survivor in Tammsvik—a bright Romanian boy of slight build who had had a thoracoplasty—taught her how to play chess and iron a shirt. She befriended other young people, took long walks and boat rides, and ate wholesome food. Owing to the generous social policies of the Swedish government, all her expenses were covered. Owing to her foresight in taking out medical insurance years earlier, while working at Söderby Sjukhus, she received a stipend of two kroner a day. In one month, she could save sixty kroner. She had more money than her hard-working sister and was not eager to leave Tammsvik.

The Schnabels sent care packages, and Herbert wrote regularly. The family left the door open for Rachel's return, but as months stretched to two years, she had time to contemplate her future; she wanted to resume school, to prepare for a career.

When she finally left Tammsvik, Rachel worked in Berta's jewelry store for a few months. In June 1953, with a stipend from the Mosaiska Församlingen (the Jewish organization provided help to refugees), she enrolled in Birkagården Folkhögskola, an adult education program that began with thirteen weeks of summer studies in its Marhålmen facility, fifty miles northeast of Stockholm on the Baltic Sea. In addition to their coursework, Principal Leonard Seth insisted that the seventy-five students learn to swim. Motivated by the five-kroner award for passing the swim test, Rachel forced herself to get into cold water each morning.

As was the case in Tammsvik, Rachel was the only Jewish woman. With dark hair and blue eyes, she attracted attention and began to feel

Elisabeth (LEFT) and Rachel (RIGHT), 1953.

confident, even exotic. She also had something to contribute. Having excelled at croquet in the convalescent home, she could now teach others the lawn game.

Following the summer program in the country, Birkagården Folk-högskola continued for twenty-six weeks in Stockholm. Rachel studied chemistry, biology, and other academic subjects. In April 1954, ten years after she was torn from her home in Sighet at age fourteen, Rachel earned her high school diploma.

Eight months later, Rachel married kind, hard-working Sidney Mermelstein, a survivor of *munkaszolgálat* (Hungarian forced labor) and a US citizen. Elisabeth, who had moved with Mike to the United States, had kept her promise to bring Rachel out to join them within the year. She had met Sidney's sisters Helen and Esther at a gathering of survivors. They remembered Rachel from Christianstadt, as did Sidney's sister-in-law, Ratza, who had worked with Rachel in the labor camp's kitchen. Sidney traveled to Sweden to meet Rachel. After their

Elisabeth (LEFT), Mike, and Rachel, just before Mike and Elisabeth left for the United States in February 1954.

Rachel and Sidney at their wedding dinner, hosted by the Schnabels, December 1954.

wedding ceremony at Stockholm's synagogue, the Schnabels hosted a celebratory dinner.

Thus began a new life, in a new country. As the wife of a kosher butcher, Rachel assumed a familiar role—as a child, she had delivered orders for her butcher grandmother; she now learned her way around Long Island suburbs. Rachel and Sidney reared two daughters, enjoyed the warmth of a synagogue community, and saved all they could. After Elisabeth died in 1982, Rachel began working as a saleswoman for Bloomingdale's, a job she proudly held for more than twenty-five years.

After Sidney died in 2011, Ruth Mermelstein (*née* Rachel Genuth) began her association with the Holocaust Memorial and Tolerance Center of Glen Cove, New York. Ever shy, she has amazed herself—as of this writing she has addressed more than two hundred school groups from around the world. She tells young people, the last generation to learn about the horrors of the Holocaust from eyewitnesses, that if they ever encounter Holocaust deniers, they should set them straight. They should stand up for those marginalized and at risk. They can overcome even grave hardship, and they should use their education to improve the world.

Ruth now knows what happened after she fell unconscious in Bergen-Belsen, how she was saved by the British Second Army, and about the man who oversaw relief efforts. She would attest to the impossible situation Glyn Hughes faced. Hughes, who at a survivors' celebration said that never, in his life, would he believe the elegantly dressed men and women before him might have been left for dead, who kept up with many survivors and took pride in their accomplishments, would have been delighted to know that one he saved went on to lead a productive life.[49]

The author, her mother, and three of her aunts who survived Bergen-Belsen, 1993. TOP ROW, LEFT TO RIGHT: Ruth Mermelstein (née Rachel Genuth), Helen Mermelstein, the author. BOTTOM ROW, LEFT TO RIGHT: Ratza Mermelstein (née Ratza Roth), Esther Weiss (née Esther Mermelstein).

EPILOGUE

November 24, 1965. One thousand survivors of Nazi death camps filled the Grand Ballroom of the Waldorf Astoria in New York City. Sitting among other invited guests (writers, scholars, and Jewish communal leaders), Glyn Hughes, the seventy-three-year-old medical director and rugby club president, had crossed the ocean to heed the trilingual directive on a twenty-foot banner hanging from the ceiling: Remember. *Zakhor* (in Hebrew). *Gedenk* (in Yiddish).[1]

Remember. The bitter winter of 1945 saw the British Second Army engaged in battles throughout northwest Germany. Hughes, its deputy director of medical services, struggled to stretch limited resources—hospitals, field ambulances, and personnel—to meet the medical needs of both civilians and vast numbers of military casualties. When he set foot in Bergen-Belsen, he encountered the filthiest of concentration camps, with ten thousand corpses, tens of thousands of barely alive inmates, and fifteen thousand recent arrivals who, though starved and dysenteric, were the only ones able to give their liberators a rousing reception.[2]

Remember. Near Hughes, on the two-tiered dais of the opulent ballroom, sat Elie Wiesel, there to receive the Belsen Association's first Remembrance Award for his *Town beyond the Wall*. And Josef Rosensaft, president of the World Federation of Bergen-Belsen Survivors, who asked those present to rise for a moment of silence that was not without sound—a symphonic ensemble played Ani Ma'amin (I believe) in muted tones. The solemn Hebrew prayer transported the elegantly dressed men and women back to a time of ineffable suffering and loss.[3]

Remember. Accurately. When the press and the BBC reported in 1945 that "even the miserable skeletons at Belsen received 800 calories [a day]," Hughes made clear in a letter to the London *Times* that the internees received nowhere near that allotment and that in the days prior to the liberation they received neither food nor water. And in 1958, when the Mission de Recherche des Victimes de la Guerre (Mission for the Search for Victims of the War) sought to exhume, reconstruct, and attempt to identify and repatriate the remains of approximately one hundred thirty French nationals who died after the liberation, which would involve disturbing three thousand corpses, Hughes appealed to President Charles de Gaulle to drop the plan and leave the dead in peace. Even at the time of burial it had been impossible to identify victims; the proposed operation, Hughes said, was medically absurd and morally without reason.[4]

The imperative to set the record straight would continue. Three years after the twentieth anniversary commemoration, Hughes refuted, in another letter to the London *Times*, Russell Barton's claim that the situation was "not so bad." Paying tribute to the medical students who came to Bergen-Belsen sixteen days after the liberation—of whom Dr. Barton was one—Hughes pointed out that by the time they arrived nine thousand inmates had already been hospitalized and at least five thousand of the survivors had died.[5]

Remember. For the occasion, for posterity, a recording was produced. Sandwiched between Yiddish songs played by Sidor Belarsky's choir and orchestra were speeches by prominent Jewish leaders: Nahum Goldmann, president of the World Zionist Organization and the World Jewish Congress; Gideon Hausner, former attorney general of Israel and prosecutor at the Eichmann trial; and Josef Rosensaft. The fourth voice, soft and warm, was that of Glyn Hughes. The brigadier began by saying that twenty years is a long time by human standards; one would expect memories to fade. Never would this be the case with Bergen-Belsen. Never would those who were there escape visions of "war and mortal misery." He said that, for the liberators, diabolical pictures have a habit of emerging . . . how much more so must this be true for those who endured the vile treatment and subhuman existence.

He said that those survivors who, despite their own condition, helped efforts to salvage lives and to ease their fellow inmates' suffering deserve the everlasting gratitude of all mankind.[6]

By the time he joined survivors at the Waldorf Astoria, Hughes had already spent time with "Belseners" in Israel and other countries. He had attended a Passover seder at the home of Norbert Wollheim, in Queens, New York, with sixty survivors who came to honor him. He had planted the first tree in Ya'ar Belsen, a forest in the Judean Hills near Jerusalem, at the ceremony of remembrance organized by Rafael Olewski to commemorate the tenth anniversary of the liberation. He had toured Israel with Wollheim and others, who noted how Hughes enjoyed his drink and how Thelma was the epitome of a lady—never breaking a sweat, despite the heat and humidity.[7]

Prior to the twentieth anniversary celebration, Hughes joined a pilgrimage to the mass graves at Belsen. Standing among thirty survivors reciting the kaddish, he wore a deep sadness. He explained to a reporter that a person "can't change in five minutes"—he saw the SS shooting people right after the liberation. And that, at the time, there was not a document to be found—the SS had destroyed them all. And that, yes, Kramer's heavy wooden desk was in his office, and, no, using it did not feel creepy.[8]

Hughes then arrived at Israel's Lydda Airport to a thunderous ovation from survivors. At a ceremony at Tel Aviv's Habima Theatre, he observed tear-filled reunions of Belseners from all over the world. He spoke of Belsen as a symbol of man's inhumanity to man. (As a constant reminder, he kept a lamp with a lampshade made of human skin in his home, a "memento" he was offered before leaving Germany.) Having seen how the committee that formed just three days after the liberation faced difficulties "with dignity, courage and persistence" and how the Bergen-Belsen DP camp became a self-governing Jewish metropolis, he regarded the "miniature state" of twenty thousand survivors as a "precursor by some years of Israel."[9]

In 1970, twenty-five years after the liberation, Hughes again joined Josef Rosensaft and others on a pilgrimage to Belsen's mass graves. Three hundred survivors commemorated their brethren's deaths with a Procession of Silence. Cantor Moishe Kraus of Johannesburg, South Africa, led them in prayer and a hymn. There were no speeches. Flowered wreaths were laid at the base of the monument. Planning to then travel to the United States, the brigadier was "stricken with an abdominal complaint." His doctor told him he needed immediate surgery. But colon cancer was not about to stop Hughes from attending the Belsen survivors' celebration. At the event, he said, "Not one of us who was not a prisoner there can ever realize what those brave people went through and endured."[10]

ACKNOWLEDGMENTS

First and foremost, I thank my mother, Ruth Mermelstein (née Rachel Genuth) for sharing her past with me since I was old enough to ask her about it. No matter how ignorant or inane or insensitive my questions, she answered them—honestly, with relevant anecdotes that captivated my imagination and gave me a sense of her experiences. Had she not made me feel as though I could always ask, I would not have been able to tell her story.

Over decades of conversations, I filled in the contours of my mother's past. Finally, I set about exploring a gap in her memory—what happened after she fell unconscious in Bergen-Belsen? I came across Hugh Llewelyn Glyn Hughes, the man most prominently associated with the liberation. Here I owe thanks to those who affirmed for me the significance of the brigadier's life, including Menachem Rosensaft, Samuel Bloch, Elie Wiesel, and Rabbi Isaac Levy. I was fortunate, too, to be able to interview Glyn Hughes's gracious daughter and son, Jean Smart and Michael Hughes, as well as several of his younger friends, before they passed away. And to meet Alan Scadding and John Higgs of Epsom College, and Peter Starling of the Royal Army Medical Corps, who were enormously helpful at the project's beginning and end—a span of fifteen years. Thank you, too, to Rebecca Jallot, Epsom College's archivist, for being so forthcoming during the final stretch.

I am grateful for the interest and help of family and friends over the very long haul. Those who read most if not all of a draft manuscript include Laurie Bennett, Erica Brown, Amelia Katzen, Robert Kegan, Ruth Kirschenbaum, Linda Kolodney, Laurie Krotman, Nancy Leipzig, Maud Mandel, Tova Mirvis, Joni Pelta, Shulamit Reinharz, Anthony

199

Rogers, Susan and Robert Shattuck, Diane Ugelow, and Linda Wells. These most wonderful beta readers suggested edits and offered insightful comments. For adding instructive marginalia, I also owe a mountain of gratitude to Kristina Nilsson.

Fellow writers and mentors who provided me with much appreciated guidance at various points include Michael Aeschliman, Nigel Hamilton, Joan Leegant, and Lesléa Newman. And had it not been for Melissa Nathanson and Elizabeth Harris, this work would not have had the benefit of such talented biographers' judgment and skill.

Early on, classes at Boston's Grub Street enabled me to learn from Amin Ahmad, Eve Bridburg, and others. The Boston Biographers Group, composed of wise and generous colleagues, has been a source of ongoing support. And Daniel Weaver and his class at Emerson College, especially Goldy Levy, offered many useful suggestions.

I owe much to my agent Sylvie Carr, for her belief in this project, her good cheer, and her wisdom throughout. Laura Davulis, my editor at Johns Hopkins University Press, embraced the idea of relaying the protagonists' journeys over five seasons, and I will be forever grateful for her expert editing. Carrie Watterson made the book much better— I could not have wished for a more attentive, professional copyeditor. Esther Rodriguez was a pleasure to work with, and I thank her and others at JHUP who contributed to the production of this book.

Colleagues and friends at Boston University and at Hebrew College, where I spent many happy years while researching and writing, lent much support. A special shout-out to Karen Bohlin and Megan Uy, with whom I worked at the forerunner to Boston University's Center for Character and Social Responsibility, and to Hebrew College's magnificent adult learning team and excellent librarian, Harvey Sukenic. Thank you, too, to Eugenia Dimant, librarian at Harvard's Widener Library, for her steadfast assistance over so many years.

For filling my life with love and joy I thank Amy, Evan, Josh and Sara, and Rachel's great-grandchildren, Isla, Ruby, Sidney, and Caleb.

Finally, I feel blessed to have a caring and thoughtful partner by my side. Those closest to biographers tolerate their obsession, witness their struggles, and often attend to what will otherwise go undone. I thank Joel from the bottom of my heart for all that he put up with and for being my in-house editor, source of balance, and best friend.

NOTES

Rachel's story was told to the author by her mother, Ruth Mermelstein, née Rachel Genuth. Most of Hughes's documents, originally found in London's Wellcome Medical Library, are now housed at the Museum of Military Medicine in Aldershot, UK. The museum is scheduled to be relocated to Cardiff in 2022.

PROLOGUE

1. *Remember: 40 Years since the Massacre of the Jews from Northern Transylvania under Horthyst Occupation* (Bucharest: Federation of Jewish Communities in the Socialist Republic of Romania, 1985), 11. After World War I (and then again, after World War II), northern Transylvania belonged to Romania. After the Hungarians entered the area in 1940, its indigenous Romanians had two weeks to leave.
2. Brasov is 390 kilometers (242 miles) south of Sighet. We do not know how Rachel's relatives traveled, but the trip likely took an entire day.
3. Today, Galicia is divided between Ukraine and Poland, and Bukovina, between Romania and Ukraine. S. Y. Gross and Y. Yosef Cohen, eds., "The Holocaust of Jewish Marmaros," trans. Moshe A. Davis, in *The Marmaros Book: In Memory of 160 Jewish Communities (Maramures Region)* (Tel Aviv: Beit Marmaros, 1983, 1996), 93–112.
4. Shoah Resource Center, "Gendarmerie," https://www.yadvashem.org/odot_pdf/Microsoft%20Word%20-%206245.pdf. The gendarmerie consisted of a police force of several thousand men charged with maintaining law and order and carrying out the Hungarian regime's anti-Jewish policies in the Hungarian countryside.
5. Randolph Braham, ed., *The Geographical Encyclopedia of the Holocaust in Hungary* (Evanston, IL: Northwestern University Press, 2013), 1:603; Elie Wiesel, *Night* (New York: Bantam Books, 1960), 5.
6. George Eisen and Tamás Stark, "The 1941 Galician Deportation and the Kamenets-Podolsk Massacre: A Prologue to the Hungarian Holocaust," *Holocaust and Genocide Studies* 27, no. 2 (Fall 2013): 208–9, 213–14,

218; Michaël Prazan, dir., "Judenfrei," *Einsatzgruppen: The Nazi Death Squads* (Netflix, 2009) (covering September–December 1941, this segment includes August 1941); Randolph Braham, "The Kamenets-Podolsk and Délvidék Massacres: Prelude to the Holocaust in Hungary," *Yad Vashem Studies* (Jerusalem) 9 (1973): 138–42; Gross and Cohen, "The Holocaust of Jewish Marmaros," 93–112; Randolph Braham and Ándras Kovacs, eds., *The Holocaust in Hungary: Seventy Years Later* (Budapest: Central European University Press, 2016), 157, 161.

7. Wiesel, *Night*, 4.
8. Gross and Cohen, "The Holocaust of Jewish Marmaros," 93–112; *Remember*, 13.
9. Wiesel, *Night*, 5.

FIRST WITNESS, THE BELSEN TRIAL

1. David Lowther, *Liberating Belsen: Remembering the Soldiers of the Durham Light Infantry* (Durham, UK: Sacristy Press, 2015), 107, 118; A. P. V. Rogers, "War Crimes under the Royal Warrant: British Practice 1945–1949," *International and Comparative Law Quarterly* 39, no. 4 (October 1990): 787–89. The British Royal Warrant, drafted at the end of October 1944 and completed and signed on June 14, 1945, was based on the royal prerogative, that is, arbitrary authority in the hands of the Crown. It enabled proceedings in any part of the world where British forces operated. The judge advocate general concluded that these were to take place in military courts. (Other nations similarly authorized trials; for example, Australia had an act of Parliament; Canada, an order-in-council under the War Measures Act; the United States, appointed military commissions.)

   Law Reports of Trials of War Criminals: The Belsen Trial, selected and prepared by the United States War Crimes Commission (New York: Howard Fertig, 1983), 129; Raymond Phillips, ed., *The Trial of Josef Kramer and 44 Others (The Belsen Trial)* (London: W. Hodge, 1949), xxiv. The Royal Warrant, according to Army Order 81/45, entitled the court to punish war crimes limited to crimes against Allied nationals. It was impossible to state the names of the tens of thousands of Belsen victims and millions at Auschwitz—all Allied nationals from various countries. At the trial, seats behind the bench were provided for representatives from ten different nations who were able to attend.

   William Hitchcock, *The Bitter Road to Freedom: A New History of the Liberation of Europe* (New York: Free Press, 2008), 258, 358. Leslie C. Green, review of *The Belsen Trial*, ed. R. Phillips, War Crimes Series, vol. 2 (London: Hodge, 1949), *Modern Law Review* 13, no. 2 (April 1950): 265–68. More than one hundred thirty affidavits, depositions, and written statements—not all of which were signed or sworn to—were admitted as evidence.

2. "Kramer and Irma Grese Will Die with 9 Others for Reich Murders," *New York Times*, November 18, 1945, 1. For the story of Irma Grese, including details about her upbringing and teenage rebellion, see Daniel Patrick Brown's *The Beautiful Beast: The Life and Crimes of SS-Aufseherin Irma Grese* (Ventura, CA: Golden West Historical, 1996).

3. Cecil E. King, in Ben Flanagan, Joanne Reilly, and Donald Bloxham, eds., *Remembering Belsen* (New York: Vallentine Mitchell, 2005), 106–7; David Bankier and Dan Michman, eds., *Holocaust and Justice: Representation and Historiography of the Holocaust in Post-war Trials* (New York: Berghan Books, 2010), 138–39.

4. Brown, *The Beautiful Beast*, 68–69, citing Playfair and Sington, *The Offenders*, 156. In late April, the Belsen guards were transferred from the Wehrmacht tank training *Kaserne* (base) to Celle for their pretrial incarceration. At this time it was decided that the legal vehicle for determining the complicity of the Belsen guards in war crimes would be a five-officer military tribunal convened with a judge advocate to serve as a legal advisor. From the beginning, British authorities proceeded in a "painstakingly judicious manner." Unless there were specific allegations of criminality, SS guards were not charged. Accordingly, thirty of the eighty-three Belsen guards (Death's Head guards, a fraction of the Waffen-SS members who served in the camps) escaped judgment. Some of the Belsen guards had succumbed to typhus. Specific charges were leveled against nine *kapos* (inmates in charge of groups of prisoners). The British officers who defended the SS incurred the wrath of people in their hometowns for aiding "enemy killers."

   Flanagan, Reilly, and Bloxham, *Remembering Belsen*, 59; *Times* in partnership with CNN, "Foreign News: Inferno on Trial," Monday, October 8, 1945, http://content.time.com/time/magazine/article/0,9171,776250,00.html; Phillips, *The Trial of Josef Kramer*, xxiv–xxv, xxii, xxxi–xxxiii; Hitchcock, *The Bitter Road*, 358; William F. Frye, "British Doctor First to Testify at Trial of Belsen," *Ogdensburg Journal* (New York), September 18, 1945, 1; Green, review of *The Belsen Trial*, 265–67; Lowther, *Liberating Belsen*, 107. Testimonies of survivors too ill to attend the trial were read to the court.

5. Tony Haggith, "The Filming of the Liberation of Bergen-Belsen and Its Impact on the Understanding of the Holocaust," in *Belsen 1945: New Historical Perspectives*, ed. Suzanne Bardgett and David Cesarani (London: Vallentine Mitchell, 2006), 89. Thirty-three rolls of film and two hundred photos were taken by the British Army's Film and Photographic Unit (AFPU). "Foreign News: Inferno on Trial."

6. Peter Dierks, "At Liberation of Belsen, British Officer's Story, 'Kramer Unashamed,'" September 19, 1945, archive.timesonline.co.uk, http:// tinyurl.galegroup.com/tinyurl/BQW9U2 (Issue 50251: 3); Hitchcock, *The Bitter Road*, 361; "Eyewitness Tells of Belsen Horror," *New York Times*, September 19, 1945.

7. Nigel Starmer-Smith, *The Barbarians: The Official History of the Barbarian Football Club* (London: Macdonald and Jane's, 1977), 213–14.

8. Starmer-Smith, *The Barbarians*, 213–14, quoting from the *Lancet*; Isaac Levy, *Witness to Evil: Bergen-Belsen 1945* (London: Peter Halban, 1995), 19; Carl Aarvold, "Thanksgiving for the Life of H. L. Glyn Hughes," St. Marylebone Parish Church, January 9, 1974.

9. Hughes's testimony appears in Phillips, *The Trial of Josef Kramer*, 30–44.

10. Phillips, *The Trial of Josef Kramer*, 31, 41.

11. Phillips, *The Trial of Josef Kramer*, 31.

12. Phillips, *The Trial of Josef Kramer*, 33.

13. Jean Smart (Hughes's daughter), conversation with the author (Worplesdon, Surrey, England, March 11, 2004). Jean spoke of her father's refusal to sit— and his consequent fatigue—on the days he testified.

14. Phillips, *The Trial of Josef Kramer*. The opening speech for the defendant Kramer is found on 145–55, and Josef Kramer's statements are recorded on 156–81.

15. Phillips, *The Trial of Josef Kramer*, 33, 39, 43, 44.

16. Phillips, *The Trial of Josef Kramer*, 40. Ben Shephard, *After Daybreak: The Liberation of Bergen-Belsen, 1945* (New York: Schocken Books, 2005), 46–47. Had Hughes had an entire division in reserve he would have been able to bring up Second Army medical units. As it was, he had only one field hygiene section with him at the time he entered Bergen-Belsen. Two days later, a second field hygiene section arrived, as did 11 Light Field Ambulance, a unit of about two hundred men trained to evacuate soldiers wounded in battle, and 32 Casualty Clearing Station, a mobile surgical unit composed of two operating teams with ancillary staff, including eight nurses.

17. Phillips, *The Trial of Josef Kramer*, 36.

18. "Belsen Shootings Seen by Britons," *New York Times*, September 19, 1945, 11; "Eyewitness Tells of Belsen Horror," *New York Times*, September 20, 1945, 5; Phillips, *The Trial of Josef Kramer*, 34–35, 43.

19. Phillips, *The Trial of Josef Kramer*, 41, 43.

20. Phillips, *The Trial of Josef Kramer*, 46.

21. Hadassah Rosensaft, *Yesterday: My Story* (Washington, DC: United States Holocaust Memorial Museum, 2004), 89; "Belsen Survivor Picks Out Nazis," *New York Times*, September 22, 1945, 5; Phillips, *The Trial of Josef*

Kramer, 74, 716. Ada Bimko's testimony can be found on 66–78, or see
bergenbelsen.co.uk/pages/TrialTranscript/Trial_Day_006.html.

22. *Law Reports of Trials*, 4, 6; Ernst Schnable, *Anne Frank: A Portrait in
Courage*, trans. Richard and Clara Winston (New York: Harcourt, Brace,
1958), 176; Phillips, *The Trial of Josef Kramer*, xxxix, xli, xl, xlii; Brown,
The Beautiful Beast, 68. Paul Holt, "How Did Irma Grese Get Like This?"
(unknown British publication, November 16, 1945, Glyn Hughes's
papers, Museum of Military Medicine archives, Aldershot, UK, RAMC
1218/2/11). Victoria Combe, "Face to Face with the Beastess of Belsen,"
Sunday Telegraph, April 16, 1995: 17; Hitchcock, *The Bitter Road*, 363;
Albert Pierrepoint, excerpts from *Executioner: Pierrepoint* (London:
Harrap, 1974), in "The Hangman's Exclusive Story," *News of the World*
(London).

23. Phillips, *The Trial of Josef Kramer*, xxxix, xli, xl, xlii; *Law Reports of Trials*,
4, 6; Willy Lindwer, *De laatste zeven maanden: Vrouwen in het spoor van
Anne Frank* (Hilvesum: Gooi & Sticht, 1988), in *Jewish Displaced Persons in
Camp Bergen-Belsen 1945–1950*, ed. Erik Somers and Rcné Kok (Seattle:
University of Washington Press, 2004), 10.

24. "Belsen Trial: Women Survivor Testifies, Blonde Beastess Is Still Smart but
Her Eyes Are Red," *Sunday Express*, September 23, 1945.

25. For Bimko's testimony, see Phillips, *The Trial of Josef Kramer*, 66–78.

26. Phillips, *The Trial of Josef Kramer*, xxxviii–xxxix, xliii, 99, 616. "Kicking of
Doomed by Nazi Described," *New York Times*, September 23, 1945, 26;
Brown, *The Beautiful Beast*, 68, 70–76, 78–81, citing Lustgarten, *Business
of Murder*, 94, 102–3, 109 and Playfair and Sington, *The Offenders*, 159–61,
164, 177, 181, 183–84, 533–35; "Inferno on Trial," *Time*, October 8, 1945,
36; "11 Accused Condemned to Death," *Times* (London), November 19,
1945, 3C; "Kramer and Irma Grese Will Die with 9 Others for Reich
Murders," *New York Times*, November 18, 1945; "Belsen Woman Guard
Weeps, Denies Guilt," *New York Times*, October 16, 1945.

27. "Belsen Trial: Woman Survivor Testifies"; "Kicking of the Doomed by Nazi
Described," *New York Times*, September 23, 1945: 26; Phillips, *The Trial of
Josef Kramer*, xxxvii; Bankier and Michman, *Holocaust and Justice*, 144.

SPRING 1944

1. Laurence Rees, *The Holocaust: A New History* (New York: Hachette
Book Group, 2017), 383; Göran Rosenberg, *A Brief Stop on the Road to
Auschwitz*, trans. Sarah Death (London: Granta, 2015), 115, 122–23.

2. *Remember: 40 Years since the Massacre of the Jews from Northern
Transylvania under Horthyst Occupation* (Bucharest: Federation of Jewish

Communities in the Socialist Republic of Romania, 1985), 15–18;
Randolph Braham, *Genocide and Retribution* (New York: Springer-Verlag,
1983), 6–18, 197.

3. Lieutenant Colonel G. S. Jackson, *Operations of Eighth Corps: Account of
Operations from Normandy to the Rhine River* (London: St. Clements Press,
1948), 9, 10, 12; H. L. Glyn Hughes, address on the eve of a memorial service for Harry, an honored member of the 8 Corps, commemorating the
twenty-fifth anniversary of the formation of the 8 Corps (Glyn Hughes's
papers, Museum of Military Medicine archives, Aldershot, UK, RAMC
1218 3/9). Hughes believed 8 Corps "must have held the record for exercises of all sorts"; "Blackcock" and "Eagle" were particularly long and
arduous.

4. H. L. Glyn Hughes, "The Medical Services" (lecture, School of Combined
Operations, August 2, 1946, Glyn Hughes's papers, RAMC 1218, 3/3);
H. L. Glyn Hughes, "The Duties of a Regimental Officer" (talk given to
RMOs, Glyn Hughes's papers, RAMC 1218 3/9); Hughes, 8 Corps twenty-
fifth anniversary address. For an exercise at Imberdon that caused the
accidental loss of life, see "Realistic Army Exercises: Live Munition Used,"
Canberra Times, April 15, 1942; *This Is Your Life*, BBC Television Theatre,
Subject 89, Monday, March 9, 1959, series 4, edition 24; letter from E. H.
Dodds, City Hall, Norwich, March 12, 1959.

5. Hughes, "Medical Services"; Jackson, *Operations of Eighth Corps*, 10.

6. Jackson, *Operations of Eighth Corps*, 2.

7. In 1940 11 General Hospital moved to Leeds and Lincoln, and then from
1942 to 1946 traveled from South Africa to Madagascar to Tripoli to Sicily.
Charles Collins (corporal nursing orderly for the No. 11 British General
Hospital, WWII, Glyn Hughes's papers, RAMC 1218/3/11), Westcliff on
Sea, England, to H. L. Glyn Hughes, March 9, 1959.

8. Helen J. McCarrick, *Nursing Times* (London), March 4, 1969, 5; H. L. Glyn
Hughes, albums, where captions beneath photos on black pages were writ-
ten in white ink (Glyn Hughes's papers, RAMC 1081/2/2). See A. J. Barker,
Dunkirk: The Great Escape (London: Dent and Knowles, 1977); Redmond
McLaughlin, *The Royal Army Medical Corps: Famous Regiments* (London:
Lee Cooper, London), 62–63; "The History of the Royal Army Medical
Corps" (War Office, 1943, Kew: National Archives, WO 32/10386);
Lieutenant Colonel A. B. Dick, RAMC, ADG, AMD 10, paper sent to
Glyn Hughes on July 16, 1946 (Glyn Hughes's papers, RAMC 1218 3/4).

9. Hughes, albums; McLaughlin, *The Royal Army Medical Corps*, 63.

10. H. L. Glyn Hughes, notes (RAC administrative conferences on December
28, 1941, January 19, 1942, and February 24, 1942, Glyn Hughes's papers).

In 1943 Hughes became deputy director of medical services for the British Second Army's 8 Corps. The British Second Army, part of Montgomery's 21 Army Group, comprised 12 Corps, 30 Corps, 8 Corps, and 1 Corps.

11. Jackson, *Operations of Eighth Corps*, 11.
12. "Preparations for Invasion," extracted from *Medical Service in the European Theater of Operations*, chapter 4, 149, https://history.army.mil/html /reference/Normandy/TS/MD/MD6.htm; Hughes, "Medical Services."
13. Hughes, "Medical Services"; H. L. Glyn Hughes, "Normandy to the Baltic from a Medical Angle" (presidential address to the Harveian Society, January 15, 1947, Glyn Hughes's papers, RAMC 1218 2/21). After the initial landing in Normandy, the British Second Army would protect the left flank of US forces.
14. Jackson, *Operations of Eighth Corps*, 11–12.
15. Jackson, *Operations of Eighth Corps*, 11–12.
16. For details on Admiral Horthy's meeting with Hitler at Klessheim Castle near Berchtesgaden and ensuing events that led to the expulsion of the Jews from the Hungarian provinces, see Rees, *The Holocaust*, 377–82.
17. Nikolaus Wachsmann, *KL: A History of the Nazi Concentration Camps* (New York: Farrar, Straus and Giroux, 2015), 319. From March 26 to October 20, 1942, approximately sixty thousand Slovakian Jews, including approximately forty-four hundred from Nitra, were deported to Auschwitz and to Majdanek (in Lublin, Poland).
18. Zoltán Singer in Randolph Braham, *The Wartime System of Labor Service in Hungary* (New York: Rosenthal Institute for Holocaust Studies Graduate Center / City University of New York; Boulder: Social Science Monographs, East European Monographs, October 15, 1995), 42–46; "After the Return Home: From the Writings of Zoltán Zelk," in *Kritika* [Criticism] (Budapest), no. 4 (1983): 6–7; Randolph Braham, "The Hungarian Labor Service System 1939–1945," *East European Quarterly*, no. 31 (1977): 13.
19. The Kolkhoz village was between Zhitomir and Korosten. Randolph Braham, *The Politics of Genocide* (Detroit, MI: Wayne State University Press, 2000), 39; Randolph Braham and Ándras Kovacs, eds., *The Holocaust in Hungary: Seventy Years Later* (Budapest, Hungary: Central European University Press, 2016), 163.
20. Braham, *The Politics of Genocide*, 39–40, 46–47; Zoltán Singer, "The History of Labor Co., No. 110/34" in *There Was Once a Time . . .* (Tel Aviv: A Dés és Vidékéröl Elszármazottak Landsmannschaftja, n.d.), 245–80. Oral testimony Protocol 875 collected by the National Committee for Attending Deportees (Deportáltakat Gondozó Országos Bizottság [DEGOB]). In

the early summer of 1945, staff at the committee's Budapest Centre collected a number of testimonies by returning deportees at hospices run by DEGOB. (In the spring of 1945, the Provincial Division of the Hungarian Association of Jewry prepared similar documents, which later also became part of the collection. The last testimony was transcribed on April 13, 1946.) Hungarian Jewish Museum and Archives (Magyar Zsidó Múzeum és Levéltár [MZSML], Budapest).

21. The men may have gone to a military hospital in Korosteny, where other survivors of the Dorosics tragedy received treatment. Braham and Kovacs, *The Holocaust in Hungary*, 163.

22. S. Y. Gross and Y. Yosef Cohen, eds., "The Holocaust of Jewish Marmaros," *The Marmaros Book: In Memory of 160 Jewish Communities*, trans. Moshe Davis (Tel Aviv: Beit Marmaros, 1983, 1996), https://www.jewishgen.org /yizkor/maramures/marh093.html; *Remember*, 26. The ghetto encompassed Timár, Kigyó, and Ipar utcak (Streets) up to Hajnal utca (Street); it would include Kamár utca, between Timár and Ipar utcak. Braham, *Genocide and Retribution*, 41. David Weiss Halivni, *The Book and the Sword* (New York: Farrar, Straus and Giroux, 1996), 40.

23. Elie Wiesel, "The Decision," *Parade*, August 28, 1995, 5; Braham, *Genocide and Retribution*, 20.

24. Braham, *Genocide and Retribution*, 40. Earlier on April 15, László Illinyi, the deputy prefect, held a meeting in Sighet with all of the county's top officials. Randolph L. Braham, ed., *The Geographical Encyclopedia of the Holocaust in Hungary* (Evanston, IL: Northwestern University Press, 2013), xlviii; Yaacov Lozowick, *Hitler's Bureaucrats: The Nazi Security Police and the Banality of Evil* (New York: Continuum, 2000), 244.

25. "The Holocaust in Northern Transylvania"(Jerusalem: Yad Vashem), citing United States Holocaust Memorial Museum (USHMM), RG 25.004M, roll 61, file 7081. https://yadvashem.org/yv/en/exhibitions/wiesel/holocaust _in_northern_transylvania.pdf; Braham, *Genocide and Retribution*, 41; Halivni, *The Book*, 48, 57–58; *Remember*, 17–20.

26. Halivni, *The Book*, 48, 57–58; *Remember*, 26.

27. Braham, *Genocide and Retribution*, 13, 20; Halivni, *The Book*, 40; Wiesel, "The Decision," 5.

28. Gross and Cohen, "The Holocaust of Jewish Marmaros," 93–112. The Nazis did not want rebellion. They had contended with the Warsaw Ghetto uprising and deceiving the Jews was now of the utmost importance. Studying the situation in one of Hungary's first ghettos, Hitler's henchmen aimed to discern how aware the Jews were of what awaited them. *Remember*, 26.

29. The sand model, created by a topography intelligence officer, was studied by 1 Airborne Division staff and 8 Corps general Richard O'Connor, who

constantly contemplated the probable course of events. Jackson, *Operations of Eighth Corps*, 14, 25.

30. Jackson, *Operations of Eighth Corps*, 14.
31. Jackson, *Operations of Eighth Corps*, 14.
32. Jackson, *Operations of Eighth Corps*, 14.
33. Jean Smart (Hughes's daughter), interviews (March 6 and March 11, 2004).
34. Jayne Hayter-Hames, *A History of Chagford* (Chichester: Phillimores, 1981); Jean Smart, interviews (March 6 and March 11, 2004); Michael Hughes (Hughes's son), letter to the author (postmarked from Seville, Spain, March 9, 2004).
35. Jean Smart, interview (March 6, 2004); Thomas P. Ofcansky and Britt L. Ehrhardt, "Men with a Mission: Early Physicians in British East Africa," *Wellcome History*, no. 41 (Summer 2009): 2; For more information on the village of Ventersburg and the region of which it was a part, see John Boje, *An Imperfect Occupation: Enduring the South African War* (Urbana: University of Illinois Press, 2015), 1–12. In 1890, of the 16,685 inhabitants of Ventersburg 7,662 were white.
36. Jean Smart, interview (March 6, 2004); Mickey Bodger and Alan Evans, interview (London, East India Club, September 24, 2010). For information on spinal carriages, see *British Medical Journal* (London), February 14, 1885, 6; Henry Ashby and George Arthur Wright, *The Diseases of Children* (London: Longmans, Green, 1889); William Blackley Drummond, *A Medical Dictionary* (London: J. M. Dent & Sons, 1918), 510.
37. Epsom College Archives. The fateful council meeting took place on October 14, 1903. Hughes was admitted under Epsom College's bylaw 24. It is unclear whether Hughes's application as a foundation scholar when he was ten—the age at which a boy normally entered Epsom College—was put on hold because of his questionable health at that time. In any case, when his application was deferred his mother took him to a restful place in Belgium to "recuperate." At the time he enrolled at Epsom, Hughes and his mother resided in Newport, the gateway city linking England and Wales.
38. Epsom College Archives; Jean Smart, interview (March 6, 2004).
39. Michael Hughes (Hughes's son), phone interview (August 4, 2004); Michael Hughes letter to the author (March 9, 2004); Jean Smart, interview (March 11, 2004).
40. Jean Smart, interview (March 11, 2004); Michael Hughes, letter (March 9, 2004); Mickey Bodger and Alan Evans, interview (September 24, 2010). Husband and wife weathered a stressful situation within a few years of moving to Kensington. See "Honour Vindicated: Doctor's Wife Faints When Case Is Dismissed," London, April 8, 1931, *Singapore Free Press and Mercantile Advertiser* (1884–1942), May 11, 1931, 3.

41. 8 Corps HQ (Medical Services) war diary (Kew: National Archives, WO 177/343); Hughes, 8 Corps twenty-fifth anniversary address.

42. Braham, *Genocide and Retribution*, 20; *Remember*, 17, 25. Dr. Lajos Meggyesi stated that Jews' money, gold, silver, jewelry, typewriters, cameras, watches, rugs, furs, and valuable paintings were to be listed in quadruplicate on a form. One copy was to be submitted to the city, one to the police, one left in the particular apartment, and one could be held by the concerned Jews. City mayors were responsible for inventorying and storing valuables until the job could be handled by the postal savings bank system. "The Holocaust in Northern Hungary," Shoah Resource Center, cited in Braham, *Politics*, 578–79.

43. "The Holocaust in Northern Hungary," in Braham, *Politics*, 578–79; Braham, *The Geographical Encyclopedia of the Holocaust*, xlvii–xlviii. To prevent corruption or leniency based on personal relationships with local Jews, the high command of the Royal Hungarian Gendarmerie sent gendarmes units to locations in other parts of the country. Fifty gendarmes from Miskolc were sent to Sighet. László Ferenczy, liaison officer, coordinated gendarmerie operations with Adolf Eichmann, head of the German Security Service.

44. Though it was one and a quarter miles from *Die Alte Shul* to the train station, it took at least two hours for the guarded thousands to walk the distance.

45. Braham, *The Geographical Encyclopedia of the Holocaust*, xlvii.

46. The trauma was so great that Rachel would not be able to swallow water for sixty years.

47. Elie Wiesel, "Pilgrimage to Sighet, a Haunted City," *New York Times*, Sunday, October 14, 1984. Sighet, a thriving Jewish community, had thirty synagogues in 1944. In 1984, but one remained. "In the space of six weeks, a vibrant and creative community had been condemned first to solitude, then to misery, and at last to deportation and death." Annette Richardson, *World War II: The Definitive Encyclopedia and Document Collection*, ed. Spencer E. Tucker (London: ABC-CLIO, 2016), 3:1426–27; Yaron Paser, *Holocaust versus Wehrmacht: How Hitler's "Final Solution" Undermined the German War Effort* (Lawrence: University Press of Kansas, 2014), 249.

48. "The Holocaust in Northern Hungary," in Braham, *Politics*, 605; *Remember*, 29, 59, 61. In 1941, Sighet had 10,144 Jews. In 1947, the town had 2,308. The town was emptied of 12,849 Jews during four days in 1944: May 16—3,007; May 18—3,248; May 20—3,104; May 22—3,490. Paser, *Holocaust versus Wehrmacht*, 249; Richard Hargreaves, *The Germans in Normandy* (Pennsylvania: Stackpole Books, 2008), 3. In the first months of 1944, Allied forces had systematically destroyed the German army's

infrastructure. By June, seventy-six thousand tons of bombs had been dropped across northwest France by low flying bombers attacking trains, trucks, and other vehicles.

49. Danuta Czech, *Auschwitz Chronicle, 1939–1945* (London: I. B. Tauris, 1990), 563–64, 622.
50. Aranka Siegal, testimony, *I Witness* (University of Southern California Shoah Foundation, November 7, 1995, Tarrytown, NY), clip 24.
51. Danuta Czech, *Auschwitz Chronicles, 1939–1945* (New York: Henry Holt, 1988), 633.

SUMMER 1944

1. For the story of the harrowing escape and the actual report, see Rudolf Vrba, *I Escaped from Auschwitz* (Fort Lee, NJ: Barricade Books, 2002); see also "Rudolf Vrba and Alfred Wetzler's 'Escape from Auschwitz, April 1944,'" *Sir Martin Gilbert*, https://www.martingilbert.com/blog/rudolf-vrba-and-alfred-wetzlers-escape-from-auschwitz-april-1944/.
2. "D-Day and the Normandy Invasion," *Strategic Thinking*, http://www.strategybydesign.org/d-day-strategy-and-the-normandy-invasion.
3. G. S. Jackson, *Operations of Eighth Corps: Account of Operations from Normandy to the River Rhine* (London: St. Clements Press, 1948), 14–17; H. L. Glyn Hughes, address on the eve of a memorial service for Harry, an honored member of 8 Corps, commemorating the twenty-fifth anniversary of the formation of the 8 Corps (Glyn Hughes's papers, Museum of Military Medicine archives, Aldershot, UK, RAMC 1218 3/9), 2–3.
4. Hughes, 8 Corps twenty-fifth anniversary address; H. L. Glyn Hughes, "Diary of D-Day Landings and Normandy Campaign," June 1944 (album covered in red moiré, Glyn Hughes's papers, RAMC 1218 2/6).
5. Hughes, "Diary of D-Day Landings."
6. 8 Corps Sitrep; Hughes, "Diary of D-Day Landings."
7. Hughes, "Diary of D-Day Landings."
8. Hughes, "Diary of D-Day Landings."
9. Jackson, *Operations of Eighth Corps*, 26–27. The two corps awaiting 8 Corps suffered appreciable casualties; Antony Beevor, *D-Day: The Battle for Normandy* (London: Viking, Penguin Books, 2009), 228–29. 8 Corps Sitrep (situation report, Kew: National Archives, WO 177/343).
10. The British called amphibious assault crafts for landing tanks on beachheads "landing craft tanks." In military terms, "headquarters" refers not only to the place in which commanders and their staff live and work, but also the actual unit comprising a commander and his staff. Hughes, 8 Corps twenty-fifth anniversary address, 2–3; Jackson, *Operations of Eighth Corps*, 18, 20, 21; 8

Corps Sitrep; Hughes, "Diary of D-Day Landings." Hughes wrote, "Well nourished [local inhabitants] were not particularly pleased to see us."

11. H. L. Glyn Hughes, "Normandy to the Baltic from a Medical Angle" (presidential address to the Harveian Society, January 15, 1947, Glyn Hughes's papers, RAMC 1218 2/21), 5, 9; Dan Van Der Vat, *D-Day: The Greatest Invasion—a People's History* (New York: Madison Press, 2013), 139. Bayeux, the first city to be liberated by 30 British Corps, fell on June 7.

12. Hughes, "Normandy to the Baltic," 5, 9; H. L. Glyn Hughes, "Precis: The Medical Services in the Field" (lecture, Glyn Hughes's papers, RAMC 1218 2/19).

13. Hughes, "Normandy to the Baltic"; John Buckley, *Monty's Men: The British Army and the Liberation of Europe* (New Haven, CT: Yale University Press, 2014), 34–35. Aligned with Montgomery's operational methods and views, Dempsey realized tactical opportunities and went about his job; he never sought the limelight.

14. Andrew Williams, *D-Day to Berlin* (London: Hodder and Stoughton, 2004), 76, 113–14. Hughes, "Diary of D-Day Landings."

15. Jackson, *Operations of Eighth Corps*, 20–23.

16. Hughes, "Diary of D-Day Landings." Hughes was not the only one who thought the plan foolhardy. After dinner and further discussion, it was modified.

17. Jackson, *Operations of Eighth Corps*, 22–23, 26–27. During the storm a floating mine sank an LCT conveying 8 Corps' 43 Division's reconnaissance regiment, resulting in a great loss of life. Ultimately, 631,000 men, 153,000 vehicles, and 689,000 tons of supplies came to the shores of Normandy. Williams, *D-Day to Berlin*, 76, 113–14; Hughes, "Normandy to the Baltic"; Yaron Pasher, *Holocaust versus Wehrmacht: How Hitler's "Final Solution" Undermined the German War Effort* (Lawrence: University Press of Kansas, 2014), 250–51.

18. Pasher, *Holocaust versus Wehrmacht*, 248.

19. Jackson, *Operations of Eighth Corps*, 27. Pasher, *Holocaust versus Wehrmacht*, 250, 256. For information on major battles in the east, see Jonathan W. Jordan, "Operation Bagration: Soviet Offensive of 1944," *World War II* magazine, July/August 2006, https://www.historynet.com/operation-bagration-soviet-offensive-of-1944.htm.

20. Pasher, *Holocaust versus Wehrmacht*, 248, 250, 256.

21. Gary Stix, "A Biologist Reconstructs the Grotesque Efficiency of the Nazis' Killing Machine," *Scientific American*, January 10, 2019, 3–5. Mathematical biologist Lewi Stone analyzed Israeli historian Yitzhak Arad's data in making these calculations. United States Holocaust Memorial Museum, "Operation Reinhard (Einsatz Reinhard)," *Holocaust*

Encyclopedia, https://encyclopedia.ushmm.org/content/en/article/
operation-reinhard-einsatz-reinhard.

22. Aranka Siegal, testimony, *I Witness* (University of Southern California Shoah Foundation, Tarrytown, NY, November 7, 1995), clips 21–22, 24; Louis Brandsdorfer, *The Bleeding Sky: My Mother's Journey through the Fire* (Scotts Valley, CA: CreateSpace Independent), 9.

23. Julie Brown (Jolan Szabo), conversation with author (North Bellmore, NY, March 16, 2011).

24. Beevor, *D-Day*, 228–29; Jackson, *Operations of Eighth Corps*, 22, 65.

25. Jackson, *Operations of Eighth Corps*, 22, 31–32.

26. Jackson, *Operations of Eighth Corps*, 28–29, 32, 39; David Lowther, *Liberating Belsen: Remembering the Soldiers of the Durham Light Infantry* (Durham, UK: Sacristy Press, 2015), 80; Hughes, "Normandy to the Baltic."

27. Jackson, *Operations of Eighth Corps*, 22–24, 27; Williams, *D-Day to Berlin*, 151.

28. Jackson, *Operations of Eighth Corps*, 36.

29. Jackson, *Operations of Eighth Corps*, 41; Beevor, *D-Day*, 232. On the second day of battle, congestion, heavy rain, and confusion slowed the attack, while 15 Scottish Division bravely fought off a Panzer counterattack. Fierce fighting occurred in several villages around Caen, especially in Cheux, where the Glasgow Highlanders lost a quarter of their strength in one day.

30. Williams, *D-Day to Berlin*, 121–23.

31. Jackson, *Operations of Eighth Corps*, 54; Hughes, "Normandy to the Baltic"; Beevor, *D-Day*, 187.

32. Beevor, *D-Day*, 187.

33. Williams, *D-Day to Berlin*, 118–19; Jackson, *Operations of Eighth Corps*, 33–37.

34. Hughes, "Normandy to the Baltic"; 8 Corps HQ (Medical Services) war diary for June 1944, appendix III (Kew: National Archives, WO 177/343). This document, written by Hughes for the purpose of "economizing manpower and maintaining maximum military efficiency," outlines how various cases of exhaustion—from "pure exhaustion," characterized by weight loss and confusion, to mild anxiety states (in fear of being hit by a bomb or shell, a man may be jittery and given to weeping, trembling, or sweating), to the acute and sudden onset of terror (under situations of great strain), to the case of the immature youth at first battle—are to be sorted out and treated. Acknowledging that it is difficult to assess whether cases are likely to recover within one to seven days or need to be evacuated to an advanced psychiatric wing, Hughes argues that "experience is the only real teacher." He also notes that the biggest rush of psychiatric cases come when there is a torrent of surgical cases, which must take priority.

35. "One cannot but admire the way in which the enemy fought and particu-
    larly the way in which he switched his anti-tank guns and defences and with
    limited resources held off such an attack as we put in with the whole weight
    of 3 Armoured Divisions in an attack East of the Orne in mid-July." Hughes,
    "Normandy to the Baltic." H. L. Glyn Hughes, "First Aid in Every Sphere"
    (lecture to the Hammersmith First Aid Society, Hammersmith Town Hall,
    February 16, 1972, RAMC 1218 3/9); Beevor, *D-Day*, 279, 281.
36. Beevor, *D-Day*, 281; Major Sam Cates, "Why Was General Richard N.
    O'Connor's Command of the British VIII Corps in Northwest Europe,
    1944 Less Effective Than Expected?" (Leavenworth, KS: School of
    Advanced Military Studies, March 2011), 41. Richard O'Connor's plans for
    8 Corps were complex and changeable. There was not always time for com-
    manders to debrief soldiers.
37. Hughes, "Normandy to the Baltic," 7–8, cited in Mark Harrison, *Medicine
    and Victory: British Military Medicine in the Second World War* (New York:
    Oxford University Press, 2004), 252–53; Williams, *D-Day to Berlin*, 262.
38. Jackson, *Operations of Eighth Corps*, 34, 52; Harrison, *Medicine and Victory*,
    253.
39. H. L. Glyn Hughes, "The Duties of a Regimental Medical Officer" (lecture
    given to RMOs, Glyn Hughes's papers, RAMC 1218 3/9).
40. See *University College Hospital Magazine* 1, no. 3 (December 1910): 124;
    1, no. 5 (April 1911): 214–16, 217, 219; 2, no. 4 (April 1912): 150–52;
    3, no. 1 (October 1912): 45; 3, no. 2 (December 1912): 88; *University
    College Hospital Magazine* 4, no. 4 (May 1914): 145.

    Hughes's ardor for the sport led to an unsurprising consequence—at
    the end of a five-month period (from October 1912 to March 1913), in
    which the UCH team played thirty-one games, he failed all of his exams
    (University College Hospital Registrars Office records). *University College
    Hospital Magazine* 3, no. 3 (February 1913): 127–28; 3, no. 1 (October
    1913): 26; 3, no. 2 (December 1913): 61; 4, no. 4 (May 1914): 145. For
    linkages between rugby and the military, see Edmund McCabe, "Rugby
    and the Great War," *Stand To! The Journal of the Western Front Association*,
    no. 52 (April 1998): 26–29.

    While in medical school, Hughes received military training with the
    Artists Rifles. For the history of this valorous regiment, founded in 1850
    by art student Edward Stirling, see Colonel H. A. R. May, CB, VD,
    Memories of the Artists Rifles (London: Howlett & Son, 1929). Colonel
    May guaranteed that each of the men he trained would comport himself
    as "an officer and a gentleman." John S. G. Blair, *Centenary History of the
    Royal Army Medical Corps* (Edinburgh: Scottish Academic Press / iynx,
    2001), 159; Ian R. Whitehead, *Doctors in the Great War* (Barnsley, UK:

Leo Cooper / Pen & Sword Books, 1999), 96–97. Document cited: PRO, War Office Instructions, January–June 1915, instruction 3, *Attendance of Medical Students at Military Hospitals*, April 1, 1915 (Kew: National Archives, WO 293/2). University College Hospital provided additional training in ambulance drills, military sanitation, and the proper treatment of injuries and ailments seen at the front, as well as instruction on the organization of the RAMC. When it had released as many professors, medical staff, and students as possible for service, teaching and medical research were put on hold. University College Hospital was among four London teaching hospitals wherein medical territorial forces were based. For the history of the Royal Army Medical Corps, see Redmond McLaughlin, *The Royal Army Medical Corps*, ed. Lieutenant General Sir Brian Horrocks (London: Leo Cooper, 1972), 18–20.

41. Whitehead, *Doctors in the Great War*, 164, 170–73. (Guidelines were issued on January 16, 1915, under Army Routine Order 554.) Hughes, "First Aid in Every Sphere."

42. Whitehead, *Doctors in the Great War*, 184–89, 228. Whitehead quoted Colonel Arthur Lee, who wrote that RMOs established aid posts in whatever shelter they could find and "as near to the firing line as was deemed safe." ("The Royal Army Medical Corps and Its Work," *British Medical Journal* 2 [1917]: 218.) In a letter to Lord Kitchener, Lee referred to reckless medical officers in France who needed to be restrained, whose acts could deprive a whole unit of his services (Sir C. Burtchaell, WIHM, RAMC 446/7: Papers: letters of Lee to Kitchener, 12 October 1914). On the other hand, see H. W. Wilson and J. A. Hammerton, *The Great War* (London: Amalgamated Press, 1915), 4:124. There were "few more splendid records than those of the eager young medicos who put regulations on one side and went where danger was the greatest."

43. Whitehead, *Doctors in the Great War*, 226; McLaughlin, *The Royal Army Medical Corps*, 55–56, 60.

44. McLaughlin, *The Royal Army Medical Corps*, 1. Hugh Shields, WIHM, RAMC 383, diary, September 25, 1914, 27, quoted in Whitehead, *Doctors in the Great War*, 185–86. Some RMOs, having seen friends being killed, were overcome by emotion and wanted to "hit back."

45. H. L. Glyn Hughes, sketch for Thelma; Captain Stanley Parker, MC, DCM, August 6, 1915 (Glyn Hughes's papers). Captain Parker was a guest on *This Is Your Life*, BBC Television Theatre, subject 89, Mon., March 9, 1959, series 4, edition 24 (the surprised subject that evening: Glyn Hughes). Parker recalled how Hughes "amputated some fellow's foot with a pocketknife."

46. See Whitehead, *Doctors in the Great War*; "Some Impressions of a Civilian at the Western Front," *British Medical Journal* 2 (1916): 502; and a report in August 1915, by Director of General Medical Services (DGMS) Sir A. Sloggett, with the BEF (British Expeditionary Force) in France, on the severe shortages of medical personnel with which the British struggled during World War I (Kew: National Archives, WO 95/44 [PRO] DGMS Diary 1915).

47. Hughes, "The Duties of a Regimental Medical Officer."

48. Hughes, "The Duties of a Regimental Medical Officer."

49. Carl Aarvold, thanksgiving for Hughes's life, St. Marylebone Parish Church, January 9, 1974; Hughes, "Normandy to the Baltic"; Antony Beevor, *D-Day*, 280–81.

50. Hughes, "Normandy to the Baltic." Of approximately six hundred exhaustion cases reviewed, 436 were returned to full duty in the line. Few relapsed. From July to September there were 8,930 exhaustion cases; throughout the entire campaign, there were 13,255 cases, comprising 15.6 percent of casualties. Hughes, "First Aid in Every Sphere."

    Hughes received the following letter from Bob, after Bob had seen "Hughie" on *This Is Your Life*:

    > You appeared just the same to me as when I joined you at H.Q. 8 Corps at Stanford Bridge, Yorkshire, as the First Corps "Trick Cyclist," and was accepted not as a mystic gent., but as "Bob." That gesture of yours gave me such confidence in being able to tackle the job, that it became possible to break down the barrier which then existed between psychiatry, medicine, and the lay mind. The point which struck me particularly was that you, as a man of courage, accepted and forgave those whose mental make-up was such that break-down under stress was unavoidable. How well I remember the days on the bridge-head [*sic*] in Normandy when I had to report to you over nine hundred "psychiatric casualties" in sixteen days, but qualified the statement by the fact that we had sent back to duty 36% . . . Again later in the campaign when we delved into the problem of "desertion in the field of battle" and returned to the line some 70% after they had served three months only of prison sentence, it pleased you immensely when it was later reported that two had acquitted themselves so well afterwards that they were recommended for the Military Medal. (at "The Hollies," Pyle, Nr. Bridgend, Glam., dated March 10, 1959, Glyn Hughes's papers, RAMC 1218/3/11)

51. H. L. Glyn Hughes, "The Medical Services in the Field" (lecture, Glyn Hughes's papers, RAMC 1218 2/19).

52. Jackson, *Operations of Eighth Corps*, 46–48, 50–53.

53. Jackson, *Operations of Eighth Corps*, 33, 44. Decisions made at the Führer's conference at Soissons were quickly disrupted and "doomed to failure." The Scotsmen referred to were from 8 Corps' 15 (Scottish) Division.

54. Jackson, *Operations of Eighth Corps*, 53, 56–57, 65; Beevor, *D-Day*, 392. Harrison, *Medicine and Victory*, 253. The mental state of the German army deteriorated sharply during the campaign.

55. Jackson, *Operations of Eighth Corps*, 52.

56. Jackson, *Operations of Eighth Corps*, 64–65.

57. Jackson, *Operations of Eighth Corps*, 61; Beevor, *D-Day*, 27, 144, 232.

58. Beevor, *D-Day*, 267–69, 271.

59. Beevor, *D-Day*, 267–69, 271.

60. Beevor, *D-Day*, 280; Jackson, *Operations of Eighth Corps*, 62–65; Van Der Vat, *D-Day*, 146.

61. Jackson, *Operations of Eighth Corps*, 64–65; Van Der Vat, *D-Day*, 146.

62. Beevor, *D-Day*, 314; Jackson, *Operations of Eighth* Corps, 68–70.

63. Beevor, *D-Day*, 307–9, 311, 314. Allied bombs were dropped by two thousand heavy bombers and six hundred medium bombers.

64. Beevor, *D-Day*, 308–9, 311, 314. Dempsey's staff assumed that Eberbach's defenses had a depth of less than three miles. Jackson, *Operations of Eighth Corps*, 74–77.

65. Beevor, *D-Day*, 316–17, 320; Williams, *D-Day to Berlin*, 164–65, 168.

66. Beevor, *D-Day*, 320–22. Major Julius Neave of Britain's 13/18 Hussars wrote of the bitter disappointment felt when British tanks were so quickly destroyed. Buckley, *Monty's Men*, 6.

67. Jackson, *Operations of Eighth Corps*, 111.

68. Hughes, 8 Corps twenty-fifth anniversary address.

69. Jackson, *Operations of Eighth Corps*, 98.

70. Harrison, *Medicine and Victory*, 252–53.

71. Hughes, "Normandy to the Baltic," 7, 9; Williams, *D-Day to Berlin*, 121–23.

72. Harrison, *Medicine and Victory*, 252–53; Hughes, "Normandy to the Baltic," 13; Hughes, "The Duties of a Regimental Medical Officer."

73. Beevor, *D-Day*, 323–24.

74. Beevor, *D-Day*, 323–24. One could hardly imagine a British or Canadian POW—whose loyalty took the form of not wanting to let their comrades down—wanting to die for Churchill or King George VI.

75. Southern Command Medical Study Week, Exercise No. 2 (Armour) and 8 Corps Medical Intelligence Summary No. 5 (July 19, 1944) (Glyn Hughes's papers, RAMC 1218 3/2).

76. 8 Corps Medical Intelligence Summary No. 5; Rex Palmer on Andrews, *This Is Your Life.*

77. Beevor, *D-Day*, 324.

78. Hughes, "Normandy to the Baltic."

79. Beevor, *D-Day*, 367, 369; Jackson, *Operations of Eighth Corps*, 114; "D-Day Overlord," in *D-Day and Battle of Normandy Encyclopedia*, https://www.dday-overlord.com/en/battle-of-normandy/allied-operations/bluecoat.

80. Danuta Czech, *Auschwitz Chronicle, 1939–1945* (New York: Henry Holt, 1990), 563–64, 664, 666. According to Danuta Czech, between May 16 and June 13, 1944, three hundred thousand Jews came to Birkenau in 113 trains. On July 12, Birkenau (Auschwitz II) held 31,406 female prisoners and 19,711 male prisoners. Auschwitz I held 14,386 prisoners.

81. "After every selection there was a lock down, that is you could not get out of the barrack. If you had to go to the latrine, you could only go in groups with a kapo." Ruth Mermelstein, email to author (January 25, 2012).

82. Siegal, *I Witness*, clip 25. Child survivor Ruth Kluger explained that during the selection "a kind of orderly chaos reigned . . . organization was superficial, because there was nothing valuable to organize or retain. We were worthless by definition." Ruth Kluger, *Still Alive: A Holocaust Girlhood Remembered* (New York: Feminist Press at the City University of New York, 2001), 106.

83. Göran Rosenberg, *A Brief Stop on the Road from Auschwitz*, trans. Sarah Death (New York: Other Press, 2012), 100–101; Nikolaus Wachsmann, *KL: A History of the Nazi Concentration Camps* (New York: Farrar, Straus and Giroux, 2015), 311; Dorota Sula, *Arbeitslager Ries* (Walbrzych: Muzeum Gross-Rosen, 2003); Bella Gutterman, *A Narrow Bridge to Life: Jewish Forced Labor and Survival in the Gross-Rosen Camp System, 1940–1945* (New York: Berghahn Books, 2008), 2, 6, 37, 57, 64, 67, 69, 71, 100, 105, 106.

84. Czech, *Auschwitz Chronicle*, 633. During the summer of 1944, some "unregistered" Hungarian Jews were selected for labor and deported from Birkenau to Gross-Rosen. Joli Hillman-Noy, testimony (University of Southern California Survivors of the Shoah Visual History Foundation, Upper Nazareth, Israel, September 2, 1988, code 46499).

85. Among other accounts, the smell of Birkenau is described in Patricia Posner, *The Pharmacist of Auschwitz* (London: Crux, 2017), 50. Helen Mermelstein, conversation with the author (July 23, 2011). Twenty-six-year-old Helen Mermelstein, from the (formerly Czechoslovakian) town of Cinadievo, registered the words of a male inmate who helped them board the train: "You are very fortunate to be leaving this place." Mildred Grun, conversation with the author (October 13, 2011). Mildred Grun, also on this transport, said

that the guard in her car told them that he would leave the doors open but that they were not to look out.

86. Helen Mermelstein, conversation with the author (July 23, 2011). Kluger, *Still Alive*, 101–2. Ruth Kluger remembers arriving at a small station with the sign "Christianstadt."

87. Dan Stone, "Christianstadt: Slave Labor and the Holocaust in the ITS Digital Archive," *Slave Labor and the Holocaust*, vol. 4 of *Freilegungen: Yearbook of the International Tracing Service* (London: Wiener Library, 2015), 78–91, citing Barbara Sawicka; "Christianstadt," in *United States Holocaust Memorial Museum Encyclopedia of Camps and Ghettos 1933– 1945*, ed. Geoffrey P. Megargee, vol. 1, *Early Camps, Youth Camps, and Concentration and Subcamps under the SS–Business Administration Main Office (WVHA)* (Bloomington: Indiana University Press, 2009), 722. Begun in 1940 as IG Farben chemical works, Christianstadt became a growing Dynamit AG explosives and munitions plant.

88. Yishay Garbasz, *In My Mother's Footsteps* (published in conjunction with the exhibit of the same name, Tokyo, 2009, by Hatje Cantz, Berlin, Germany, 2009; exhibited also at the Northwood University International Creativity Conference in Midland, MI, in 2010), 86, 90; Kluger, *Still Alive*, 116–17. Siegal, *I Witness*, clip 26. When she first arrived in Christianstadt, Aranka Siegal took ten showers a day. (The showers were outdoors.) She washed her clothes and roamed about. Gutterman, *A Narrow Bridge to Life*, 147, 149, 161. After Ravensbrück and Stutthof, Gross-Rosen had the largest population of women prisoners. In January 1945 there was a total of 76,728 prisoners in the Gross-Rosen system; 25,524 of these were women. The total number of concentration camp prisoners was 706,650, of whom 198,522 were women.

89. Zsabo Jolan (Julie Brown), conversation with the author (March 16, 2011).

90. Kluger, *Still Alive*, 101–2; Rosenberg, *A Brief Stop on the Road from Auschwitz*, 100–101; Wachsmann, *KL*, 311. Vera Hájková-Duxová, "Such Was Life," in *The World without Human Dimensions: Four Women's Memories* ("The Menorah" Series, Publication of the State Museum in Prague, 1991), 103. In Auschwitz, inmates were issued clogs.

91. Gutterman, *A Narrow Bridge to Life*, 102, 234–35, 241; Kluger, *Still Alive*, 114; Wachsmann, *KL*, 311.

92. Accounts of the diet in Christianstadt can be found in Hájková-Duxová, "Such Was Life," in *The World without Human Dimensions*, 103–4; Kluger, *Still Alive*, 118; Garbasz, *In My Mother's Footsteps*, 92.

93. Joli Hillman-Noy, *I Witness* (University of Southern California Shoah Foundation Institute, interview conducted on September 2, 1998, in Upper Nazareth, Israel), code 46499. Joli Basch worked in the factory

making bullets. She claimed "there was a lot of sabotage." Eva Hillman, conversation with the author (January 15, 2012). Eva Hillman, daughter of Joli Basch, said that her mother reported that she and others urinated into vats used to prepare munitions. Hájková-Duxová, *The World without Human Dimensions*, 103. Describing the hall in which women worked with "hot grey mush," Hájková-Duxová wrote, "It was like hell there." Stone, "Christianstadt," 88. Weapons produced at Christianstadt were substandard. For one, women filled them with insufficient powder.

94. Hájková-Duxová, *The World without Human Dimensions*, 104; Stone, "Christianstadt," 88.

95. According to Rachel, Elisabeth worked in an asbestos mine. A type of work that covered women in gray dust is described in Franziska Faktorová, *The World without Human Dimensions*, 208–9; and Siegal, *I Witness*, clip 26.

96. Doraneni's formal name was Mrs. Teszler-Reich.

97. Hájková-Duxová, *The World without Human Dimensions*, 107. This occurred in the first week of August 1944, shortly after Rachel's arrival. Helen Mermelstein, conversation with the author (March 4, 2012). Helen Mermelstein recalled that "they were always asking who was pregnant." She never again saw those who admitted to this condition.

98. Rachel was especially vulnerable because of her age. Wachsmann, *KL*, 310, citing Kubica, "Children," 205, 217, 289; Buser, *Überleben*, 116–21; and Pohl, *Holocaust*, 106–7. Between 1942 and 1945, approximately two hundred ten thousand children were deported to Auschwitz, and almost all under the age of fourteen were gassed upon arrival. Fewer than twenty-five hundred Jewish children survived the initial selections. (This figure excludes deportees from Theresienstadt.)

99. Siegal, *I Witness*, clip 26. Aranka Siegal recalls the moment she, like Rachel, was picked to work in the kitchen. Aufseherin Luci asked, "Does anyone speak German?" Every hand went up. Aranka flashed her biggest smile, hoping to be chosen. She described the women in charge of the camp as "unreal." They displayed seriousness only when male officers were around. Martha, the big one who was the boss, was always laughing. Gerta, the little one, never smiled. Luci, of medium height and fair with blue eyes, was a "giggler."

100. Jackson, *Operations of Eighth Corps*, 140; Van Der Vat, *D-Day*, 167; Stuart Hills, MC, *By Tank into Normandy: A Memoir of the Campaign in NW Europe from D-Day to VE Day* (London: Cassell, 2002), 144. Beevor, *D-Day*, 462; Hughes, "Normandy to the Baltic"; Lowther, *Liberating Belsen*, 81. John Buckley, *Monty's Men*, 182. The Allies were forced to use bulldozers. See also "Normandy: Armaggedon on a Country Lane," *London Telegraph*,

August 7, 2004, https://www.telegraph.co.uk/travel/destinations/europe/
france/730930/Normandy-Armageddon-on-a-country-lane.html.

101. Hills, *By Tank into Normandy*, 144; Van Der Vat, *D-Day*, 167.
102. Jackson, *Operations of Eighth Corps*, 142–43.
103. Jackson, *Operations of Eighth Corps*, 142–44.
104. Jackson, *Operations of Eighth Corps*, 145.
105. Hughes, "Memorial service for Harry"; Jackson, *Operations of Eighth Corps*,
     141. According to Buckley, between D-Day and the end of August, three
     hundred thousand Germans were killed or wounded; two hundred and
     eight thousand were taken prisoner. Allied losses amounted to two hun-
     dred thousand killed or wounded; sixteen thousand died or went missing.
     Buckley, *Monty's Men*, 182.
106. Hughes, "The Duties of a Regimental Medical Officer."

FALL 1944

1. Dan Stone, "Christianstadt: Slave Labor and the Holocaust in the ITS
   Digital Archive," *Slave Labor and the Holocaust*, vol. 4 of *Freilegungen:
   Yearbook of the International Tracing Service* (London: Wiener Library,
   2015), 4:83, citing *Survivors Report on Gross-Rosen* 1.1.11.0/82111220/
   ITS. In August/September 1987, three women from Prague who had been
   in Christianstadt submitted a report saying that one thousand women had
   come from Auschwitz to the labor camp: five hundred on July 8, 1944, and
   five hundred at the end of August / beginning of September; most of the
   latter had been in the Łódź ghetto. (Rachel's records indicate that she and
   about two hundred fifty others came at the beginning of August.)
2. Aranka Siegal, testimony, *I Witness* (University of Southern California
   Shoah Foundation, Tarrytown, New York, November 7, 1995), clip 27.
3. Czech female surnames took the suffix -ová. Siegal, *I Witness*, clip 27.
4. Bella Gutterman, *A Narrow Bridge to Life: Jewish Forced Labor and Survival
   in the Gross-Rosen Camp System, 1940–1945* (New York: Berghahn Books,
   2008), 140; Stone, "Christianstadt," 84, 88–89. Others' accounts of tortures
   endured at Christianstadt mentioned roll calls as

> an opportunity to belittle us, to punish us, and to torment us. At
> the slightest perceived infraction, the guards would hold a so-called
> Strafappell or punishment roll call . . . [T]he commonest cause for
> one was as punishment for a prisoner covering herself with her blan-
> ket during roll call . . . for the cold was unbearable . . . Anyone who
> fainted . . . had cold water thrown over them by a guard. The victim
> then had to stand up again in her wet dress, even when it was frosty.

5. David Wyman, *The Abandonment of the Jews: America and the Holocaust, 1941–1945* (New York: Pantheon Books, 1984), 292–307; G. S. Jackson, *Operations of Eighth Corps: Account of Operations from Normandy to the River Rhine* (London: St. Clements Press, 1948), 145.

6. Jackson, *Operations of Eighth Corps*, 145–47.

7. H. L. Glyn Hughes, address on the eve of a memorial service for Harry, an honored member of 8 Corps, commemorating the twenty-fifth anniversary of the formation of the 8 Corps (Glyn Hughes's papers, Museum of Military Medicine archives, Aldershot, UK, RAMC 1218 3/9).

8. H. L. Glyn Hughes, "Diary of D-Day Landings and Normandy Campaign," June 1944 (album covered in red moiré, Glyn Hughes's papers, RAMC 1218.2/6); Redmond McLaughlin, *The Royal Army Medical Corps*, ed. Lieutenant General Sir Brian Horrocks (London: Leo Cooper, 1972), 91–92; John Buckley, *Monty's Men: The British Army and the Liberation of Europe* (New Haven, CT: Yale University Press), 296–99, 302; H. L. Glyn Hughes, "Normandy to the Baltic from a Medical Angle" (presidential address to the Harveian Society, January 15, 1947, Glyn Hughes's papers, RAMC 1218 2/21).

9. Hughes, "Normandy to the Baltic"; David Lowther, *Liberating Belsen: Remembering the Soldiers of the Durham Light Infantry* (Durham, UK: Sacristy Press, 2015), 84; Jackson, *Operations of Eighth Corps*, 149–50. The Belgian frontier was crossed on September 6. Jean Smart (Glyn Hughes's daughter), interview with the author (March 6, 2004).

10. Jackson, *Operations of Eighth Corps*, 150–52. Dan Van Der Vat, *D-Day: The Greatest Invasion—a People's History* (Bloomsbury: Madison Press, 2003), 226–27. The British would need to move twenty thousand vehicles across a single road in sixty hours.

11. Jackson, *Operations of Eighth Corps*, 153–55. H. L. Glyn Hughes, "Germany, 1945: The Assault and After" (lecture, St. Mary's Hospital Medical Society, February 14, 1946, Glyn Hughes's papers, RAMC 1218 2/21).

12. John S. G. Blair, *In Arduis Fidelis: Centenary History of the RAMC* (Edinburgh: Scottish Academic Press, 1998), 306–8. One of the hospitals took in 5,825 in thirteen days. Jackson, *Operations of Eighth Corps*, 156.

13. McLaughlin, *The Royal Army Medical Corps*, 93–94.

14. H. L. Glyn Hughes, sketch for Thelma (Glyn Hughes's papers). The American Airborne Division had been put under Hughes's command. Jackson, *Operations of Eighth Corps*, 155–56.

15. Hughes, sketch for Thelma. The driver in the jeep just ahead was captured.

16. Hughes, sketch for Thelma. The tanks that arrived "were not very clever in their positioning and were almost all knocked out by bazookas."

17. Hughes, sketch for Thelma.

18. Were a soldier to win a second Distinguished Service Order, the award would be indicated by an actual bar beneath his original medal. In his account for Thelma, Hughes explained, "The incidents connected with my second Bar which came as the greatest surprise were involved with the Battle of Arnhem and the failure of 30 Corps (led by Lieut.-General Horrocks) to relieve the Airborne Forces which had carried out the attack." Jackson, *Operations of Eighth Corps*, 155–56. Hughes and others were caught on their way back from Nijmegen on account of a sudden thrust by 107 Panzer Brigade and infantry, aiming to cut 30 Corps' axis. Peter Starling, "Brigadier Hugh Llewelyn Glyn Hughes CBE DSO MC: His Life and Work" (lecture, Belsen Commemoration and Study Period, Hohne, Germany, April 15, 1998, Museum of Military Medicine archives). During World War II only eighteen "second bars to the DSO" were awarded to members of the Royal Army Medical Corps.

19. McLaughlin, *The Royal Army Medical Corps*, 100; Alan Scadding (former head of history and politics at Epsom College), conversation with the author (March 2004); G. H. Swindell wrote that he first met Glyn Hughes at "Plug St" in 1915. "[H]e became a legend in our Division (25th), a brave man whose life in the trenches would be summed up in these words, 'Selfless devotion to duty' " (Museum of Military Medicine archives, RAMC 1218 1/11).

20. Hughes, sketch for Thelma.

21. *Thiepval July 1916* (document in Glyn Hughes's files on the First World War, Glyn Hughes's papers); Hughes, sketch for Thelma; "War Honours," *British Medical Journal* (September 6, 1916): 337; Starling, "Brig. H. L. G. Hughes"; *The History of The Royal Army Medical Corps*, War Office, May 1943. The statistic on the survival rate of those awarded the VC is found at the Museum of Military Medicine.

22. Helen J. McCarrick, "One Man in His Time" (document on *Nursing Times* stationery, London, Little Essex St., March 4, 1969, private collection). In recounting his part in "a bit of a scrap with a group of Prussian guards trying to break out of their trenches," Hughes demonstrated for nurse Helen J. McCarrick, in 1969, how he "lobbed Mills bombs" (simple, rugged, and effective hand grenades). Hughes, sketch for Thelma; Chronicle of 1st Wiltshire's activities (Museum of Military Medicine archives). After serving with 1 Wiltshires for ten months, Hughes was considered by the brigade and divisional commanders to be the most experienced officer in the battalion. They instructed incoming Colonel Williams to consult Lieutenant Hughes on any problems that arose.

23. Hughes, sketch for Thelma. During this period Lieutenant Colonel S. S. Ogilvie commanded the brigade.

24. Starling, "Brig. H. L. G. Hughes"; McLaughlin, *The Royal Army Medical Corps*, 54.
25. Hughes, sketch for Thelma.
26. Hughes, sketch for Thelma.
27. Letter from Private Swindell (Hughes, private collection). This letter, prompted by the *This Is Your Life* television event (*This Is Your Life*, BBC Television Theatre, Subject 89, Mon., March 9, 1959, series 4, edition 24) came from a first private in the 77 Field Ambulance who had "presented" himself at Hughes's regimental aid post "just up the trench from Seven Trees." A victim of "Our War," he was now in a hospital. When nurses there asked him whether he knew Glyn Hughes, "the Dr. of T.V. last night," he grinned and told them that he "had not only heard of him but had the honour of serving in the trenches with him." In Mr. Swindell's reminiscences he, like Mr. Edwards, referred to men with whom both he and Hughie had served, including Paddy Stevens, who was killed on March 21, 1918, and Major Lescher, whose leg was blown off at Thiepval and who in his last years suffered a stroke and mental instability, "always rambling about the War." And he described his reactions to seeing Hughes, after so many years, on television:

> When I think of the loss of Paddy, & then you yourself, being
> wounded, I recall that not only the 1st Wilts, but the 77th F.ct,
> were stunned . . . [I] never heard of you again till last night, it was
> a proud moment, when I realized who I was gazing at, & how glad
> I felt, that Life had been spared to you, & when the band played,
> I stood to attention, as a token of my respect for you, but also of
> the Spirit of Service you instilled into us . . . Thank you Sir, for that
> glimpse of you, & I am sure all those wounded you attended to &
> all the old 77th F.ct. men who saw you, had one thing in common
> last night, & that was Pride, that we had the honour to gaze on one
> of the 25 Divisions [*sic*] greatest Men, the Huns placed us fifth on
> their list of great Divisions only being led by two Scottish & Irish,
> & it was Men like you that inspired us.
>
> > Yours in humble gratitude,
> > 37789 Ex. Pte. G H Swindell of 77 Field Ambulance,
> > 7 Brigade, 25 Division, B.E.F. France 1915 x 1918.

28. For details pertaining to their last actions of the war, see the chronicle of 1 Wiltshire's activities. Mr. A. J. Edwards, M.BE (20 Fairway, Leigh-on-Sea, Essex, March 10, 1959, Hughes, private collection).

29. H. L. Glyn Hughes, "The Duties of a Regimental Medical Officer" (lecture given to RMOs, Glyn Hughes's papers, RAMC 1218 3/9). In encouraging RMOs to take an interest in military matters, Hughes said they would thus "do good" for the RAMC and for themselves as well. He emphasized the advantages of involvement, commitment, and knowing others' jobs. One might more readily "get one's way." Hughes, sketch for Thelma.
30. Jackson, *Operations of Eighth Corps*, 156; Hughes, "Normandy to the Baltic," 11; Lowther, *Liberating Belsen*, 84.
31. McLaughlin, *The Royal Army Medical Corps*, 94; Hughes, "Normandy to the Baltic," 12. September 26 saw the final evacuation of 2,163 injured men. In all, the 25 Division evacuated 2,800.
32. The Battle of the Dukla Pass, for the strategic mountain crossing between Poland and Czechoslovakia, was among the bloodiest battles on the eastern front. (The author's uncle, Alexander Mashek, took part in this battle.) See Erich Kulka, *Jews in Svoboda's Army in the Soviet Union: Czechoslovak Jewry's Fight against the Nazis during World War II* (Lanham, MD: University Press of America, 1987), 333–51.
33. Mindi is a pseudonym for the older teenager who features in several parts of Rachel's story.
34. Neither Rachel nor Ratza could imagine the hardships to come. Nor the workings of providence. Eleven years later, in Lakewood, New Jersey, they would celebrate Passover as sisters-in-law. (Their husbands-to-be were brothers.) Ratza told her daughter, Ruth, that Rachel was always afraid. Ruth Kirschenbaum, conversation with the author (April 2016).
35. Aranka Siegal, conversation with the author (December 2018); Gutterman, *A Narrow Bridge to Life*, 159, 237.
36. Ruth Mermelstein, email to author (January 27, 2012): "[My birthday celebration] sure [was] the best part of my horrible experience. If I would not have had that experience, if I only had the sad stories about being separated from my family and the hardship of surviving I would never have been able to open up to you to tell you about my life. I think that my Christianstadt experience also gave me strength to go on. It was just a lucky break for a short time."
37. Isak Arbus, "Roza Robata: A Heroine of the Auschwitz Uprising, "*Jewish Currents*, October 6, 2015, https://jewishcurrents.org/articles/roza-robota -a-heroine-of-the-auschwitz-uprising. See also Shlomo Venezia, *Inside the Gas Chambers: Eight Months in the Sonderkommando of Auschwitz* (Malden, MA: Polity Press, 2009). The revolt came after months of planning and the involvement of female slave laborers, who smuggled explosives from the

nearby Union munitions factory. Ian Kershaw, *The End: The Defiance and Destruction of Hitler's Germany, 1944–1945* (New York: Penguin Group, 2011), 86–87, 89. On September 21, Himmler told defense district commanders that "if the enemy should break in somewhere, he will encounter a fanatical people, fighting like mad to the end, that he will certainly not get through." In truth, but a small minority of the Volkssturm, meant to "embody the true Nazi revolution," were ardent Nazis. Most, very young and old, "trudged unwillingly and fearfully" into the service. See Kershaw for ways in which the "entire frontier population" was being called upon "to ensure the freedom of [the German] homeland."

38. Hughes, "Normandy to the Baltic," 20.
39. Hughes, "Normandy to the Baltic," 13.
40. Hughes, "Normandy to the Baltic," 12.
41. Hughes, "Normandy to the Baltic," 11, 13.
42. Jackson, *Operations of Eighth Corps*, 157–59; Hughes, "Normandy to the Baltic," 12.
43. Hughes, "Normandy to the Baltic," 12.
44. Hughes, "Normandy to the Baltic," 12.
45. Hughes, "The Assault and After"; Hughes, "Normandy to the Baltic," 12.
46. Jackson, *Operations of Eighth Corps*, 160–61.
47. Jackson, *Operations of Eighth Corps*, 161, 163.
48. Jackson, *Operations of Eighth Corps*, 164.
49. Hughes, "Normandy to the Baltic," 7, 12; H. L. Glyn Hughes, "The Duties of a Regimental Officer" (lecture to RMOs, Hughes's papers, RAMC 1218 3/9).
50. H. L. Glyn Hughes, "Medical TEWT—Tactical Exercise without Troops—14–16 Oct. 45: DS Notes on Requirement 2" (Paper 7, Hughes's papers); Jackson, *Operations of Eighth Corps*, 66. Hughes, 8 Corps twenty-fifth anniversary address, 4. "Throughout the entire campaign [Army Commander General Dempsey] said—'I seem always to see the White Knight in the forefront and I am glad to pay my tribute to a great Corps.'"
51. Hughes, "Normandy to the Baltic," 7, 12; Hughes, "Duties of a Regimental Officer"; Jackson, *Operations of Eighth Corps*, 64–65.
52. Jackson, *Operations of Eighth Corps*, 163–64.
53. Ruth Mermelstein, conversation with the author (May 18, 2012). The four other girls who went on the outing: Aranka Siegel, the daughters of Roubitscheková and Hoffmanová, and the middle of the three sisters who shared a room with Rachel. Rachel believed Luci intended to treat the young prisoners, to show them the town of Christianstadt. Göran Rosenberg, *A Brief Stop on the Road from Auschwitz*, trans.

Sarah Death (New York: Other Press, 2012), 100–101. The camp was located at *Schwedenwall*, "Sweden wall," in the forest west of the town of Christianstadt, then in eastern Germany. After the war, the town became part of western Poland and changed its name to Krzystkowice.

WINTER 1944–1945

1. John Buckley, *Monty's Men: The British Army and the Liberation of Europe* (New Haven, CT: Yale University Press), 259–60.
2. Buckley, *Monty's Men*, 259, 260; H. L. Glyn Hughes, "Germany 1945: The Assault and After" (lecture, St. Mary's Hospital Medical Society, February 14, 1946, Glyn Hughes's papers, Museum of Military Medicine archives, Aldershot, UK, RAMC 1218 2/21), 1; H. L. Glyn Hughes, lecture, Fleet (March 27, 1946, Glyn Hughes's papers, RAMC 1218 2/18), 2–3; G. S. Jackson, *Operations of Eighth Corps: Account of Operations from Normandy to the River Rhine* (London: St. Clements Press, 1948), 164–65; H. L. Glyn Hughes, address on the eve of a memorial service for Harry, an honored member of 8 Corps, commemorating the twenty-fifth anniversary of the formation of the 8 Corps (Glyn Hughes's papers, RAMC 1218 3/9), 2, 4. General O'Connor left to assume another post at the beginning of December. Hughes said that "8 Corps must have had the record in number of Commanders," Lieut. General Sir Evelyn "Bubbles" Barker being the last of eight.
3. See B. J. Copeland, "Ultra: Allied Intelligence Project," *Encyclopaedia Britannica*, https://www.britannica.com/topic/Ultra-Allied-intelligence-project, for information about the location and work of Ultra. Buckley, *Monty's Men*, 259, 260. The "bulge" extended into East Germany. Hughes, Fleet lecture, 2–3; Hughes, "Germany 1945." See Simon Worrall's "The Real Reason Hitler Launched the Battle of the Bulge," *National Geographic*, December 31, 1969, for an interesting analysis of Hitler's motives.
4. Hughes, "Germany 1945," 1; Hughes, Fleet lecture, 2–3.
5. Hughes, "Germany 1945," 1–2; Hughes, Fleet lecture, 4.
6. Hughes, "Germany 1945," 1.
7. Hughes, "Germany 1945," 1–2; Hughes, 8 Corps twenty-fifth anniversary address, 2, 4; Jackson, *Operations of Eighth Corps*, 165.
8. Hughes, "Germany 1945," 1–2.
9. Bella Gutterman, *A Narrow Bridge to Life: Jewish Forced Labor and Survival in the Gross-Rosen Camp System, 1940–1945* (New York: Berghahn Books, 2008), 3. Gutterman quotes Primo Levi, who wrote, in *The Drowned and the Saved*, of the victims' relentless struggle to avoid punishment, to act in their own defense: "Immediate needs pinned their eyes to the ground."

10. Dan Stone, "Christianstadt: Slave Labor and the Holocaust in the ITS Digital Archive," in *Slave Labor and the Holocaust*, vol. 4 of *Freilegungen: Yearbook of the International Tracing Service* (London: Wiener Library, 2015), 4:84; Vera Hájková-Duxová, "Such Was Life," in *The World without Human Dimensions: Four Women's Memories* ("The Menorah" Series, Publication of the State Museum in Prague, 1991), 106; Ruth Kluger, *Still Alive: A Holocaust Girlhood Remembered* (New York: Feminist Press at the City University of New York, 2001), 128.

11. Gutterman, *A Narrow Bridge to Life*, 192, 195, 199.

12. Hájková-Duxová, in *The World without Human Dimensions*, 108. Sometime in the second half of January, SS men came to the camp, and there was talk of evacuating it. Gutterman, *A Narrow Bridge to Life*, 195–96; Daniel Blatman, *The Death Marches: The Final Phase of Nazi Genocide*, trans. Chaya Galia (Cambridge, MA: Belknap Press of Harvard University Press, 2011), 98–99, 103.

13. Kluger, *Still Alive*, 126.

14. H. L. Glyn Hughes, diary and notes, 2nd Army, January–February 1945 (Glyn Hughes's papers, RAMC 1218 2/8); Buckley, *Monty's Men*, 258; Peter Caddick Adams, *Snow and Steel: The Battle of the Bulge, 1944–45* (New York: Oxford University Press, 2015), 659; Redmond McLaughlin, *The Royal Army Medical Corps* (London: Leo Cooper, 1972), 97–98. See also Har Gootzen and Kevin Conner, *Battle for the Roer Triangle (Operation Blackcock—January 1945)* (Glasgow: Creative Colour Bureau, 2006).

15. Buckley, *Monty's Men*, 258. The latest advances in the treatment of disease also benefited soldiers. McLaughlin, *The Royal Army Medical Corps*, 97. See also Michael Snape, *God and the British Soldier: Religion and the British Army in the First and Second World Wars* (New York: Routledge, 2005).

16. Buckley, *Monty's Men*, 259.

17. Jackson, *Operations of Eighth Corps*, 165; Mark Harrison, *Medicine and Victory: British Military Medicine in the Second World War* (New York: Oxford University Press, 2004), 263.

18. Nikolaus Wachsmann, *KL: A History of the Nazi Concentration Camps* (New York: Farrar, Straus and Giroux, 2015), quoting Yehuda Bauer, 554, 556–57, 559.

19. Stone, "Christianstadt," 85–86, 89; Edith Birkin, cited in Anton Gill, *The Journey Back from Hell: Conversations with Concentration Camp Survivors* (London: Harper Collins, 1994), 429; Kluger, *Still Alive*, 129; Aranka Siegal, testimony, *I Witness* (University of Southern California Shoah Foundation, November 7, 1995, Tarrytown, NY), clips 29–30. Rose Mermelstein (née Ratza Roth), Survivors of the Shoah Visual History

Foundation, Visual History Archive (University of Southern California, New Jersey: December 14, 1995), code 10139. Ratza described how the food for pigs tasted delicious.

20. Hájková-Duxová, in *The World without Human Dimensions*, 108–9; Gutterman, *A Narrow Bridge to Life*, 199, 216.
21. Siegal, *I Witness*, clip 29.
22. Joli Hillman-Noy, Survivors of the Shoah Visual History Foundation (Upper Nazareth, Israel: September 2, 1988), code 46499. Joli Basch felt satisfaction knowing that this vital German city had been bombed. Yishay Garbasz, *In My Mother's Footsteps* (published in conjunction with the exhibit of the same name, Tokyo, 2009, by Hatje Cantz, Berlin, Germany, 2009; exhibited also at the Northwood University International Creativity Conference in Midland, MI, in 2010), 116. *The World without Human Dimensions*, 111.
23. Headquarters British Army of the Rhine (Medical TEWT—Tactical Exercise without Troops—October 14–16, 1945) (Secret) Paper 6, studied at Major General N. Cantlie, "Southern Command Medical Study Week" (Depot & TE RAMC, Crookham, February 17–21, 1947, Museum of Military Medicine archives, RAMC 1218 3/2).
24. H. L. Glyn Hughes, "Normandy to the Baltic from a Medical Angle" (presidential address to the Harveian Society, January 15, 1947, Glyn Hughes's papers, RAMC 1218 2/21), 14; Lieutenant Colonel R. L. MacPherson, "Casualty Evacuation in the Battle of the Rhine" (Museum of Military Medicine archives, RAMC 1218 3/8); Cantlie, "Southern Command Medical Study Week."
25. Hughes, "Normandy to the Baltic," 14; "Operation Plunder and the Sequaelae" (HQ British Army of the Rhine, Medical TEWT, 15/16 Oct. 1945, Museum of Military Medicine archives).
26. Harrison, *Medicine and Victory*, 263, 265.
27. Harrison, *Medicine and Victory*, 263, 265.
28. War diary, 8 Corps (Kew: National Archives, WO 177/343); Peter Starling, former director of RAMC Museum, conversation with the author (March 18, 2004).
29. Hughes, "Normandy to the Baltic," 15–16.
30. Hughes, "Normandy to the Baltic," 15–16; Cantlie, "Southern Command Medical Study Week."
31. Hughes, "Normandy to the Baltic," 15–16.
32. Hughes, "Germany 1945," 3.
33. Garbasz, *In My Mother's Footsteps*, 18, 112; *The World without Human Dimensions,* 114–15.
34. Garbasz, *In My Mother's Footsteps*, 18, 112.

SPRING 1945

1. Some groups of evacuees may have been deposited at Flossenbürg. *The World without Human Dimensions: Four Women's Memories* ("The Menorah" Series, Publication of the State Museum in Prague, 1991), 115–16; Yishay Garbasz, *In My Mother's Footsteps* (published in conjunction with the exhibit of the same name, Tokyo, 2009, by Hatje Cantz, Berlin, Germany, 2009; exhibited also at the Northwood University International Creativity Conference in Midland, MI, in 2010), 124.

2. Daniel Blatman, *The Death Marches: The Final Phase of Nazi Genocide*, trans. Chaya Galia (Cambridge, MA: Belknap Press of Harvard University Press, 2011), 105; Michael Berenbaum, "Death Marches," *Encyclopaedia Judaica*, 2nd ed. (Farmington Hills, MI: Gale Group, 2008); Joseph Freeman, *The Road to Hell: Recollections of the Death March*, ed. Donald Schwartz (St. Paul, MN: Paragon House, 1998); Lusia Haberfeld, testimony, *I Witness* (University of Southern California Shoah Foundation, Melbourne, Australia, Oct. 13, 1996), clip 37.

3. Sandra Solotaroff Enzer, *Anne Frank: Reflections on Her Life and Legacy*, ed. Aaron Enzer (Chicago: University of Illinois Press, 2000), 54; Melissa Müller, *Anne Frank: The Biography* (London: Bloomsbury, 1998), 262.

4. H. L. Glyn Hughes, "Germany, 1945: The Assault and After" (lecture, St. Mary's Hospital Medical Society, February 14, 1946, Glyn Hughes's papers, Museum of Military Medicine archives, Aldershot, UK, RAMC 1218 2/21), 2. Not until early March was the entire area of the Reichswald Forest cleared. Lieutenant Colonel R. L. MacPherson, "Casualty Evacuation in the Battle of the Rhine" (Museum of Military Medicine, RAMC 1218 3/8).

5. Joanne Reilly, *Belsen: The Liberation of a Concentration Camp* (London: Routledge, 1998), 11; Nikolaus Wachsmann, *KL: A History of the Nazi Concentration Camps* (New York: Farrar, Straus and Giroux, 2015), 335, 565–66. Gisella Perl, *I Was a Doctor in Auschwitz* (New York: International University Press, 1948), 166.

6. Wachsmann, *KL*, 565, 567. Hanna Lévy-Hass, a resistance fighter who arrived in Bergen-Belsen the previous summer, described the new arrivals in a February 1945 diary entry. Babey Widutschinsky-Trepman, *What Makes Babey Run?* (Montreal: Concordia University, Montreal Institute for Genocide and Human Rights Studies, December 1995); Aranka Siegal, testimony, *I Witness* (University of Southern California Shoah Foundation, Tarrytown, New York, November 7, 1995), clip 30.

7. Garbasz, *In My Mother's Footsteps*. According to Salla, who was in Rachel's transport, the group was placed in the quarantine section of the camp.

8. Dan Van Der Vat, *D-Day: The Greatest Invasion; A People's History* (Bloomsbury: Madison Press, 2003), 308; H. L. Glyn Hughes, medical conference (HQ British Army of the Rhine, October 15–16, 1945, Glyn Hughes's papers).

9. Van Der Vat, *D-Day*, 308; Hughes, conference; Hughes, "Germany, 1945," 2; Christopher Woody, "74 Years Ago, US Troops Got Their First Foothold in Nazi Germany—Here Are 8 Photos of the Battle for Remagen," March 7, 2019, https://www.businessinsider.com/us-troops-capture-bridge-at -remagen-entering-nazi-germany-in-wwii-2017-3.

10. Hughes, "Germany, 1945," 2.

11. H. L. Glyn Hughes, "Normandy to the Baltic from a Medical Angle" (presidential address to the Harveian Society, January 15, 1947, Glyn Hughes's papers, RAMC 1218 2/21), 13, 15–16; H. L. Glyn Hughes, "First Aid in Every Sphere" (lecture given to the Hammersmith First Aid Society, Hammersmith Town Hall, February 16, 1972, RAMC 1218 3/9).

12. Mark Harrison, *Medicine and Victory: British Military Medicine in the Second World War* (New York: Oxford University Press, 2004), 265; Hughes, "Normandy to the Baltic," 31.

13. Lieutenant Colonel M. W. Gonin (Special Order of the Day thanking all ranks of the 11 Light Field Ambulance and 567 Coy American Field Service Unit for work since coming to Bergen-Belsen on April 17, 1945). With 6 Guards Armoured Brigade and the Americans, Gonin's field ambulance shared in the capture of Münster.

14. Hughes, "Normandy to the Baltic," 15, 17, 31. When the airfield was shelled, the RAMC had to resort to staging posts. Hughes, "First Aid in Every Sphere."

15. Hughes, "Germany, 1945." British hospitals had more advanced surgical techniques and promoted conservative treatments. John Buckley, *Monty's Men: The British Army and the Liberation of Europe* (New Haven, CT: Yale University Press, 2014), 290.

16. Hughes, "Germany, 1945," 4.

17. H. L. Glyn Hughes, lecture, Fleet (March 27, 1946, Glyn Hughes's papers, RAMC 1218 2/18), 8–9; Hughes, "Germany, 1945," 4.

18. Hughes, Fleet lecture, 10; Hughes, "Normandy to the Baltic," 16–17; Buckley, *Monty's Men*, 290; Hughes, "Germany, 1945," 5.

19. Hughes, Fleet lecture, 10; Hughes, "Germany, 1945," 5.

20. Hughes, Fleet lecture, 6–8; Hughes, "Germany, 1945," 5.

21. Hughes, Fleet lecture, 6–8; Hughes, "Germany, 1945," 5.

22. Hughes, Fleet lecture, 6–8; see also Greig Watson, "Operation Gomorrah: Firestorm created 'Germany's Nagasaki,'" BBC News, https://www.bbc.com/

news/uk-england-43546839; and David H. Lippman, "Allied Aerial Destruction of Hamburg during World War II," Historynet, https://www.history net.com/allied-aerial-destruction-of-hamburg-during-world-war-ii.htm.

23. Hughes, "Germany, 1945," 4, 8.
24. Hughes, "Germany, 1945," 4, 8.
25. Hughes, "Germany, 1945," 3; Hughes, Fleet lecture, 6.
26. For an account of how some Jews observed Passover in Bergen-Belsen, see Eugene Pogany's *In My Brother's Image* (New York: Penguin, 2000).
27. Esther Mermelstein (told to the author by her aunt). Also described by survivor Alice Lok Cahana, in her oral testimony: "Alice Lok Cahana Describes Arrival at Bergen-Belsen" (transcript), United States Holocaust Memorial Museum, https://encyclopedia.ushmm.org/content/en/oral-history /alice-lok-cahana-describes-arrival-at-bergen-belsen.
28. Fania Fénelon, *The Musicians of Auschwitz* (London: Michael Joseph and Atheneum, 1977), 253–55; David Grynberg, testimony, *I Witness* (University of Southern California Shoah Foundation, Melbourne, Australia, January 16, 1997), clip 172; Ernest Levy, testimony, *I Witness* (University of Southern California Shoah Foundation, London, England, December 29, 1996), clip 19. As of 2019, the USC Shoah Foundation has made available online approximately two hundred fifty oral testimonies pertaining to Bergen-Belsen.
29. Leonard Berney, *Liberating Belsen Concentration Camp: A Personal Account*, ed. John Wood (n.p.: Amazon Digital Services, 2015), 14; Reilly, *Belsen*, 25; Cecily Goodman, quoted in Leslie Hardman, *The Survivors: The Story of the Belsen Remnant* (London: Vallentine Mitchell, 1958), 9; Branko Lustig, testimony, *I Witness* (University of Southern California Shoah Foundation, Los Angeles, CA, January 31, 1999), clip 16.
30. Anita Lasker-Wallfisch, *Inherit the Truth: A Memoir of Survival and the Holocaust* (New York: St. Martin's Press, 1996), 95.
31. Helen Mermelstein, interview with the author (May 18, 2007); Abel J. Herzberg, *Between Two Streams: A Diary from Bergen-Belsen*, trans. Jack Santcross (New York: I. B. Tauris, 1997), 207.
32. Flaster described Bergen-Belsen as "the last of the last, and the worst of the worst." Mendel Flaster, testimony, *I Witness* (University of Southern California Shoah Foundation, San Diego, CA, December 11, 1995), clip 31.
33. Joseph Kessel, *The Man with the Miraculous Hands* (New York: Farrar, Straus and Cudahy, 2004), 152–53, 209–16; Charles Schwab (Hillel Storch's grandson) in *God, Faith & Identity from the Ashes*, ed. Menachem Z. Rosensaft (Vermont: Jewish Lights, 2015), 189; In this 2013 speech at a Westchester, New York, synagogue, Hillel Storch's grandson describes his grandfather's

efforts to save lives. Himmler countermanded orders for Bergen-Belsen to be blown up on April 8. See http://www.larchmonttemple.org/Uploads/ file/Kristallnacht_Commemoration_Larchmont_Temple_11_8_13_One _Hillel_Storch_Rescue_Effort.pdf. Göran Rosenberg, *A Brief Stop on the Road from Auschwitz* (New York: Other Press, 2012), 136. Himmler had more than one person influencing his decision not to destroy Bergen-Belsen. See Joanne Reilly, *Belsen: The Liberation of a Concentration Camp* (London: Routledge, 1998), 23. Kurt Becher, an aide to Himmler who had visited Bergen-Belsen on April 10, recommended that he turn the typhus-infected camp over to the approaching British army. See also Jon Bridgman, *The End of the Holocaust: The Liberation of the Camps* (Portland, OR: Areopagitica Press, 1990), 47–49.

34. Hela Blumenthal, testimony, *I Witness* (Sea Point, South Africa, June 9, 1996), clip 50. Magda Bloom and Hadassah Bimko saw the SS burning papers. Of Magda's barracks of one thousand, only thirty-seven survived. Her mother died on April 14, one day before the liberation. Magda Bloom, testimony, *I Witness* (Birmingham, England, August 4, 1998), clip 62; Hadassah Rosensaft, *Yesterday (My Story)* (Washington, DC: United States Holocaust Memorial Museum, 2004), 49.

35. Samuel Stern's statement in Bernice Lerner, *The Triumph of Wounded Souls: Seven Holocaust Survivors' Lives* (Notre Dame, IN: University of Notre Dame Press, 2004), 113–14.

36. There is some variance in accounts of the handover. (Berney, for example, wrote that two emissaries appeared.) Schmidt produced a map marking a proposed no-fire zone of five by three and a half miles around the camp. Berney, *Liberating Belsen*, 1–2. The three emissaries: Colonel Schmidt, second in command at Bergen-Belsen; Lieutenant Colonel Bohnekamp; and a medical officer. Accompanying them was a translator. Mark Celinscak, "The Final Rescue? Liberation and the Holocaust," in *Unlikely Heroes: The Place of Holocaust Rescuers in Research and Teaching*, ed. Ari Kohen and Gerald J. Steinacher (Lincoln: University of Nebraska Press, 2019), 66–67. Celinscak wrote that Colonel Schmidt approached the British with other members of Germany's 1 Parachute Army. Derrick Sington, *Belsen Uncovered* (Bristol: Burleigh Press, 1946); Colonel E. E. Vella, MD, FRC Path, L/RAMC, "Belsen: Medical Aspects of a World War II Concentration Camp," *Journal of the Royal Army Medical Corps* 130 (1984): 34.

37. Richard Williams, "Discovering Belsen," in *Perspectives: Journal of the Holocaust Centre* (Beth Shalom) (Summer 2001): 11; Ben Shepherd, *After Daybreak: The Liberation of Bergen-Belsen 1945* (New York: Schocken Books, 2005), 22; 63rd Anti-Tank Regiment, RA war diary (Kew: National

Archives, WO 171/4773), appendix B, "Belsen Concentration Camp"
(April 13, 1945); "Agreement with Regard to Belsen Concentration Camp
Made by Chief of Staff, 1, Para Army, Military Commandant Bergen
and BGS, 8 Corps." The agreement is also found among Hughes's papers
(RAMC 1218 2/12); H. L. Glyn Hughes, "German Concentration
Camps—Early Measures at Belsen" (lecture, Interallied Conference on War
Medicine, June 4, 1945, Glyn Hughes's papers, RAMC 1218 2/15); David
Woodward, "Prison Camp's Fate: Truce to Decide: British to Take Charge,"
On the Aller, *Manchester Guardian*, April 13, 1945; Wachsmann, *KL*, 580;
Berney, *Liberating Belsen*, 1–2.

38. Berney, *Liberating Belsen*, 1; Second Army war diary (Kew: National
Archives, WO 171/3952); Hughes, "Early Measures at Belsen"; Hughes,
"First Aid in Every Sphere," 8. Hughes, "Normandy to the Baltic," 32;
8 Corps HQ (Medical Services) war diary (Kew: National Archives,
WO 177/343).

39. Hughes, "Early Measures at Belsen"; Ben Flanagan and Donald Bloxham,
eds., *Remembering Belsen: Eyewitnesses Record the Liberation* (London:
Vallentine Mitchell, 2005), 6; Shepherd, *After Daybreak*, appendix A;
Michael John Hargrave, *Bergen-Belsen 1945: A Medical Student's Journal*
(London: Imperial College Press, 2014), 43.

40. Wachsmann, *KL*, 580; Berney, *Liberating Belsen*, 1–2; Kew: National
Archives PRO: WO 171/4184 11th Armoured Division. G; PRO: WO
177/343, DDMS 8 Corps in Shepherd, *After Daybreak*, 7.

41. Major Dick Williams, "The First Day in the Camp," in *Belsen 1945: New
Historical Perspectives*, ed. Suzanne Bardgett and David Cesarani (London:
Vallentine Mitchell, 2006), 27–30; *50th Anniversary of the Entry of the
British Troops into Bergen-Belsen* (report by Major W. R. Williams, RASC,
S and T Branch 8 Corps, January 30, 1995, Imperial War Museum archives,
London), 1; Williams, "Discovering Belsen," 11.

42. Williams, "Discovering Belsen," 2; Williams, text for a talk on the 50th anniversary of the entry of British troops to the camp, April 1945 (Imperial War
Museum archives); Dick Williams, phone interview with the author (April
16, 2007). Why did H. L. Glyn Hughes insist on using the term "displaced
persons"? Williams's answer: "We had no information at that time as to who
these people were. Other than being able to tell who was male or female,
they looked absolutely alike. All the camp records had been destroyed
by the SS." Wachsmann, *KL*, 577. During April and early May 1945 the
concentration camp system collapsed. Allied forces reached the remaining
satellite camps and main camps, including Buchenwald and Dora (April 11),
Bergen-Belsen (April 15), Sachsenhausen (April 22–23), Flossenbürg (April
23), Dachau (April 29), Ravensbrück (April 30), Neuengamme (May 2),

Mauthausen-Gusen (May 5), and Stutthof (May 9). A total of two hundred fifty thousand prisoners were liberated from concentration camps during these five weeks, with Bergen-Belsen containing the largest number, fifty-five thousand. Robert J. Philips (former Lieutenant Colonel RAMC), "I Was There," "Triumph over Belsen," The Hollies, Pyle, Glamorgan (Imperial War Museum archives). After a "tour of inspection" with Lieutenant Colonels R. Gwyn Evans (ADMS) and A. M. Mitchie (ACH), Lieutenant Colonel Phillips wrote, "No single [event] was more exhausting, sickening, stirred up so much bitterness and resulted in such disturbing and lasting memories than that associated with conditions at Belsen concentration camp." He conducted two further tours of inspection on May 10 (three weeks post-liberation) and May 30 (six weeks postliberation) and made reports to Glyn Hughes.

43. Williams, 50th anniversary, 2–3; Perl, *I Was a Doctor*, 166. Even the SS called Bergen-Belsen a "dung heap."

44. "The two SS escorting me had no compunction in shooting two DPs who had tried to approach me. I was most apprehensive and vulnerable at this uncalled for action." Report by Major W. R. (Dick) Williams, RASC (S and T Branch, 8 Corps HQ, January 30, 1995, Hatch End, Pinner MedX, HA 4EJ, Imperial War Museum archives). Williams, 50th anniversary, 2–3. Dick Williams recounted these same facts at the Yad Vashem UK commemoration in April 2007, honoring H. L. Glyn Hughes. Williams described the stench. During the battles of the Falaise Gap there were many casualties and "a lot of bloated [dead] animals"—the "smell of death was in the air." Williams, conversation with the author (2007). Despite repeated warnings, the Hungarian guards continued shooting at inmates for two days after the British army arrived.

45. Williams, 50th anniversary; Williams, "Discovering Belsen."

46. John Randall, phone interview with the author (April 17, 2007); Sington, *Belsen Uncovered*, 19; Reilly, *Belsen*, 23–24, Lieutenant Colonel R. I. G. Taylor, report on Belsen Camp (Appendix "J" Folio 1, Museum of Military Medicine archives); Flanagan and Bloxham, *Remembering Belsen*, 6–7; "Belsen," *British Zone Review* (Chief, Public Relations and Information Services Control Group, Control Commission for Germany, [B.E.]: Printing & Stationery Services, BAOR), October 13, 1945; Robert Collis and Han Hogerzeil, *Straight On* (London: Methuen, 1947), 51; Berney, *Liberating Belsen*, 3, 5, 7. For an account of the order of the arrival of various units at Bergen-Belsen, see Mark Celinscak, *Distance from the Belsen Heap: Allied Forces and the Liberation of a Nazi Concentration Camp* (Toronto: University of Toronto Press, 2015), 31–37.

47. Berney, *Liberating Belsen*, 2.

48. Brigadier H. L. Glyn Hughes, RAMC, DDMS 2nd Army, BLA, "German Concentration Camps—Early Measures at Belsen" (remarks given at the Inter-Allied Conference, June 4, 1945, Museum of Military Medicine archives, RAMC/1218 2/15); Imperial War Museum (05/44/1).

49. Brigadier H. L. Glyn Hughes, "Belsen Camp, April, 1945," in Samuel Bloch, ed., *Holocaust and Rebirth: Bergen-Belsen 1945–1950* (20th anniversary book; Association of Survivors from the British Zone, 1946–1947, Bergen-Belsen Memorial Press of the World Federation of Bergen-Belsen Associations, 1965), 94–96; Hughes, "First Aid in Every Sphere," 8; Hughes, "Germany 1945," 16.

50. Brigadier H. L. Glyn Hughes, PRO WO 235/24, in Flanagan and Bloxham, *Remembering Belsen*, 12–13.

51. Hughes in Flanagan and Bloxham, *Remembering Belsen*, 12–13; Sington, *Belsen Uncovered*, 23.

52. Reilly, *Belsen*, 24; Toby Haggith, "The Filming of the Liberation of Bergen-Belsen and Its Impact on the Understanding of the Holocaust," in Bardgett and Cesarani, *Belsen 1945*, 89, 94, 98; IWM Sound Archive accession nos. 4579/06 reel 4 and 19588/4 reel 3, Imperial War Museum archives; Siegal, *I Witness*, clip 35.

53. Hughes, "Belsen Camp," 94–96; Hugh Stewart, interview by Carol Hurst (Denham, Buckinghamshire, January 11, 1998, USHMM videotapes, 3977240121). Stewart, one of the liberators, went around the camp with Hughes when they first arrived. He noted how the brigadier was "terrifically moved . . . almost in tears . . . shattered by it."

54. Hughes, "German Concentration Camps"; Berney, *Liberating Belsen*, 104.

55. Collis and Hogerzeil, *Straight On*, 49–50; Shepherd, *After Daybreak*, 43.

56. Sington, *Belsen Uncovered*, 43, 140; George Leonard's account in Martin Wells, "We Found Mounds of Bodies Stacked Three to Five Feet," *South Wales Echo*, August 14, 2000, 12; Rosensaft, *Yesterday*, 52.

57. 8 Corps war diary.

58. Reilly, *Belsen*, 23–24. Lieutenant Colonel Taylor had received written instructions from the Brigadier General Staff, 8 Corps, that he was to assume control of the area around Belsen "as per the agreement with the Wehrmacht." Hughes, "Germany, 1945." Hughes decided to tour the camp in a jeep followed by army vehicles as a show of British force. Michael John Hargrave, *Bergen-Belsen 1945: A Medical Student's Journal* (London: Imperial College Press, 2014), 42–44.

59. Derrick Sington was commander of 14 Amplifier Unit, Intelligence Corps. Flanagan and Bloxham, *Remembering Belsen*, 9; Reilly, *Belsen*, 23–24.

60. Helen Mermelstein, conversation; Hagit Lavsky, *New Beginnings: Holocaust Survivors in Bergen-Belsen and the British Zone in Germany, 1945–1950*

(Detroit, MI: Wayne State University Press, 2002), 42; Anita Lasker-Wallfisch, *Inherit the Truth: A Memoir of Survival and the Holocaust* (New York: St. Martin's Press, 1996), 95; Martin Gilbert, *The Day the War Ended: VE-Day 1945 in Europe and Around the World* (London: HarperCollins, 1995), 18; Raye David, conversation with the author (July 20, 2009).

61. Suzanne Bardgett, "What Wireless Listeners Heard: Some Lesser Known BBC Broadcasts About Belsen," in Bardgett and Cesarani, *Belsen 1945*, 131–33. Sington, *Belsen Uncovered*, 27–28.

62. Taylor, Report on Belsen Camp.

63. Sington, *Belsen Uncovered*, 47–48; Jo Reilly et al., eds., *Belsen in History and Memory* (London: Frank Cass, 1997), 146–47.

64. Perl, *I Was a Doctor*, 174–75; Hughes, Irgun She'erit Haplitah, 94–96; Frances Epstein, "Roundtrip" (unpublished memoir, 1975). Frances Epstein, a Czech inmate, saw Hughes—the "distinguished medical officer"—crying.

65. Berney, *Liberating Belsen*, 9–11.

66. Siegal, *I Witness*, clip 33.

67. Reilly, *Belsen*, 27–28, 34; Berney, *Liberating Belsen*, 30.

68. Elly Trepman, "Rescue of the Remnants: The British Emergency Medical Relief Operation in Belsen Camp 1945," *Journal of the Royal Army Medical Corps* 147 (2001): 282.

69. Paper by Lieutenant Colonel Gonin, 11 (Br) Light Field Ambulance (Imperial War Museum archive, Documents.3713).

70. Rosensaft, *Yesterday*, 43–44; Gonin paper, 21–22. Hughes had won three DSOs.

71. Hadassah Rosensaft in Brewster Chamberline and Marcia Feldman, eds., *The Liberation of the Nazi Concentration Camps 1945: Eye Witness Accounts of the Liberators* (Washington, DC: United States Holocaust Memorial Museum, 1987), 153; Rosensaft, *Yesterday*, 52–53.

72. Hughes, "Germany, 1945," 5.

73. Leslie H. Hardman in Cecily Goodman's *The Survivors: The Story of the Belsen Remnant* (London: Vallentine Mitchell, 1958), 1, 10, 20; Hughes, "German Concentration Camps."

74. Major T. D. Prescott, "Reflections of Forty Years Ago—Belsen 1945," *Journal of the Army Medical Corps* 132 (1986): 48–51. (Prescott was second in command of 11 Light Field Ambulance; it was the job of two privates from his unit to spray anyone who entered the camp with anti-louse powder.) Muriel Knox Doherty, *Letters from Belsen, 1945: An Australian Nurse's Experiences with the Survivors of War*, ed. Judith Cornell and R. Lynette Russell (Australia: Allen & Unwin, 2000), 170; Olga Horak, "Bergen-Belsen: A Survivors' Memoir of the Death Camp," in *Together: American Gathering of Holocaust Survivors and Their Descendants* (New York:

Together, January 2005). Olga recalled how the British brought in DDT by the truckload. Flanagan and Bloxham, "Remembering Belsen" (typescript, BBC Written Archives Center, London, WRU C7726), xi.

75. Flanagan and Bloxham, *Remembering Belsen*, xi–xiii.

76. Hughes, "Germany, 1945," 6; Flanagan and Bloxham, *Remembering Belsen*, xii; Roger Boyes in Belsen, Northern Germany, "When Belsen Was Liberated, the Holocaust Hit Home in Britain," *Times* (London), April 16, 2005.

77. Flanagan and Bloxham, *Remembering Belsen*, xi–xiii (from a typescript held at BBC Written Archives Center, WRU C7726); Roger Boyes, "When Belsen was Liberated, the Holocaust Hit Home in Britain," *Times* (London), April 16, 2005; David Lowther, *Liberating Belsen: Remembering the Soldiers of the Durham Light Infantry* (Durham: Sacristy Press, 2015), 117. The British nation tuned into Dimbleby's BBC broadcast on April 19, "a landmark in the history of broadcasting."

78. Flanagan and Bloxham, *Remembering Belsen*, 13–14; Gonin paper, 29–30; Pt. E. Fisher, "A Soldier's Diary of Belsen" (7406789, 32 CCS, Museum of Military Medicine archives, RAMC, British Liberation Army, 4/17/1945). Fisher's eyes filled with tears when he carried "these human wrecks" into their beds.

79. "Belsen," *British Zone Review*, 16; Berney, *Liberating Belsen*, 9–11.

80. "Belsen," *British Zone Review*, 16; Berney, *Liberating Belsen*, 12–13; Williams, 50th anniversary, 3; Levy, *I Witness*, clip 19.

81. Hughes, "Germany, 1945," 6; Reilly, *Belsen*, 26. See "Belsen," *British Zone Review*, for details on the "normal" diet as well as three "hospital diets" for the sick, allowing for incremental increases of food as patients gained strength. Hughes, "Normandy to the Baltic," 19.

82. Flanagan and Bloxham, *Remembering Belsen*, 31; "Belsen," *British Zone Review*.

83. "Belsen," *British Zone Review*, 8.

84. Others mentioned the Scottish entertainers (the "incongruous sight"), including Aranka Siegel, *Grace in the Wildnerness* (New York: Farrar, Straus and Giroux, 1985), 13; Lustig, *I Witness*, clip 17; Edith Baneth, testimony, *I Witness* (University of Southern California Shoah Foundation, London, England, January 27, 1998), clip 253.

85. Major Alexander Smith Allan, 113 Light Anti-Aircraft Regiment (Imperial War Museum Sound Archive 11903/2), in Flanagan and Bloxham, *Remembering Belsen*, 31.

86. Isaac Levy, phone interview with the author (June 2, 2004; Levy resided in London). Glyn Hughes, "a man of great heart," was concerned with the physical welfare of the people; he was a doctor and "not a politician."

Harrison, *Medicine and Victory*, 268, citing Brigadier Glyn Hughes, "Report on Medical Aspects of Belsen" (Museum of Military Medicine archives, CMAC RAMC 1218/2/13), 10; Celinscak, *Distance from the Belsen Heap*, 164–65.

87. Berney, *Liberating Belsen*, 9–11, 16–17; Hughes, "Early Measures at Belsen."

88. Hughes, "Early Measures at Belsen"; Reilly, *Belsen*, 33, 34, 73, 74; "Belsen," *British Zone Review*; Rosensaft, *Yesterday*, 54.

89. Flanagan and Bloxham, *Remembering Belsen*, 21–22; Gonin paper, 21–22.

90. "Belsen," *British Zone Review*, 7–8; Trepman, "Rescue of the Remnants," 283; Berney, *Liberating Belsen*, 18; Reilly, *Belsen*, 44, citing PRO WO 171/4604: 10 Garrison Report, 18–30 April, App. E, and Hankinson, "Belsen."

91. Gonin paper, 20; Anny Pfirter (head of medical personnel, International Committee of the Red Cross), *Memories of a Red Cross Mission: Bergen Belsen 1945* (Geneva: International Committee of the Red Cross). Anny Pfirter sent her notes, "Memories of Belsen," to Brigadier Glyn Hughes, "who did so much to save so many," on August 15, 1960 (Glyn Hughes's papers, RAMC/1218 2/18). Molly Silva Jones, "The Medical Relief Effort: Eyewitness Accounts," in Bardgett and Cesarani, *Belsen 1945*, 56, 62, 65. Though an ever-wider swath of country was combed for supplies, shortages at Belsen persisted.

92. Jo Reilly, David Cesarani, Tony Kushner, and Colin Richmond, eds., "Belsen in History and Memory," *Journal of Holocaust Education* 5, nos. 2/3 (1996): 4.

93. H. L. Glyn Hughes, notes for a speech (Museum of Military Medicine archives).

94. Martin Wells, *South Wales Echo*, August 14, 2006; Rosensaft, *Yesterday*, 55. Rosensaft (née Bimko) believed that the handling of the victims by their murderers, "even at the last moment," was a sacrilege. Michael Hughes, interview with the author (August 4, 2004). Though Hughes shared little with his family about Bergen-Belsen, he did tell his son how the SS were forced to handle the dead with their bare hands. He also conveyed his utter disdain for the "self-styled master race." Eli Stern, testimony, *I Witness* (University of Southern California Shoah Foundation, Monsey, New York, March 24, 1996), clip 138; Williams report, 4.

95. Reilly, *Belsen*, 28; Prescott, "Reflections," 48–51; Hughes, "Normandy to the Baltic," 18.

96. Levy, *Witness to Evil*, 12; Isaac Levy, testimony (University of Southern California Shoah Foundation, London, January 30, 1996), clip 31.

97. Gonin paper, 24–25; Gonin, in Flanagan and Bloxham, *Remembering Belsen*, 24–27.

98. Gonin, in Flanagan and Bloxham, *Remembering Belsen*, 24–27.

99. Gonin paper, 20. Patients came from the horror camp "completely naked and wrapped in blankets."

100. Hillman-Noy, Oral history (University of Southern California, September 2, 1998, Northern Israel, VHA 46499), cited in Dan Stone, "Christianstadt: Slave Labor and the Holocaust in the ITS Digital Archive," in *Slave Labor and the Holocaust*, vol. 4 of *Freilegungen: Yearbook of the International Tracing Service* (London: Wiener Library, 2015), 4:91.

101. "The Medical Relief Effort: Eyewitness Accounts; Soldier Major Ben Barnett, Nurse Molly Silva Jones and Medical Student Gerald Raperport," in Bardgett and Cesarani, *Belsen 1945*, 54–57.

102. Private Fisher E., 32 CCS, RAMC, British Liberation Army, "A Soldier's Diary of Belsen" (Museum of Military Medicine archives 17/4/45).

103. Berney, *Liberating Belsen*, 15; "Hun Mayors—and 'Mike'—Tour Belsen: Stern Rebuke on Loudspeakers," *Evening News* (London), April 25, 1945.

104. Trepman, "Rescue of the Remnants" 281–93; Paul Kemp, "Relief of Belsen," in Bardgett and Cesarani, *Belsen 1945*, 31; Levy, *Witness to Evil*, 11.

105. Gonin considered Hughes to be "one of those men, like Churchill, that Britain produces in times of crises." Gonin, in Flanagan and Bloxham, *Remembering Belsen*, 24.

106. Gonin, in Flanagan and Bloxham, *Remembering Belsen*, 27; Jo Reilly et al., "Belsen in History and Memory," 140; Vella, "Belsen," 46, 54; Jones in Bardgett and Cesarani, *Belsen 1945*, 57; "British Relief Teams in Belsen Concentration Camp," in Bardgett and Cesarani, *Belsen 1945*, 68; Flanagan and Bloxham, *Remembering Belsen*, 35; Private Emmanuel Fisher, 32 CCS, RAMC, BLA, Trepman, "Rescue of the Remnants," 286; Pfirter, *Memories of a Red Cross Mission*, 17.

107. Jones in Bardgett and Cesarani, *Belsen 1945*, 57, 66; "Belsen," *British Zone Review*, 7–8; H. Roberts and P. Potter in Vella, "Belsen," 46.

108. Hughes, "Normandy to the Baltic," 19; Reilly, *Belsen*, 26; Hargrave, *Bergen-Belsen 1945*, 30. "Belsen," *British Zone Review*, 7–8.

109. Pfirter, *Memories of a Red Cross Mission*, 8, 11; Cyril J. Charters, letter (to "my darling," May 15, 1945), in Flanagan and Bloxham, *Remembering Belsen*, 38–39. Charters wrote of "the ghost-like army that . . . fill the rooms of Belsen . . . They lie in their beds mute and helpless, with fleshless limbs grotesquely protruding from under blankets. Lifeless eyes glare out of hollow spaces devoid of flesh; their necks are thinner than my wrist . . . Try to picture a skeleton covered with skin alone; try to picture thousands like it ravaged with typhus, dysentery and even worse diseases—picture that in your mind and you know, in part, the truths of Belsen."

110. Collis and Hogerzeil, *Straight On*, 73; Berney, *Liberating Belsen*, 18–19; Shepherd, *After Daybreak*, 112–14.

111. Shepherd, *After Daybreak*, 131; Hughes, "Normandy to the Baltic," 18.

112. Shepherd, "The Medical Relief Effort at Belsen," in Bardgett and Cesarani, *Belsen 1945*, 39.

113. Hargrave, *Bergen Belsen 1945*, 13, 17, 25–29, 32; Trepman, "Rescue of the Remnants," 285. Other drugs used in Belsen included opium, albucid, sulphapyradine, sulphathiazole, and kaolin. Bardgett and Cesarani, *Belsen 1945*, 43; T. C. Gibson, *London Hospital Gazette* 48 (1945): 148, in Vella, "Belsen," 47–49.

114. Hargrave, *Bergen Belsen 1945*, 19, 66; Vella, "Belsen," 50, 54.

115. Hargrave, *Bergen Belsen 1945*, 19.

116. Hargrave, *Bergen-Belsen 1945*, 29, 32.

117. Dr. L. W. Clarkey (St. Bartholomew's Medical School), in Flanagan and Bloxham, *Remembering Belsen*, 51. Clarkey described how in the evenings "one got rebound," laughing more than one normally would. Vella, "Belsen," 54, 58.

118. Hargrave, *Bergen-Belsen 1945*, 37–39.

119. Hargrave, *Bergen-Belsen 1945*, 43.

120. Trepman, "Rescue of the Remnants," 290; Dr. D. C. Bradford (former St. Bartholomew's medical school student), in Flanagan and Bloxham, *Remembering Belsen*, 52.

121. Hargrave, *Bergen-Belsen 1945*, 81.

122. Trepman, "Rescue of the Remnants," 290; G. Raperport, "Expedition to Belsen," *Middlesex Hospital Journal* 45 (1945): 21–24, in Bardgett and Cesarani, *Belsen 1945*, 59, and in Vella, "Belsen," 54. A tribute by the military medical commander, Glyn Hughes, Brigadier, DDMS, Second Army, in Vella, "Belsen," 130.

123. Raperport, in Bardgett and Cesarani, *Belsen 1945*, 59; Vella, "Belsen," 130. For an explanation of how typhus is contracted, see Gonin, in Flanagan and Bloxham, *Remembering Belsen*, 24–25. Letter to Brigadier H. L. Glyn Hughes from R. J. Phillips (psychiatrist). Phillips copied a memorandum from Brigadier General S. Baynes-Hines, dir., USA Typhus Commission, Office of the Surgeon General, Washington, DC, July 9, 1945, Subject: Typhus Fever in British Medical Students (Museum of Military Medicine archives, RAMC 1218). Leslie Silverstone, interview with the author (Boston University Health Services, June 4, 2004). Dr. Silverstone, who was one of the medical school students sent to Bergen-Belsen from Kings College, London, said that one from his group, Arthur Pimbler, died of typhus contracted in Bergen-Belsen.

124. Berney, *Liberating Belsen*, 20–22.

125. Berndt Horstmann, conversation with the author (October 11, 2013). The Bergen-Belsen historian said patients were separated in the hospital area according to their degree of debilitation.

126. The Allies divided liberated Germany and Austria into "occupation zones," with the Americans, the British, and the French occupying the west, and Russia, the east of Germany. Known to take revenge by raping German women, the Russians were very much feared. See Lucy Ash, "The Rape of Berlin," BBC News, Berlin, May 1, 2015, https://www.bbc.com/news/magazine-32529679.

127. Hughes, Fleet lecture, 11–12; Hughes, "Normandy to the Baltic," 17; Michael Hughes, interview (August 4, 2004). After the war's end, Hughes's family eagerly awaited his return home. On May 8, VE day, his wife and daughters, who had left London for the safety of the countryside, went out to celebrate. His fourteen-year-old son Michael, too young to go to a bar, invited a friend over; they broke into the liquor cabinet and had their own drunken revelry. Redmond McLaughlin, *The Royal Army Medical Corps* (London: Leo Cooper, 1972), 104.

128. Hargrave, *Bergen Belsen 1945*, 69.

129. Hargrave, *Bergen Belsen 1945*, 70. Some accounts indicate that it was Block 47 that was set ablaze. Each hut had been set afire after it had been evacuated; at this point, some administrative huts and the watchtowers were still standing. Pfirter, *Memories of a Red Cross Mission*; Sington, in Flanagan and Bloxham, *Remembering Belsen*, 38; Sergeant Bert Hardy of No. 5 AFPU, BU 6674 (Imperial War Museum archives, May 21, 1945); Hagit Lavsky, "The Day After: Bergen-Belsen from Concentration Camp to the Centre of the Jewish Survivors in Germany," *German History* 11, no. 1 (1993): 45–46; see also Shepherd, *After Daybreak*, 124–26, for a description of the ceremonial burning of the hut and the celebration in its aftermath.

130. Ben Shepherd, in Bardgett and Cesarani, *Belsen 1945*, 45. Johnston issued his last report the previous day.

131. Lavsky, "The Day After," 46. Though hope was rekindled within survivors, they were preoccupied throughout the summer of 1945 with the fate of relatives. Trepman, "Rescue of the Remnants," 288; Collis and Hogerzeil, *Straight On*, 73–74; Flanagan and Bloxham, *Remembering Belsen*, 32–33. In a letter dated May 18, 1945, C. J. Charters, 37 Kinema Section, RAOC, wrote that the sun was warm and strong and there were more signs of life in the camp.

132. Hughes, "Germany, 1945," 18; Major R. J. Phillips, advisor in psychiatry, Second Army, to Brig. H. L. Glyn Hughes, May 31, 1945 (Museum of

Military Medicine archives, RAMC 1218 2/4). After three visits to the
Belsen camp, Phillips concluded that "these poor unfortunates were
reduced to frightened, inarticulate children and . . . the re-education process
and rebuilding of their personalities will take a very long time."
133. Trepman, "Rescue of the Remnants," 290–91. Lieutenant Hodges, a welfare
officer, initiated an elementary school. Collis and Hogerzeil, *Straight On*,
74; Martha Golan, testimony, *I Witness* (University of Southern California
Shoah Foundation, April 20, 1995, Point Piper, Sydney, Australia), clips
40–41.
134. Miss Margaret Wyndham Ward, British Red Cross Society, letter of June 23,
1945, in Flanagan and Bloxham, *Remembering Belsen*, 91.
135. Avinoam J. Patt and Michael Berkowitz, eds., *We Are Here: New Approaches
to Jewish Displaced Persons in Postwar Germany* (Detroit, MI: Wayne State
University Press, 2010). In 1946 there were more than 1,070 weddings in
the British Zone. Hughes, "Belsen Camp," 97.
136. Lavsky, *New Beginnings*, 77. "Kazet," pronounced "Katzet," stands for KZ.
Under the leadership of director Sami Feder, the Kazet Theatre, by and
for survivors of concentration camps, developed from former inmates'
clandestine activities during their incarceration. Joseph Wolhandler, "On a
Concentration Camp Stage," *New York Times*, June 30, 1946, 11.
137. Flanagan and Bloxham, *Remembering Belsen*, 88–89. Anita Lasker-Wallfisch
described the July 30, 1945, Yehudi Menuhin concert.
138. Judith Petersen, "Belsen and a British Broadcasting Icon," *Holocaust Studies:
A Journal of Culture and History* (London) 13, no. 1 (Summer 2007):
19–43.
139. Lavsky, *New Beginnings*, 64–70; Peter Starling, RAMC, email to author
(November 2, 2010). It seems that Glyn Hughes visited Belsen regularly for
several months. In his role as director of medical services, he is mentioned
only six times for the year beginning June 1945 in 21 Army Group war dia-
ries (he was either chairing meetings or signing reports). The last time he is
mentioned is on November 4, 1945, when he chaired a meeting to discuss
the reorganization of medical services field units. During his testimony at
the Belsen Trial, on September 19, 1945, Hughes stated that he was still
visiting the DP camp. Glyn Hughes, notes for talk at the 20th anniversary
commemoration of the liberation of Bergen-Belsen, Habima State Theatre,
Tel Aviv, Israel, July 13, 1965 (Glyn Hughes's papers). The Jewish committee
in nearby Celle published the first issue of *Unzer Sztyme* (Our Voice). The
DP camp was becoming a vibrant enclave, with its own publications, police
force, barbershops, and workshops, and organized activities for three hundred children, many of whom were sick and without family. Hughes would

be especially delighted to visit the children's block, where he beheld the love and devotion of women volunteers and the children's "increasing happiness." One year later he was glad to learn that many of the children were distributed among *kibbutzim* in Palestine. Boaz Cohen, "And I Was Only a Child: Children's Testimonies, Belsen 1945," in Bardgett and Cesarani, *Belsen 1945*, 153. Among the few children who survived Bergen-Belsen were fifty-two Dutch children (whose families were in the diamond trade) and thirty children from Poland and Slovakia. Quote is by Dr. Yaffa Singer, who was born in the Glyn Hughes Hospital. Menachem Rosensaft, ed., *God, Faith & Identity from the Ashes: Reflections of Children and Grandchildren of Holocaust Survivors* (Woodstock, VT: Jewish Lights, 2015), 258.

140. For more information on "Jewish organizational efforts in Bergen-Belsen" and those who served on the postliberation Jewish committee, see Lavsky, *New Beginnings*, 63–77; William Hitchcock, *The Bitter Road to Freedom: A New History of the Liberation of Europe* (New York: Free Press, 2008), 339, 348; Patt and Berkowitz, *We Are Here*, 230; Menachem Rosensaft, conversation with the author (April 13, 2004); Hitchcock, *The Bitter Road to Freedom*, 339, 347.

141. Patt and Berkowitz, *We Are Here*, 237–39; Chuck Olin, Chick Cooper, and Matthew Palm, dirs., *In Our Own Hand: The Hidden Story of the Jewish Brigade in WWII* (Chuck Olin Associates Films, 1998).

142. H. L. Glyn Hughes, "Belsen and After" (lecture, Glyn Hughes's papers). In this speech, Hughes speaks of the "tradition of Jewish unity" developed in the Bergen-Belsen DP camp. He pays tribute to Josef Rosensaft, who was "the real creator of the new Jewish enclave," and Hadassah, whom he put in administrative charge of the hospital of fourteen thousand beds. He felt great joy when they wed and, more recently, when he and his wife attended their son Meni's bar mitzvah in Israel. (Menachem was born in the Glyn Hughes Hospital.)

143. Levy, *Witness to Evil*, 19; Zippy Orlin, Erik Somers, and René Kok, *Jewish DPs in Camp Bergen-Belsen 1945–1950: The Unique Photo Album of Zippy Orlin* (Seattle: University of Washington Press in association with Netherland Institute for War Documentation, 2004), 119; H. L. Glyn Hughes, speech given at the 20th anniversary commemoration of the liberation of Bergen-Belsen, Habima State Theatre, Tel Aviv, Israel (Glyn Hughes's papers).

SEASONS AFTER

1. H. L. Glyn Hughes, "Germany, 1945: The Assault and After" (lecture, St. Mary's Hospital Medical Society, February 14, 1946, RAMC 1218 2/21), 5.

2. Helen Mermelstein, letter to her brother Hershu ([who was at the time a military officer in Zatec, Czechoslovakia], Karlstad, Sweden, 1945, Washington, DC: United States Holocaust Memorial Museum archives).

3. Mermelstein, letter; Hagit Lavsky, "The Day After: Bergen-Belsen from Concentration Camp to the Centre of the Jewish Survivors in Germany," *German History* 11, no. 1 (1993): 50. The Swedish government offered to take seven thousand of the sick former inmates for six months.

4. See Sgt. Evans, No. 5 Army Film & Photographic Unit, BU 9231 (War Office, Second World War Collection, July 20, 1945, Imperial War Museum, London) for a rare photo of displaced persons being evacuated to Sweden. Mermelstein, letter; Robert Collis and Han Hogerzeil, *Straight On: Journey to Belsen and the Road Home* (London: Methuen, 1947), 155–56.

5. Mermelstein, letter.

6. The trip to Katrinehölm took more than five hours.

7. David Lowther, *Liberating Belsen: Remembering the Soldiers of the Durham Light Infantry* (Durham, UK: Sacristy Press, 2015), 106–7.

8. Raymond Phillips, ed., *The Trial of Josef Kramer and 44 Others (The Belsen Trial)* (London: W. Hodge, 1949), xxxvi; "Members of Lueneberg Court Visit Belsen Camp to Investigate Nazi Crimes on the Spot," Jewish Telegraphic Agency Archive, September 24, 1945.

9. "Jews from Fifty Camps in Germany Discuss Their Problems at Conference in Bergen-Belsen," Jewish Telegraphic Agency, September 27, 1945; Menachem Z. Rosensaft, "Bergen-Belsen: The End and the Beginning" (*Children and the Holocaust* symposium presentation, Center for Advanced Holocaust Studies, Washington, DC: United States Holocaust Memorial Museum), 128.

10. "Jews from Fifty Camps," Jewish Telegraphic Agency, September 27, 1945; Hagit Lavsky, *New Beginnings: Holocaust Survivors in Bergen-Belsen and the British Zone in Germany, 1945–1950* (Detroit, MI: Wayne State University Press, 2002), 75–76.

11. "Jews from Fifty Camps," Jewish Telegraphic Agency, September 27, 1945; Lavsky, *New Beginnings*, 75–76; Muriel Knox Doherty, letter dated September 27, 1945, in Ben Flanagan, Joanne Reilly, and Donald Bloxham, eds., *Remembering Belsen* (London: Vallentine Mitchell, 2005), 88–89.

12. Rosensaft, *Bergen-Belsen*, 128; Jo Reilly et al., eds., *Belsen in History and Memory* (London: Frank Cass, 1997), 168; "Jews from Fifty Camps," Jewish Telegraphic Agency, September 27, 1945.

13. Flanagan and Bloxham, *Remembering Belsen*, 84–85. See also Avinoam J. Patt and Michael Berkowitz, *We Are Here: New Approaches to Jewish Displaced Persons in Postwar Germany* (Detroit, MI: Wayne State University Press, 2010), 237–40.

14. "Jews from Fifty Camps in Germany," Jewish Telegraphic Agency, September 27, 1945; Ben Shephard, in Suzanne Bardgett and David Cesarani, *Belsen 1945: New Historical Perspectives* (London: Vallentine Mitchell, 2006), 46; Ben Shephard, email to the author (February 5, 2004). Hughes did not share the anti-Semitism of many middle-class English of his day. In contrast, General Sir Frederick Morgan, who ran UNRRA from September 1945 to August 1946, did not conceal his anti-Semitism, which was "quite unexceptional among the British military and officialdom." See Morgan's autobiography, *Peace and War: A Soldier's Life* (London, UK: Hodder & Stoughton, 1961).

15. Zvi Asaria-Helfgott, *We Are Witnesses* (Jerusalem: Yad Vashem, 2010), 157.

16. Leslie C. Green, review of *The Belsen Trial*, ed. R. Phillips, War Crimes Series, vol. 2 (London: Hodge, 1949); *Modern Law Review* 13, no. 2 (April 1950): 267–68; Phillips, *The Trial of Josef Kramer*, 520, 537.

17. *Law Reports of Trials of War Criminals: The Belsen Trial* (London: United Nations War Crimes Commission, 1947), 2:19–20; "Sensation Slated for Belsen Trial," *New York Times*, September 30, 1945, 39.

18. Anita Lasker-Walfisch, *Inherit the Truth: A Memoir of Survival and the Holocaust* (New York: St. Martin's Press, 1996), 124.

19. Green, review of *The Belsen Trial*, 267, 268; "Lord Wright at Trial," *New York Times*, October 18, 1945, 15S; Phillips, *The Trial of Josef Kramer*, 717; William Hitchcock, *The Bitter Road to Freedom: A New History of the Liberation of Europe* (New York: Free Press, 2008), 357.

20. Phillips, *The Trial of Josef Kramer*, xxv; "Belsen Trial Continues," *New York Times*, October 24, 1945, 10; Brooks Atkinson, "Moscow Sees 'Softness' to Nazis in U.S. Zone and at Belsen Trial," *New York Times*, November 4, 1945, 29; "Belsen Trial Criticized," *New York Times*, October 15, 1945, 5; "Russians Denounce Trials at Lueneberg," Moscow, October 25, *New York Times*, October 27, 1945, 6.

21. Daniel Patrick Brown, *The Beautiful Beast: The Life & Crimes of SS-Aufseherin Irma Grese* (San Marino, CA: Golden West Historical, 1996), 79–81, citing Playfair and Sington, *The Offenders*, 181, and "11 Accused Condemned to Death," *Times* (London), November 19, 1945, 3C; "Kramer and Irma Grese Will Die with 9 Others for Reich Murders," *New York Times*, November 18, 1945; Peter Lantos, *Parallel Lines* (London: Arcadia Books, 2006), 105–6; Geoffrey Wheatcroft, "A Good Kill," *Boston Globe*, January 21, 2007, F1–F3; Brown, *The Beautiful Beast*, 87, citing Pierrepoint, *Executioner: Pierrepoint* (London: George Harrap, 1974), 150.

22. "Jews in Poland Protest 'Mildness' of Sentences Imposed at Belsen Trial," Jewish Telegraphic Agency (Warsaw, November 25, 1945). The Central

Committee of Polish Jews "sharply attacked" the verdicts rendered at the trial. Shlomo Samson, *Between Darkness and Light* (Jerusalem, Rubin Mass, 1998), 367.

23. Hadassah Rosensaft, *Yesterday: My Story* (Washington, DC: United States Holocaust Memorial Museum, 2004), 91–92.

24. Hughes's papers (Museum of Military Medicine archives, RAMC 1218 3/1). Hughes copied in his own hand his letter requesting a regular commission and the response.

25. Hughes's papers; Peter Starling, conversation with the author (March 18, 2004); Starling, email to the author (April 28, 2007); Rowan MacAusland, interview with the author (April 16, 2007).

26. Hughes wrote the letter to the general on November 20, 1945, from the RAMC depot in Crookham, Aldershot (Hughes's papers, RAMC 1218 3/1). H. L. Glyn Hughes obituary, *British Medical Journal* 1 (January 19, 1974): 122.

27. Sári Stein, from Munkacs, Czechoslovakia, survived the war with her two older sisters.

28. Eli Getreau, "Praktisk pedagogik I ett skolhem: Erfarenheter från arbetet bland ungdom som varit i koncentrationläger" [Practical pedagogy in a boarding school: Experiences from work with youngsters liberated from concentration camps], trans. Ruth Mermelstein (née Rachel Genuth), *Pedagogisk Tidskrift* 80, nos. 3–6 (September 29, 1952): 39–126.

29. Getreau, "Practical Pedagaogy in a Boarding School."

30. Getreau, "Practical Pedagaogy in a Boarding School."

31. Getreau, "Practical Pedagaogy in a Boarding School."

32. Alika was from Satmar, Romania. Valli was from Munkacs, Czechoslovakia. Eli Getreau had come from Germany to Sweden before the war.

33. Göran Rosenberg, *A Brief Stop on the Road from Auschwitz*, trans. Sarah Death (New York: Other Press / London: Granta, 2015), 191.

34. Obituary of H. L. Glyn Hughes, *Lancet* 302, no. 7841 (December 8, 1973): 1340–41. For a view into Hughes's work as director of the South-East London General Practitioner Centre, see Brigadier H. L. Glyn Hughes, "The South-East London General Practitioner Centre," *Postgraduate Medical Journal* (London) 38 (June 1962): 329–33.

35. H. L. Glyn Hughes, "Some Reflections on the National Health Service: Its First Ten Years" (lecture, Glyn Hughes's papers, Museum of Military Medicine archives, Aldershot, UK).

36. Hughes, "Some Reflections on the National Health Service"; H. L. Glyn Hughes, "Disappearing G.P. Hospitals," *British Medical Journal* 1, no. 5279 (March 10, 1962): 709. Helen J. McCarrick, "One Man in His Time" (draft

on *Nursing Times* stationery sent to Glyn Hughes on March 4, 1969). The training of medical students in hospitals was a "new concept." Hughes, "The South-East London General Practitioner Centre," 329–33.

37. Hughes and Armorel had divorced in 1947. Michael Hughes, letter to the author (postmarked March 9, 2004). Jean Smart, interview with the author (March 11, 2004). Mickey Steele Bodger and Alan Evans, interview with the author (September 24, 2010). Hughes "worshipped" Thelma. Alan Hagdrup, letter to author (May 11, 2007). Thelma was "formidable."

38. McCarrick, "One Man in His Time"; H. L. Glyn Hughes, "Message from the President" (Christmas/seasonal greetings), in Eric Claxton, *The Struggle for Peace: The Story of Casualties Union in the Years Following the Second World War* (London: Book Guild, 1992), 107–8, 206, 229–30.

39. BBC (British Broadcasting Company) telephone message for Mr. Leslie Jackson, giving him instructions for speaking with Glyn Hughes about the discussion with Anthony Craxton and Rex Alston, the meeting at Broadcasting House, and then the ruse to bring him to the stage of *This Is Your Life* (Glyn Hughes's papers).

40. *Radio Times*, March 6, 1959: 14, on the challenge of surprising subjects. *This Is Your Life*, B.B.C. Television Theatre, subject 89, Mon., March 9, 1959, series 4, edition 24. Hughes did not smile. Nor did he let on that he was embarrassed by the accolades and unhappy being the subject of attention. Bodger and Evans, interview. Feeling "trapped," Hughes "was livid" about the *This Is Your Life* surprise. Ronald Hancock spoke of Hughes's playful side, interview with the author (Epsom College, March 8, 2004). Hughes would hold on to the Red Book that captured stories told that evening, as well as letters and telegrams from viewers both known and unknown to him, who expressed joy at seeing him being honored and who relayed information about their own lives and old friends (Glyn Hughes's papers).

41. Bodger and Evans, interview; H. L. Glyn Hughes, "Evacuation of Casualties" (lecture, Dublin, February 5, 1957, Glyn Hughes's papers, RAMC 1218 3/8). Hughes detailed steps, protocols, and provisions needed in the event of a nuclear bomb. Jean Smart, interview with the author (March 11, 2004).

42. Menachem Rosensaft, conversation with the author (August 13, 2004).

43. H. L. Glyn Hughes, *Peace at the Last: A Survey of Terminal Care in the United Kingdom* (London: Calouste Gulbenkian Foundation, 1960); "Peace at the Last: Security Love, and Adequate Care" (review of Hughes's book), *Glasgow Herald*, July 8, 1960.

44. Jonathan Rosen, "The Final Stage," *New York Times Magazine*, December 26, 2004, 14.

45. Cicely Saunders, "Peace at the Last," *Nursing Times*, July 15, 1960, 879. The title for Glyn Hughes's *Peace at the Last* was taken from the sixteenth-century prayer, "lord grant us safe lodging . . . and peace at the last." "Many Private Nursing Homes Unsatisfactory: Care of the Dying Often Inadequate," *Guardian*, July 1960, 5; "Lack of Care for the Dying," *Times* (London), July 7, 1960; "Peace at the Last: Security, Love, and Adequate Care," *Glasgow Herald*, July 8, 1960.

46. Jean Smart, interview with the author (March 6, 2004).

47. Editorial, *Journal of the Royal College of General Practitioners* 24 (1974): 83–84; Jean Smart, interview with the author (March 6, 2004); Bodger and Evans, interview; H. E. Robson, obituary of H. L. Glyn Hughes, *British Journal of Sports Medicine* 2–3 (August 8, 1974): 73 (PMC 1859479).

48. Jörgen Lehmann, FCCP, "The Treatment of Tuberculosis in Sweden with Para-aminosalicylic Acid (PAS): A Review," *American College of Chest Physicians CHEST Journal* 16, no. 6 (December 1949): 684–703; R. McLaren Todd, MD, MRCP, DCH, "Treatment of Primary Pulmonary Tuberculosis with P.A.S.," *British Medical Journal*, June 6, 1953, 1247.

49. Menachem Rosensaft, conversation with the author (August 13, 2004). Hughes absolutely knew the condition of survivors in April 1945. Belle Eisenberg, testimony, *I Witness* (University of Southern California Shoah Foundation, West Bloomfield, MI, May 21, 1996), clip 30; Brigadier H. L. Glyn Hughes, "Belsen Camp, April, 1945," in Samuel Bloch, ed., *Holocaust and Rebirth: Bergen-Belsen 1945–1950* (20th anniversary book; Association of Survivors from the British Zone, 1946–1947, Bergen-Belsen Memorial Press of the World Federation of Bergen-Belsen Associations, 1965), 94–96. Of seeing survivors of Bergen-Belsen, Hughes wrote that whether or not he knew them personally, "it gave [him] a wonderful feeling to realise that they had been saved from certain death and were now . . . leading normal constructive lives."

EPILOGUE

1. Hughes had helped the event organizers by requesting news clippings covering the period of the liberation of Bergen-Belsen from the following media outlets: the *Times* (London), the *Daily Telegraph*, the *Guardian*, the *Daily Express*, the *Evening Standard*, the *Evening News*, the *Sunday Times*, and the *Observer* (Glyn Hughes's papers, Museum of Military Medicine archive, Aldershot, UK).

2. Lavsky, *New Beginnings*, 42.

3. "1,000 Nazi Death Camp Survivors Meet Here," *New York Times*, November 25, 1965. With Hughes on the dais sat Rabbis Joel Halpern and Israel Olewski, survivors of Auschwitz, Buchenwald, and Bergen-Belsen.

4. H. L. Glyn Hughes, The Bath Club, SW. 1, "Calories at Belsen" (letter to the editor, *Times* (London) (Hughes's papers). "This despite the fact that ample supplies and personnel to distribute them were readily available to the Germans." Menachem Z. Rosensaft, "The Mass Graves of Bergen-Belsen: Focus for Confrontation," *Jewish Social Studies* 41, no. 1 (Winter 1979): 159, 169, 199. Rabbis and scientists were consulted. When the Comité de Liaison de la Résistance (the coordinating committee for fifty-three French organizations) condemned the suspension of exhumation operations, tensions escalated. President Charles de Gaulle was about to contact Chancellor Konrad Adenauer to expedite proceedings. Glyn Hughes addressed the matter in a letter to Rosensaft that was published in the *Jewish Chronicle* (London), July 10, 1959, 24. Hughes later said that the mass graves at Bergen-Belsen could not be compared to those of unknown soldiers or war cemeteries—"they were symbolic of something else."

5. Dr. Russell Barton, "Belsen," in *History of the Second World War* (London: Purnell & Sons, in cooperation with the Imperial War Museum.) 7, no. 15, 3/6 (1968): 3081–85. Glyn Hughes marked up this article, correcting facts and figures. His letter refuting Barton's claims was published in the London *Times* on November 30, 1968 (Issue 57422: 11).

6. Sam Bloch, ed., *Holocaust and Rebirth 1945–1965* (New York: Bergen-Belsen Memorial Press of the World Federation of Bergen-Belsen Associations, 1965), 312.

7. Arie Olewsky, conversation with the author (June 4, 2016); Ruth Wollheim Wachter-Carroll, email to author (June 23, 2016); Engelina Billauer, conversation with the author (June 10, 2016).

8. Donald Brittain, dir., John Kemeny, prod., *Memorandum* (National Film Board of Canada, 1966).

9. H. L. Glyn Hughes, speech at the Habima State Theatre, July 13, 1965 (Glyn Hughes's papers); Macabee Dean, "Hugh Glyn Hughes, 'Liberator of Bergen-Belsen,' " "Visitors' Gallery," *Jerusalem Post*, July 15, 1965 (submission by Hadassah Rosensaft, US Holocaust Memorial Museum archives, CZA A140/130, S.8–9); H. L. Glyn Hughes, "Belsen and After" (lecture, Glyn Hughes's papers); Menachem Rosensaft, conversation with the author (May 28, 2013); Mickey Steele Bodger and Alan Evans, interview with the author (September 24, 2010). For a view into Hughes's allegiance to Israel, see "Anglo-Jewry's Anatomy Is Examined: Brigadier and Youth Leader Disagree," *Jewish Chronicle*, April 26, 1963; Rosensaft, *Yesterday*, 147.

"BBC Commemorates the Liberation of Bergen-Belsen Camp by Allies," *Jewish Telegraphic Agency*, April 13, 1965.

10. "Gen. Hugh Hughes, Freed Belsen Camp," *New York Times*, November 30, 1973; *Editorial Journal of the Royal College of General Practitioners* 24 (1974): 83–84; "300 Jews Mark Death Camp End," *Palm Beach Post*, July 2, 1970, A6. In 1970, there was also a commemoration of Belsen's liberation in Montreal. Jean Smart, interview with the author (March 6, 2004).

INDEX

Page numbers in *italics* indicate a photograph or other illustration.